DIGITAL HEMLOCK

TARA BRABAZON was born and educated in Perth, Western Australia. She has lived and worked throughout Australia and New Zealand, and is currently a senior lecturer in Cultural Studies at Murdoch University, Perth. She has won a National Teaching Award for the humanities, along with other awards for cultural studies teaching and disability education. Tara is also a wide-ranging commentator on feminism, men's studies, teaching and cultural history. Her previous books, *Tracking the Jack: A Retracing of the Antipodes* and *Ladies who Lunge: Celebrating Difficult Women* were both published by UNSW Press.

THIS BOOK IS DEDICATED TO
KEVIN BRABAZON,
WHO KNOWS MORE THAN I WILL EVER LEARN.

DIGITAL HEMLOCK

INTERNET EDUCATION
AND THE
POISONING OF TEACHING

Tara Brabazon

UNSW PRESS

A UNSW Press book

Published by
University of New South Wales Press Ltd
University of New South Wales
UNSW Sydney NSW 2052
AUSTRALIA
www.unswpress.com.au

© Tara Brabazon 2002
First published 2002
Reprinted 2004

National Library of Australia
Cataloguing-in-Publication entry:

Brabazon, Tara.
Digital hemlock: Internet education and the poisoning of teaching.

Includes index.
ISBN 0 86840 781 X.

1. Internet in higher education.
2. Education, Higher — Effect of technological innovations on.
I. Title.

378.17344678

Designed by Di Quick
Printed by Dbooks

CONTENTS

PREFACE:
HEMLOCK IN THE HARDWARE

Little is known of Socrates. Although remembered as the greatest of teachers, he wrote nothing that survives to this day. We know him only through the words of his students. Socrates remains a beacon for educators, and not because he provided the answers to complex theorems or conducted the perfect proof. Instead, he had the courage to ask difficult questions. It is a potent — if mythic — image of a bare-footed Socrates wandering around ancient Athens interrogating those he meets with urgent inquiries like 'What is truth?', 'What is self?', 'Why are you doing that?', or indeed, 'How did we get here?'.

An answer to the last question is the trigger for my words. This is a book with an agenda: it stands for dissent, critique and political change. At this moment, governments in the United Kingdom, United States and Australia are proclaiming that their university systems are 'in crisis'. While they may be correct, it is these same governments that have *created* the crisis they are now decrying. At the very point when more students are attending higher education than at any point in history, governments have removed funding from the sector. Elite universities were and are properly resourced, but the new, over-populated universities are desperately peddling their wares to the corporate sector and/or alumni philanthropists to make up for the shortfall in cash. In this environment of turmoil and confusion, universities have become the convenient fall guy for the bullying bullish market.

Once an aura of crisis is established in the sector, those who triggered the troubles offer a grab bag of solutions and medications. The dense irony, which would be darkly funny if it was not so serious, is that at the very moment when money has been removed from universities, governments have demanded more control over management, strategy, curriculum, teaching and research. The piper is calling the tune without paying for the privilege. The rationale for this turnaround needs to be located, and quickly.

We have now moved to a consumer model of education, requiring the establishment of university league tables. Cambridge, Harvard and Melbourne Universities are at the top: local, regional and new colleges fill out the base of the structure. To determine such an order, rigorous and intensive surveillance and monitoring of the sector is required. In the United Kingdom, the Quality Assurance Agency (QAA) visits all universities and departments, with the aim of regulating teaching standards. The Australian Universities Quality Agency (AUQA) has a similar function. The aim is to equalise the levels of teaching and learning across higher education. While such a goal may seem laudable, there are major consequences. Content is standardised so that a law degree offered at Manchester Metropolitan University is 'equivalent' to that granted from Cambridge. Academic specialities are lost in the desire for a common core of necessary units. Invariably, the elite universities continue to dominate the desirable curriculum standards, trading on reputation, while innovation and politically critical studies are devalued and dismissed. In this environment, teaching becomes even more conservative and backward looking, as the pedagogic panopticon values, judges and erases change and originality.

Once a league table is established, students are transformed into consumers who can choose the 'best' teaching and learning environment, as determined by the government of the day. The information utilised to assemble this league table of universities includes student questionnaires, (business-inspired) generic skills and graduate competencies. Students — obviously — will not reward a course that tests or questions them, or that may actually fail them. Tough courses with demanding lecturers who care passionately about their subject area are lost from this system. Rigour and discipline are not popular and are not assessed positively by students who require maximum results from minimum efforts. Discussions of graduate skills and attributes encourage the most simple of marking methods and a 'tick a box' monitoring of achievement. The profoundly significant moments in life cannot be assessed in the short term. What a student may find difficult, arduous and irrelevant at age eighteen may be revelatory in the long term. Universities are institutions offering insight for decades, not a day, a week or a term. At this time, they are swaying in the breeze of rapid-fire ministerial briefings and policy changes.

Meanwhile, some things never change. Elite universities have always regulated themselves. Oxford, Sydney or Princeton Universities did not and will not allow governments to meddle in their business. Only when the university sector expanded — and working-class students started to attend — did surveillance become necessary. The free market economy has worked in the interests of a few elite institutions. But governments require more than for this privileged group to train a select few. Mass education reduces unemployment figures and shifts the expense of training from employers to tertiary teachers. Elite universities therefore conduct their teaching and research in the free market — charging high fees and gaining large research contracts. Those universities lower on the league table gain neither time nor money for research, and have their teaching regulated to suit transitory governmental initiatives.

These are the debates confronting higher education. Should the system remain the same? Should it be regulated or deregulated? Should it instruct an elite or a majority? It is these polarised arguments that have led the push into e-learning. Online education is not the cause of, nor the solution to, a university's 'problems'. It is a smokescreen and conservative bandaid to replace students with paying customers. The problem is that very few people know what universities actually do. During the years of elitism, a minority of lucky students experienced a revelatory journey through ideas, thought and knowledge. The university that has opened its car parks, libraries and lecture theatres to 'the masses' is a dilapidated structure, being propped up by exhausted academics. Staff, students and administrators spend their time attempting to maintain the system, rather than aiming for higher goals and future-oriented strategies. Students are not gaining a higher education at the moment; they are queuing at a McUniversity drive-through. The only problem is that the fries have run out.

Government regulators provide one version a university's aspirations, goals and function; this book provides a different view. Through much of their history, universities were a closed world to most people — closed to the taxpayers who funded them. They were elite organisations with few restrictions. Now that they have rightly opened their doors to women, the working class, the mature aged, and those of diverse races and differing physical capacities, regulators have loudly imposed their goals over the sector. Alternative histories, trajectories and options are being quashed.

This book brings the people back to universities. It is intentionally, deliberately written in a way that appears strange to the page, with arguments interspersed with emails, vignettes and stories of a teaching life. I want to open out the university to discussion, debate and critical commentary. This type of book used to be common. Sylvia Ashton-Warner made a career telling the stories of her teaching life in Maori classrooms throughout New Zealand. At the moment, feature films are presenting a very damaging portrayal of the academic. Ponder *The Wonder Boys* and *Good Will Hunting*. Both feature ageing scholars with some form of drug dependency, wandering around the campus self-absorbed and self-loathing. The notion that women or people of colour actually attend and succeed at university as either staff or students does not cross the palette of the contemporary film vista.

To provide a dissenting view of this vision, I welcome readers into my classroom, introducing my students and presenting the daily events that form an academic life and working day. In these pages, readers will discover many versions of a university. Intense humour and well-deep sadness seep out of these paragraphs and pages. Universities are the places where the brightest of a nation train their mind, with the aim of moving into the world and making it a better place. Perhaps that is the primary lesson of this book: universities are not 'about' making money, they are 'about' making a difference.

Governments do not want stroppy academics like me offering dissent. I have been — and will be — dismissed as romantic or nostalgic, out of touch with the 'real world'. But Jon Savage once stated that 'History is made by those who say "No"'.[1] We are at a historical moment where those of us who care about universities need to stop the nonsensical meetings where administrators inform teachers about teaching; we need to tear up the well-funded policy documents calling for budgetary restraint. I am only one worker of thousands in the education system, a system that is being relentlessly attacked for its poor standards and inept teaching. There is nothing particularly 'special' about me as a teacher, academic or thinker. Like so many, I do care deeply for students and the knowledge that we create, teach and nurture. That is why, through these pages, I have let readers behind one particular Wizard's curtain, to see the relentless and corrosive work that makes Oz function. We have wonderful teachers in the current system who are rarely acknowledged for their expertise and influence. I have a single aim: to demonstrate the importance of universities to national and cultural life, showing what can be improved and what is destroying the work that we do. Particularly, I place attention on technology. There is a reason for this focus.

For the last five years, money has been poured into online teaching, as a solution for overcrowded lecture theatres and laboratories. At the same time, more of our students are forced into part-time employment, caused by fees and the fact that an increasing number are not financially supported by their family. They require 'flexibility' away from a rigid university timetable. Tenured staff are also difficult to control by regulation and government guidelines. These workers are dangerous: possessing institutional memory, they can see a wheel being re-invented, and intervene. The simplest solution to all these problems is to employ casual staff to write courses for the web. Students are removed from the campus, easing the strain on library resources and facilities. They complete courses between work commitments, and those tenured staff fight for their jobs, rather than for social justice and social responsibility.

There was only one problem with this solution: students did not enrol for online courses. Millions of dollars have been wasted on the creation of an infrastructure that is barely used. What regulators and governments did not recognise is that students quite rightly want 'the university experience' of intense debate, social interaction, drinking, dancing and profound, life-changing learning. The list of high profile universities that welcomed the dot com educational initiative and have been burned by it is growing. The University of California and New York University have simply closed down their online divisions. Columbia University and the London School of Economics do not charge for their e-courses, using them only for promotion of the conventional learning environments. My task — at this historical moment of institutional failure — is to present the messy history of Internet teaching that few talk about, and even fewer commit to print. I summon the spirit of Socrates, wandering around cyberspace asking the difficult questions.

We are all intellectuals, thinking and creating new interpretations of our reality. Whatever our formal occupations, we teach and learn from those around us. The task of an intellectual — in the best sense

— is to offer alternatives. The dissenting intellectual who is prepared to agitate for change in twisted times is not supported by the workplace, media, schools, universities or government funding models. We live in clean times of crisp, ruthless economic decisions overshadowing the convoluted enactment of social justice imperatives. Supposedly, if disempowered groups can gain *access* — another of those buzzwords — to universities, computers, or employment, then their future will be assured. This panacea for poverty and inequality leaves me restless and unconvinced.

I have been teaching in universities for over a decade, commencing work when I was three years older than my students. This decade of my working life has seen an entrepreneurial explosion of Internet-inflected education. Much has been promised. New phrases punctuate schools and universities, such as flexible delivery, life-long learning, student-centred teaching, managerialism, strategic planning, convergence, synergetic futures and economic rationalism. Teachers who do not march in step with this digital drum are demeaned as neo-luddites, reactionaries or has-beens.

The Internet is a new deity. We worship our back-lit screens as our ancestors once made offerings to statues of higher powers. Our eyes flit across the monitor as hands float across the keyboard. It is a seductive combination for an ashen era. Those who trash this neo-mystical relationship between a user and their inbox express a new sacrilege. It is important to note that Socrates was sentenced to death not only because he lead the young astray, but because he neglected the Gods. By doubting the self-evident benefits of the information age, dissenters abandon — like Socrates — (digital) deities.

My words do not shun technology or present a pessimistic denunciation of Internet-based learning. Instead, I reveal other trajectories that will make the current teaching environment better and stronger. Most importantly, the Internet is placed into a far longer history of education, media, teaching and learning. This book is structured around four core issues. The first section presents the political 'realities' and challenges of contemporary education. The second segment works through the debates encircling literacy: I investigate the purposes of reading and writing, and the role of the library within higher education. The third part explores student motivation, giving attention to the (frequently assumed) link between teaching and learning. I also show why the disembodied virtual university has not worked, and why teachers have bodies that matter. The fourth component probes social justice, ensuring that an attention to efficiency and productivity does not efface more important concerns with reparation and representation.

I am not against technology. After all, technology is everywhere: a toaster, a ruler and a pencil are devices that extend the limits of human behaviour and actions. I do believe that we must *start* with teaching and learning goals, and then determine how technology can assist these functions. Teachers currently feel as if we are trapped in a Monty Python sketch. We are living the opening scene of *The Meaning of Life* where, through the 'miracle of birth', the medical administrator remains most impressed by the machine that goes ping rather than the arrival, before his eyes, of new life. Far too many educational administrators gravitate towards the ping, missing the magic being woven by teachers with little more than a voice, enthusiasm and energy.

Socrates was sentenced to death for his crimes against society. The greatest teacher of all, whose questions were too radical for his time, drank the hemlock and died. Educators must mind this lesson. Those who dissent, those who offer resistance, may suffer a similar fate. The crushing of alternatives, the ignorance of history and the avoidance of political debate will cut the heart out of education. Without attention to social justice, critical literacy and social change, our students will know how to send an email, but have nothing to say in it.

PART I

ASSUME THE
POSITION

1

DO YOU WANT FRIES WITH THAT?
INTERNET TEACHING AND THE
ADMINISTRATION OF KNOWLEDGE

Settle down, people. Welcome to ERE 102. This course, colloquially known as Selling Silicon Snake Oil, provides an introduction to an Economically Rationalist Education. I teach you how to use the Internet, not for the purposes of critical thinking or creative mobilisations of hypertext, but to administer knowledge. For those with busy lifestyles, you are encouraged to leave the lecture theatre right now and buy a long black at the library coffee shop. Everything I am about to say will appear in my PowerPoint demonstration, which is downloadable from the website. Please do not contact me if you have difficulty logging onto the course site. Your access is not my responsibility. So, if this is the last time I see you in this lecture theatre, I thank you for enrolling in ERE 102. I look forward to receiving your emails. Have a nice life.

In keeping with our bullet-point culture, I will now dim the lights and attempt to activate my PowerPoint presentation. Hopefully the projector will work. As I have not prepared a lecture, I will talk to the slides, filling in the space between the headings with banal comments and self-evident nonsense. You will, however, see some attractively coloured graphs. These are downloadable from the course website. Well, they would be, but they are rather large documents and cannot be saved to a floppy disc. I am certain, though, that most of you have a CD Rom burner in your homes; it will be necessary to get the most out of ERE 102. After all, there is no textbook and not much reading. Everything you need to complete the assignments is found in my PowerPoint bullet points. Copying them down accurately will determine the calibre of your grade in this course.

So starts an imaginary, dystopic university course. Readers may recognise fragments of this spiel, either from their own teaching, the work of others, or from fashionably superficial budgetary briefings and marketing meetings. While this imagined course is crudely configured, it does provide an entry into the concerns of this book. Now that the practices and principles of web-based teaching are experiencing a boom (of spin doctoring if nothing else), it seems timely to unpick the digital fabric of education. At the end of our academic career, when we have returned the last telephone call, answered the last email and closed our office door for the final time, we will not list our major teaching success as training efficient administrators. Most of us hope to teach prime ministers, community workers, journalists and filmmakers who will make a difference to the world. Certainly the modern university, as one ideological arm of the nation state, is a bureaucratic, corporate, capitalist organisation. This volatile role for the university triggers a new vocabulary of excellence, standards, flexibility and efficiency.

In keeping with the era, I will track the shape of the argument around a critical vocabulary of five banal terms. These words push five over-pressed keypads of the policy keyboard: crisis, teaching, management, flexibility and literacy. My critical initiative is not meant to discount Internet-based education. Instead, I attack the justifications of web-inflected learning, suggesting that teachers may be major losers in the — clichéd — virtual university. This chapter introduces the recurrent motifs of my book. A frame is established, and an argument commenced.

UNIVERSITIES IN CRISIS?

It is densely ironic that universities have entered a period of crisis at the very time when women, mature-aged students and ethnic minorities are entering the institution. In such an environment, a 'national curriculum' makes little sense. Currently, the desire for traditional values and skills and the needs of the competitive marketplace have affiliated the goals of neoconservatives with those of neoliberals. Both these ideologies mock and ridicule popular culture and the truths of everyday life. Michael Apple has suggested that:

> what counts as knowledge, the ways in which it is organized, who is empowered to teach it, what counts as an appropriate display of having learned it, and — just as critically — who is allowed to

ask and answer all these questions, are part and parcel of how dominance and subordination are reproduced and altered in this society.[1]

In many nations these questions about the value of knowledge are trapped within a rigid market orientation. For example, the changes in Australia's education policy in the mid-1980s coincided with John Dawkins becoming a Commonwealth minister in 1987, during the era of a Labor — supposedly leftist — government. The White Paper of 1988 expressed the aims of higher education within the most rei-fied of economic languages: efficiency, accountability, productivity and competition. As Janice Dudley and Lesley Vidovich recognised, the point of the Commonwealth policy was to 'harness ... higher education as an instrument of micro-economic reform to drive eco-nomic recovery'.[2] Post-compulsory education was a safety valve on the labour market, and a mechanism to temporarily reduce unem-ployment levels. Gripped between notions of productivity and com-petition, the university sector was tempered with, and tempted by, questions of immediate social, economic and political relevance.

This '"one-stop" educational mall'[3] does not address or assist the needs of scholarship or training. If education is considered in this way, then much time and effort is spent keeping the customer satis-fied, or else they may 'shop around' for other courses. Satisfaction is not the basis of social or personal transformation. If we are satisfied, then we do not agitate for change. If we are satisfied, then we do not need to think. Satisfaction breeds mediocrity, compliance and banal-ity. Through undergraduate and postgraduate education, academics build long-term knowledges, skills and research expertise.[4] Dissatisfaction breeds questioning, agitation and research. The net-work of peer review reinforces these processes. While most of our students do not end up working in a university, they have the right to a considered, consolidated body of knowledge, rather than an ill-organised jigsaw puzzle of what a future employer may desire.

The dual motifs of crisis and economic rationalism are framing the current movement into Internet-based teaching. Crisis is an unfortunate and inappropriate trigger for technological innovation. Through these changes, the academy has been both resilient and compliant. The shift in logos, from the 'ivory tower' to the 'real world', has downplayed and demeaned the critical role of scholars. The desire for concrete knowledge that will serve pressing economic concerns is promoted by both neoliberals and conservative leftist governments. Not surprisingly, David Whittle, an IBM executive and cultural commentator, has stated that:

> over the years, I've learned far more online about how things really work than I learned about how things should work in theory in six years of higher education as an undergraduate and graduate student.[5]

Cyberspace becomes the virtual library and university — and the fount of all knowledge. Such a stance decentres the role and expertise of librarians and academics. I am not suggesting that a solution to the crisis of knowledge is a return to intellectual elitism. Instead, I believe that all educators should be given credit for their expertise, rather than the market rate for their knowledge. Lucas was correct when he showed that 'if there is a true crisis in American higher education today, it is chiefly a crisis of purpose'.[6] The university has always been much more than a trade school for the workplace or a site for professional credentialing. Obviously, there has never been consensus by governments, scholars or the (broadly defined) public domain on the undergraduate curricula at universities. Life-long learning is not examinable or compartmentalised into semester-length units. Traditionally, to teach well is to deny closure. To teach well in the current system is to administer marking criteria.

Internet-based learning is a response to consumerism and the reduction in government funding. This has been an unfortunate context for the expansion of online pedagogy. The language of computer-based systems — cost savings, efficiency and productivity — has masked the public interest and investment in information technologies. For example, while outlay in computers increased an average of 24 per cent per year through the 1980s, investment in other business equipment declined.[7] Technology is driven by the competitive business sector, and while the Internet simplifies the management of educational tasks, it poses very specific challenges for university teachers. This technocratic consciousness has meant that, as Aronowitz and Giroux have realised, 'the central question regarding learning is reduced to the problem of management'.[8] In this milieu, a teacher's behaviour is controlled, scrutinised and evaluated. Radical ideas and expansive research are crushed into modules, criteria and bullet points, being rendered consistent, predictable and banal.

TEACHER: ROLES AND EXPECTATIONS

There are multiple meanings derived from the term 'teacher'. The skills currently being stuffed into the educational package include how to teach larger classes and be more entrepreneurial. The four pillars of academic life — teaching, research, administration and community service — are the post-war foundations of this system. The market-inflected 'innovations' in the academy, when accompanied by vocationalism and the rise of structural youth unemployment, have altered the requirements of teachers and teaching. Polarised institutional and educational priorities trigger statements of 'compet[ing] effectively for additional students while maintaining the same or a smaller faculty'.[9] Therefore, technology is framed as a cheaper, more efficient replacement for university teachers.

A radical reworking of teaching has taken place in the last ten years. As teachers become facilitators, and lectures transform into workshops, the notion of effective education has morphed. A Curtin University of Technology website has proclaimed: 'good teaching practices tend to work as partnerships between teachers and students, creating student-centred learning. The teacher's role thus becomes less central, but definitely not unimportant'.[10]

Teachers, as the group responsible for curriculum, methodology and assessment, are not only 'not unimportant', but absolutely critical to the reputation and success of students and universities. Internet-based learning actually 'increase[s] academic workloads'.[11] *Somebody* needs to design the content and layout.[12] *Somebody* needs to write the webpages. *Somebody* needs to ensure that hypertext links are up-to-date.[13] *Somebody* needs to create evaluative criteria. *Somebody* needs to moderate students' results. Therefore, student-centred learning is not only rhetoric, but also an ideological mask to deflect attention away from the power that teachers hold and the increased workload necessary to construct a web-based education. As Stephen Brookfield has suggested, 'students know teachers have particular expertise ... to pretend otherwise is to insult students' intelligence and to create a tone of mistrust from the outset'.[14] Students are not equal to teachers: instead, teachers need to create a structured chance for disempowered groups to speak. While a staff member assigns a grade and awards a degree, teachers and students are never 'partners in constructing knowledge'.[15] Ironically, at the moment when student-centred learning has become a cliché, students are (overtly) evaluating teachers' abilities.[16] While staff may state that students are responsible for their own learning, students are blaming staff for their results. Consider the answers to the following student survey question:

> What advice would you give to teaching staff planning to create a web-based learning course?

- Don't disregard the human factor for tutorials and labs

- Use it as a tool but don't use it as the only means of communication — maintain word-of-mouth explanations as central to the course

- Make it easy to follow and colourful; make it interesting so people stay attentive

- Think about the students first and from the students' perspective. You are a teacher first.

- You have to be enthusiastic about what you are doing[17]

None of these respondents ask teachers to give students more responsibility. Students instead demand — alongside Internet-based materials — face-to-face contact as 'central to the course'. If these students required face-to-face discussion, why were they enrolled as online students? Also, with many universities locked into bland, unforgiving educational platforms and templates, such as Blackboard and WebCT, making sites look 'colourful' is difficult. Students also feed off staff enthusiasm: the bits and bytes are not replacing the jokes and jibes. The point of Internet-based education is to relieve staff of some face-to-face teaching, so that universities become cheaper to run and more productive. What has actually happened is that teachers have continued to run traditional programs and correspondence courses, and have also been responsible for developing online units alongside the conventional workload demands. In other words, Internet teaching is a time-consuming add-on to already full working days.

The transformation of students into consumers of knowledge and customers of the academy has major consequences for teachers. As Smith and Webster have suggested, 'today, the university is ... expected to treat its students as consumers, and so students have begun to blame their teachers for their failures'.[18] Such an attitude ignores the complex process of learning. To read, remember, understand, synthesise and interpret knowledge is often drudgery. To learn with effectiveness requires repetition, practice and failure. Simplifying the convoluted, arduous but rewarding intellectual journey into a cycle of disappointment and blame undermines the activity of learning — and teaching. This change has been caused because knowledge has been transformed into competence. While computers are seen to promote access to education, there are substantial structural problems to address. Angela Benson and Elizabeth Wright reported that over 20 per cent of their students found that access to computers and the Internet actually hindered the completion of assignments.[19] Internet-based education is not replacing conventional lectures and tutorials. Instead, web-based teaching is becoming one more site of writing and administration. Daniel Petre and David Harrington, as software designers, demonstrate little understanding of (Internet) teaching. They stated: 'responding to an e-mail is not very time-consuming and doesn't encroach on one's personal space'.[20]

I have always been an early starter, entering my office by 7:30 am. When I first arrived at Murdoch University — a campus situated in Perth, Western Australia — during 1997, I was able to complete two hours of research and administration before my teaching day started at 9:30 am. By 1999, these two hours were filled with answering emails. After teaching in the morning, though, I was able to go the library some afternoons. By the middle of semester one, 2000, I was unable to complete *any* reading or administration through the course of a working day. Between the (necessary) student consultations and over 240 emails every day, it takes me up to four hours to handle these queries. As a touch-typist, each email only takes a few moments to answer. With effective filters and clear folders, I rarely confront spam or a glut of ill-organised messages. However *the number* of emails has permanently changed the shape of my working day. Hour-long blocks are set aside to read and reply to an ever-increasing stream of professional, academic, research and teaching inquiries. Administration and research are now conducted early in the morning, late at night and on weekends. I no longer bother bringing my briefcase to work. My story is not unusual. But this change in the pattern of my working day — within four years — has reduced and decentred intellectual tasks to competency and generic skills.

The Internet has increased student access to the instructor. While such access can be framed as beneficial to students and education broadly defined, it has emerged during the very period when research and administrative responsibilities have also increased. Some theorists question why staff lack motivation and resist Internet-based teaching.[21] For the first time, staff place overt attention on delivery management systems. In the past, they wrote study guides but did not have to think about how these publications were photocopied and distributed. Now, they not only write teaching materials but structure them within templates, keep hypertext links current and address queries when students cannot access a site. Michelle Vachris's realisation is very serious in terms of teachers' time, and career: 'Because the online technology promotes a more cooperative learning environment, this interaction is more costly in terms of instructor time than is the case of a traditional classroom'.[22] While the working conditions are saturated with economic imperatives, university structures are still reliant on the vocationalism and goodwill of academics.[23] There is an assumption that teachers will complete work and training for which they are not paid. Teachers take time away from research, marking and in-class preparation to develop a new site of learning. Lynne Shrum has presented the framework of a Californian-based scheme:

> Teachers voluntarily gave up one month of the summer to learn about new technologies to improve instruction. For four weeks, these teachers lived in dormitories, attended classes, and prepared lessons from early morning until late at night. They developed skills in many areas of teaching and technology. In return for their commitments, the teachers received a stipend that included room and board, a small cash award or the equivalent sum toward the purchase of a microcomputer, and a limited amount of software.[24]

Many university scholars have freely given time to develop Internet sites that have increased their own workload.[25] The long-term consequence of computer ubiquity is that organisations and individuals are committed to the endless updating of hypertext links and software upgrades. Such activities have transformed teachers into managers of information and designers of websites.

ADMINISTRATION, MANAGEMENT
AND DESIGN

The management of the learning environment is part of the administrative revolution of the academy. At its best, 'the administration of Internet-based learning (IBL) is a process of negotiation and collaboration between individual academics, colleagues, and university structures'.[26] This 'collaboration' is not compatible with my experience of web-based development.

> I currently provide a unit at Murdoch University that is offered at both second- and fourth-year levels. The course is available internally, through correspondence modes and via the web. That means that six distinct versions of the course run, all with different assessment and all requiring continual monitoring and updating. It is simply assumed that the sites will be available, internal and distance education study guides delivered and a collection of readings developed. I had no decision-making role in extending this internal course to distance education in 1998, to the web in 1999 and to fourth-year level in 2000. Every time I change a reading, develop a new section of a lecture and update the content and interpretation — which is every semester of every year — six different study guides and sites are altered. There is currently no workload-based recognition of online courses or the updating of materials through multiple modes. That means I am not paid for work that fills weeks of my working life every semester of every year. In other words, this is work not acknowledged as work.

While good teachers recognise that learning can only take place if students feel comfortable to make mistakes, the institutional framework does not encourage such an imperative. If teachers are granted a lecture theatre then they are able to ensure that the students have access to the learning environment. However, this power is removed from teachers through the desire for flexibility and facilitation. If a university server is down, if the WebCT platform has disenabled guest account creation and thereby blocked student entry into the website, then the instructor becomes responsible for a situation over which they can do little except write placating emails.

HTML (Hypertext Markup Language) offers enormous potential for the development of innovative educational architecture. This simple format for both representing and linking documents is an outstanding opportunity to create new types of referencing, writing and reading. The repercussions of hypertext for those who teach and assess the work of others is also far-reaching. John Scigliano, Jacques Levin and Greg Horne assert that there is the capacity for 'immediate questioning and feedback on work'.[27] Once more, a clash emerges between the potential of the technology and the reality of teachers' lives. 'Immediate feedback' is also possible through written essays, but a one-to-two-week turnaround is the standard. The potential of hypertext raises the possibility of an essay being marked the moment it arrives — either through the tracking function in Word, or via Notepad. Invariably, this 'immediate feedback' does not happen.

> In my courses I allow students to choose the form of their first assignment — video presentation, audio tape, government research paper or website. One year, with 133 students enrolled in a course, I received three web-based assignments. While there was the potential for 'immediate feedback', I treated these assignments the same as the others. Needless to say, the three students repeatedly sent me emails asking if I had looked at their webpage. This interest was not matched by the other 130 students. They granted me seven days to complete the marking.
>
> I do not have Internet access at home. I have always argued that I bring enough work into my private life without needing the added expense and distraction of clearing emails late in the night. So these three web-based assignments were the last marked. I went into work on a Sunday afternoon and proceeded to 'mark' them. I was not impressed with what was presented, as the students merely wrote written reports and then converted the documents to HTML. The characteristic of webpages is hypertext, and there were numerous links possible in this assignment. To start them off, I had provided twenty-two sites for the students. But this left me in a difficult position. They had completed a mediocre assignment and placed it on the web, assuming that they would gain points for innovation. Yet they had used linear writing modalities in a convergent medium. All received a credit. All were disappointed. My statement that they did not use the potential of the medium did not really gel with them. I described

the equivalent as a student submitting a video presentation in which they stood in front of a camera and read an essay to the lens. They did not grasp the parallel.

The managerial makeover of the contemporary university has resulted in a re-evaluation of curricula. As Trevor Kerry and Janice Tollitt-Evans have realised, 'those of us who came into the teaching profession a while back had no inkling that the job of the teacher would develop into one with such a heavy load of administrative work'.[28] In evaluating the virtual curriculum, questions should be raised about both teacher education and professional development. The managerialism of the current university system has meant that Internet-based pedagogy has been focused on design issues rather than rationale, intentions or applications. The laissez-faire attitude to teacher training has relied on 'gifted amateurs' rather than structural change to initiate Internet-based education. Too often, the major managerial decision-makers mouth the phrase 'flexible learning' without any sense of the consequences for teachers, students or education. Some instructors, shadowing the language of the market, attempt to protect their area from cost-cutting by streamlining units and making their courses 'economically viable'. For example, consider Graham Seal's course, LCS12 Australian Literature:

> In its first year of online operation only 1 of 9 students enrolled in the course worked in its online mode. Dr Seal emphasizes that the creation of the website will enable the course to run economically in future with such small numbers. The course will also be ready as more students go online.[29]

Pedagogical or political rationales were irrelevant to the web-based transfer of LCS12 Australian Literature. With such a tiny enrolment, online education was a desperate act to keep the course feasible. The excessive work involved in creating this course *for one student* was an implicit presence in this review.

The polarised impact of information technology within universities can be attributed to a lack of training in the mid-to-late 1990s.[30] While most institutions made Internet training 'available', they did not reduce the workload to enable staff to take up this opportunity. I have been endlessly frustrated that training sessions have been scheduled during semester and term times, without any reference to the fact that *teachers* are *teaching* during *teaching weeks*. That early absence of (proto) just-in-time instruction has resulted in a lack of critical reflexivity and familiarity on reading and writing for the web, and an over-emphasis on the technology 'itself'. While technology continues to 'advance', it will not be used appropriately unless crafted within pedagogy.

FLEXIBILITY AND EXCELLENCE

The two motifs of the university — flexibility and excellence — have also marked Internet studies and Internet-based instruction. A student questionnaire, probing the rationale for web-based teaching, hinted at the pressures confronting academics to adapt. The far-reaching demands of students in this new environment perhaps foreshadow the future of university education. Consider a few of the student comments:

> I would be worried if lecturers ... feel that because they made the effort to put their work online their job is finished.

> To perhaps have a time when e-mails can be answered quickly.

> Must be available by e-mail, phone, fax and personally for contact still.[31]

These are not self-regulated learners. These student responses are not strong endorsements for the benefits of the Internet for learning, teaching or the credibility of a university. The desire for students to contact staff whenever — and however — they desire would be unexpected in most business environments. Such desires from students not only appear ungracious, but are treating academic staff like a customer service agency. Through the increased meeting and managerial load on academics, there will be less hours in the day when students can see teachers or have their calls answered. Even though materials have been put online, and the potential of asynchronous communication mobilised, students want emails to be answered *quickly*. Similarly, staff are to be available by email *and* phone *and* fax *and* in person. Most online students describe flexibility in study as the great advantage of Internet-based education.[32] The cost of student flexibility is staff productivity. The major justification for staff to promote Internet-based education is that it 'increase[s] students' responsibility of their own learning'.[33] However, student evaluations demonstrate that the reverse is taking place.[34] Online education has created a new problem, which will fragment the university further, and make an academic's workday less efficient.

The desire for flexibility, as a justification for the increasing role of the Internet in teaching, comes at the loss of other, older imperatives of university education. Part of the project of *Digital Hemlock* is to provide a memory trigger — not to celebrate past educational systems — that affirms the structures and ideas from the past that are still important. As bell hooks has realised, 'there is not much passionate teaching or learning taking place in higher education today'.[35] The point of flexibility was — politically — highly useful. It was a way to transform universities into sites of lifelong learning. It has now transformed into a strategy to shorten three-year degrees, normalise course overloads and cheapen what is being taught. Learning always exists in a social situation. Application of knowledge creates a link between doing and thinking. This connectivity can occur in any media at any time. However, it does take intellectual discipline on the behalf of a student. Learning — challenging learning — is rarely pleasant. It is confronting to re-theorise the realities impressed from parents, friends, religious organisations and governments. The stakeholders in technology education are myriad: from governments to university administrators and employers. It is the teachers who make the virtual classroom — with all its practicalities — actually function.

The notion of good practice, let alone best practice, in educational delivery remains a vexed question. Obviously, instructional design, curriculum development and technology are integrated modes of communication. The language of Roger Atkinson needs to be monitored, critiqued and problematised: 'Online learning offers attractive ways to enhance the flexible delivery of vocational education and training'.[36] The terminology — attractive, enhance, flexible, vocation, training — is telling. The key question is whether or not valuing flexibility above all other attributes is a stable foundation for our higher education sector.

LITERACY AND CULTURAL CAPITAL

The final section of this introductory chapter inflects the two terms of literacy and cultural capital with the antagonistic ideologies of the university sector. Clearly, encryption is both a metaphor and metonymy of our teaching and learning lives. But who possesses the key to unlock these codes? Literacy standards have been a tenet of neoliberal ideologies. The changes to literacy demand compromises to both the humanities and the education system. The corporate aims of the university signal a movement from cultural capital to dollars and cents. It is clear, as Gregory Rawlins has realised, that 'Adam Smith outran Karl Marx'.[37] Western institutionalised education has built civilisation by advancing industrialisation.

If I could un-invent one software programme, it would be PowerPoint. Without exception, the worst presentations, lectures and budget briefings I attend are conducted using this tragic package. Presenters break all the rules of public speaking — repeating verbatim the words on the screen; letting the technology determine the pace and order of the presentation; and even requiring a darkened room. Also, many of these presentations either do not run, or start late, because of 'problems with the technology'. For students, new problems emerge. An example is a site offering advice to teachers using PowerPoint:

> Once you use presentation software to create your overheads, you then have the ability to archive all your overheads on your course Web-site. This way, students can review and check their own notes against the exact overheads you used in class. Students often comment upon how useful it is to have this resource.[38]

This kind of system has major problems. Students desire access to the overheads of a lecture — this access means that they do not have to attend the lecture. More seriously, the students who 'check' their notes against the PowerPoint slides will invariably copy down any points they missed — word for word. This is not critical thinking: in fact, it is not even thinking.

This decentring of critical thinking will result in the systematic mark(et)ing of the sciences and economics over the humanities. Further, the illusion of access promoted by computers creates confusion between the presentation of information and the capacity to use, sort and interpret it. Students have difficulty matching research needs with indexes: such a difficulty is only intensified through databases. Cerise Oberman demonstrates the clear intellectual gap between information and knowledge within the university library:

> The reference staff strategically placed corresponding print and CD-ROM indexes next to each other. The ERIC index was placed next to the ERIC CD-ROM and Psychological Abstracts

was placed next to PsychInfo, and so on ... the idea behind jux-taposing the print index to the electronic one was simple. We were trying to encourage students to use the print index as a starting point for their research. From the reference staffs' point of view, this experiment was a total and complete failure. Students preferred to wait in line for the omniscient computer rather than to consult print indexes even when librarians pointed out their availability and appropriateness.[39]

Information is therefore not the issue: the methodologies avail-able to assess it must be granted more attention. A librarian told me a story about students' lack of critical skills, demonstrating how the profession has been effected by the rushed introduction of web-based education. PowerPoint is framed as an effective way to convey information in lectures. Many staff make these PowerPoint 'slides' available to students. The size of these files means that students can-not download them onto floppy discs. Librarians are pestered every day with complaints from students whose attempts to save to a disc 'do not work'. The idea of using a pen and paper to *write their notes* is not viewed as an option. Some technologies are obviously more important — and determinant — than others.

We must continue to ask what is the purpose of higher educa-tion, and how much of this conservative ideology should be allowed to determine the agenda for the sector. Dennis Hayes has recognised the dangers inherent in an implicit acceptance of the narrative of computer-generated improvement:

> Every era has its heresies. Perhaps there is no greater contempo-rary heresy than the notion that computers have betrayed us. Yet betrayal — and fundamental failure — is what the record quietly shows.[40]

The religious tones of his words are poignant. It is a time of here-sies, betrayal and failure. This narrative — of alternatives, question-ing, fear and concern — should not be dismissed as dystopic or anti-technology. Instead, we need to prevent the flattening of public debate. The next chapter continues my critique by presenting the intertwining histories of the Internet and teaching. I will show how teachers and teaching are being challenged and undermined through the Internet. Learning is not technologically dependent. It is reliant on commitment, interest and passion.

2

LET'S MAKE LOTS OF MONEY: DIGITAL DEALS AND TRAFFICKING TRUTH IN THE VIRTUAL CLASSROOM

I've got the brains
You've got the looks
Let's make lots of money.

'Opportunities', Pet Shop Boys[1]

Writing about Internet teaching is like being trapped in the *Blair Witch Project*. All the stones have changed position, the compass does not work, odd screams erupt from the dead of night and we desperately need a tissue to wipe up the mess. There is the sensation of travelling in circles bereft of a map, being endlessly interrupted by a pesky documentary filmmaker urgently attempting to separate the myth from the reality and the truth from the lies.

This chapter tells some truths, and some lies, about the current educational system. It takes as its trigger the powerful directive of Paul Willis, demanding educators to do better and be better:

Insofar as education/training becomes ever more subordinated to technical instrumentalism and to the 'needs' for industry, it will be seen as a necessary evil to be tolerated in order to obtain access to the wage in order to obtain access to leisure and consumption and their cultural energies … We need an altogether new approach to education.[2]

He creates a compelling avowal for difference, critique and resistance. Unfortunately, Willis's words were published in 1990; unfortunate because these new approaches have not been sketched, and education has been even more tightly enfolded into technical instrumentalism and the workplace, compounded through the proliferation of the web and the Internet. It is now even more urgent to summon different needs, goals and emphases in education. Instead of attacking narrow, skill-based training — and affirming wider, broader and stronger political goals — teachers are trapped in the chorus of the Pet Shop Boys' 'Opportunities'. Education has the brains, the workplace has the looks: together they make lots of money. What is forgotten is that this lyric was ironic, superficial and playful — affirming the necessity for alternatives in the era of big shoulder pads and high unemployment. This chapter therefore gets our hands dirty in the troubled terrain of the contemporary school and education system, providing a new way to ponder Internet-based learning. The first section presents a brief history of the Internet and the web, followed by the major challenges confronting teaching and teachers. The final section shows how the directive to 'get courses on the web' is corroding the professionalism and workplaces of teaching staff. The chapter is a position paper that pokes and probes the unfashionable, obstinate, difficult, volatile, angry and passionate parts of an education that are slipping away from us in the movement towards templated learning.

INTERNET 101, OR THE LIE OF THE RUG

I built the first electronic digital computer and the prototype
was finished up in October or November 1939.

John Vincent Atanasoff

He lies like a rug.

J Presper Eckert[3]

Reading about the proto-world wide web history of the Internet is like reliving a Monty Python sketch. Harvard scientists, rather than Yorkshiremen, fight an intense battle to prove that *they were there* at the impoverished beginning, the *real* beginning — rather than a pseudo-scientific run to the US Patent Office — and that other physicists, mathematicians and writers lie like a rug. Books have been written about the origins of computer-mediated communication. The most bizarre and fascinating is Joel Shurkin's *Engines of the Mind*, which features eleven chapters, each detailing a possible 'origin' of the Internet. Pinpointing historical beginnings, like endings, is a messy business. For example, the decadent and convoluted stories of Ada Byron Lovelace and Charles Babbage become lost in the muscular narrative of masculine progress and development.[4] Contestations over remembering and forgetting continue at the digital frontier. This volatile chronology demonstrates that we are still in the process of making a history of the Internet that can be used in the present. The Internet is not a static object to be assessed and discussed; it is a thinking space that allows meanings to be made.

Twenty years ago David Lowenthal argued that the past is a foreign country.[5] Increasingly the present has become a tourist destination. The most significant analytical task for contemporary critics is to disrupt the dual ideologies punctuating the now: inevitable technological change, and progress. The notion that technology may actually make our lives *worse* — less productive, less political, less potent — seems beyond the discursive pale. The potentials and problems of the digital and analogue environments must be oriented into critical theories of information, knowledge, entertainment, pleasure and education. The ideologies of the analogue, invoking constant, subtle movement and continuity, are marked against the discontinuous structure of digitisation. The two states — on/off — are mirrored by the profound simplicity of the binary-based computer language: 0 and 1. In reified — Shelleyfied — frameworks, digitisation may appear to be a frightening manifestation of crazed science, but this new world order has major advantages. Digital information is networkable and dense. These advantages simplify into the clichéd term of our time: convergence. While seeming to solve the problems created by inter-media transference, the benefits of digitisation can be over-stated. Technological obsolescence is a major concern, but so is application and usability. It will be several years, and perhaps a decade, before videodisc technology is able to surpass the convenience and economy of analogue tapes. The transformation of analogue media into bits and bytes often appears as an inevitable formation. In response, libraries, offices, archives and educational establishments are altering their budget and training structures. The Internet is networking change.

The Internet is a linkage of millions of computers and thousands of networks. These terminals and systems are able to share information because of a coding system that allows computers to electronically mark and categorise data — TCP/IP (Transmission Control

Protocol/Internet Protocol). This language has been described as 'the Esperanto of the Internet'.[6] Put basically, the Transmission Control Protocol breaks data into packets, which are enclosed in a digitised envelope, with clearly marked (web)[7] addresses for the sender and receiver. The Internet Protocol determines how the data passes from sender to receiver. Different packets of information may utilise different paths to their designation. The TCP determines, at the end of the journey, whether the data is still intact and able to be re-assembled into its original formation. Through this process, a client–server model of data exchange is established.

It is straightforward to describe how the Internet moves information through cyberspace by breaking it into components that are then reassembled at the destination. Such a movement is made possible because the 'home' and 'destination' systems share the TCP/IP. This simple Internet narrative is unravelled when we consider how information transfer is used and accessed. Software gives human signs, codes, genres and languages to computers. Therefore, the technical components of the Internet become less relevant. Just as a car can be driven without a working knowledge of a six-cylinder engine, so can the Internet be negotiated without a grasp of how information is packaged and processed. Similarly, the Internet — and the web even more so — utilises much of the vocabulary and iconography of earlier technological forms. Webpages, home pages and WebTV confirm the convergence of media.[8] To discuss the interplay and similarities between older and newer media is to undermine the arguments of those who desire a computer revolution.

Marshall Soules asks: 'is technology neutral?'.[9] When considered politically, technology, like any other formation, cannot be placed outside ideology. All sites are read in a way that negotiates with the social experience of the reader and user. There is no unmediated text, or unmediated reading. Soules, following on from Michel Foucault, argues that 'technology is the instrument of our governance'.[10] Nodes of power and resistance saturate the Internet. It is not autonomous or self-standing. To stress technology above all other cultural and social formations is to transfer men and women into homo faber (toolmakers and users). This stance also provides a tidy method to separate social structures and consciousness from technology and objectivity. It is too easy to argue that computers, convergence or digitisation will create a revolution in society. Such a notion is promoted by Michael Rosenthal, who stated that 'digitized text will change everything'.[11] The teleological clichés of the 1990s — the death of books, the paperless office and the end of libraries — did not eventuate. 'Everything' has not changed: we still have libraries and books, and we are still drowning under the deadweight of reports, agendas and application forms. By focusing on the technological mode of delivery, the concepts that underlie professional practice and the mode of production are deflected from discussion.

Any protocol-based history of technology requires careful commentary. The Internet's 'backbone' — the main lines that carry most of the information — is formed through the biggest networks on the system. These are owned by the largest Internet Service Providers: America Online's ANS Sprint, UUNet, GTE and MCI. These networks connect to each other, preventing redundancy. This means data can be redirected from one part of the route, which may have been damaged or corrupted, to another part of the network. The routes that are within the physical territory of the United States have less redundancy and are more reliable. The maxim that the Internet exists nowhere and everywhere decentres discussion of the physical infrastructure that formulates the system. Particular countries and regions have a high level of Internet connectivity: others are minimally affiliated with the network.[12] There is obviously a commercial stake in promoting the scale and scope of the matrix. The United States remains the centre of the Internet, in both physical and geographical terms. There are enormous financial advantages gained from this domination:

> Information technology is important to the nation not only because of its value in advancing science and technology and U.S. competitiveness, but because of the ubiquity of the technology and its effect on all aspects of citizens' lives.[13]

The 'global' nature of the Internet depends on the calibre of the telephone system. The 'globe' that the Internet spans is not only dominated by America, but is saturated with its presence, language and politics. This leverage is not surprising. Formed in the United States, the Advanced Research Projects Agency Network (ARPANET) was a 1960s scientific experiment with a military inflection. In 1967 Lawrence Roberts published this plan for a wider audience.[14] His packet switching allowed governmental, educational and research sites to be connected via a high-bandwidth network.[15] This more complex history is embedded in the myth that the Internet would allow the

United States to fight and survive a nuclear war. Monitor the function of this myth as Bruce Sterling restates this 'origin': 'Some thirty years ago, the Rand Corporation, America's foremost Cold War think-tank, faced a strange strategic problem. How could the US authorities successfully communicate after a nuclear war?'.[16] A simplification of technology, and the power invested in it, is present in his words. A desire to slot the Internet into a simple model of cultural imperialism and cold war directives is a way to control a very convoluted and complex history. The Internet is more than the ARPANET, NSFNET[17] or USENET. It *was* all these systems, but it *is* more than these matrixes. There are consequences of the intense Americanisation of the Internet, and these are addressed in the final section of this book.

Considering the exclusivity of this history and the cultural capital necessary to be a part of the pre-www Internet, it is odd that, as Quarterman and Carl-Mitchell have realised, 'lots of people really want to believe that the Internet is very large'.[18] The desire to map the Internet, and focus on the growth, is also a way to strategically forget the American domination of the sources of information, communication and education. It is simply too convenient, at a time when the United States is the core for 'a new world order' (to poach George — without the double ya — Bush's phrase) to argue that suddenly 'real' space and 'real' geography no longer matter. A narrative of the Internet is being written to suit contemporary political needs. Depending on the shading of this history, a myriad of great men can be the 'founders' of the Internet: Bob Kahn, Bob Taylor, Larry Roberts, Vint Cerf, Wes Clark and Bolt Beranek. *Wired* magazine is particularly effective in building the reputations of these mythic men.[19] American men have dominated and (re)written the history of the Internet. Ironically, this 'tradition' changes when considering the world wide web. Tim Berners-Lee claims popular cultural originator status, having worked on the project at the European Particle Physics Laboratory (CERN). While the Internet is a network of computers, the web is a network of hypertext links. As Berners-Lee realised, 'the Web made the net useful because people are really interested in information ... and don't really want to have to know about computers and cables'.[20] The web browser software allows a connection to an Internet service provider. The innovation of the web is the hypertext markup language that allows a hyperlinking of documents. This language developed the first graphical user interface: the web browser, Mosaic. Marc Andreessen then founded Netscape Communications in April 1994.

It is easier to discuss protocols and languages than power and domination. It is crisply convincing to displace geography and history while focusing on packet switching and great men. The binary language of computer-mediated communication allows a smooth transference of data, but meaning systems are not exchanged as easily. Theorists need to ask more useful questions, rather than allow applications to mask politics. A significant query, for example, explores *who* is using this digital material and *why*. While the Internet is a wide-ranging social phenomenon, its uses are frequently reduced to email and the most basic of search engines. A socio-technical approach provides modes of thought and meaning for the challenges of digitalisation. Using this framework, the Internet can be considered as an interrelated system of power relationships, rather than as a politically neutral carrier of knowledge. Obviously, this politicised network provides a volatile setting for education.

TEACHING 102 OR, BRING ON THE BUNNY

Non-Australian readers may not be familiar with this abusive cricketing catchcry from the cheaper seats of famous sporting venues. When Australian bowlers have removed nearly all of the opposing team's batsmen, which they do with predictable regularity, and the number 11 player — the worst batsman of the opposing team — strides out to the crease, the crowd mantra 'Bring on the bunny' washes across the field. That is, here comes the most inept player that we will see today. Bowl him a bouncer, do him an injury and finish the innings.

Such a catchcry has profound resonance for teachers of large first-year courses. Invariably, the least experienced graduate students are selected to conduct first-year teaching, which is the most difficult and committed of educational tasks. Bringing on the bunny to conduct this pedagogically demanding role is a test by fire for the soon-to-be-scorched rabbits. I know this catcall well — I have been cooked medium rare a few times myself. This practice is common, not only in Australia and New Zealand, but in the United Kingdom, Canada and the United States. As Christopher Lucas reported:

> Ironically, graduate students who are the least experienced are most often assigned to teach the largest introductory-level courses, presumably on the theory that so-called entry-level courses demand the least pedagogical skill or expertise.[21]

The reason for this bizarre state of affairs is that, for most academics, research is the priority and the basis of intellectual culture. Dedication to teaching takes quality time away from archival searches and writing. Students rarely see male professors anymore. Most of my students think that universities are dominated by women. They simply cannot believe that there are more male academics than female. They never see them. While teaching is frequently invisible or demeaned by administrators and researchers, much of the financial viability of all these research institutions is built on the economic contribution of undergraduate teaching.

My first full-time teaching experience was as a bunny, teaching a large first-year course. Since that time, I have always taught first-year students, as a choice and privilege, not as a duty or sacrifice. It is hard work. Staff become a combination of mother, boss, disciplinarian, counsellor, friend and mentor. Working in the blast furnace of first-year university teaching means that I have lived through the daily changes to education in the last decade without hiding behind research grants, teaching buyouts or sabbaticals. As an intellectual on the feet — and a teacher on the move — I have transformed from a wide-eyed bunny staring at an oncoming cattle truck into a wise rabbit who knows the rules of the road. This section therefore charts some of the challenges to the education sector, which made the system vulnerable to an Internet-inflected productivity revolution.

Teaching has multiple meanings and conveys myriad applications. It can be only understood in precise contexts — in both space and time. Very often, teaching is evaluated through two dominant interpretations: a focus on what a teacher is doing, *the tasks conducted,* or a result-oriented approach, *what has been achieved.* Actually, teaching is an art and a craft, formulated to communicate, create and critique ideas and ideologies. Communication skills are integrated into the acquisition of all discipline-specific knowledges. Education therefore requires the application of a wide range of communicative technologies: not only threaded discussion groups or email, but aural, oral, verbal and bodily literacies must be deployed. Too many teachers are maligning these other modes of exchange in the rush to (once more) affirm the misguided notion that the medium is the message:

> Everything is going 'virtual' from traditional college classes to business training sessions over the telephone and the Internet! The 'old ways' of learning are quickly being replaced.

> Telecommunication technologies are fast becoming the 'main-stream' in the new age, and traditional educational institutions are presently straining to keep up! One result: we can learn virtually anything from the very source of the information![22]

Anything can be learned virtually, except non-verbal behaviour, tactile and olfactory communication and analogue modes of thinking. Also, emotional and affective skills and experiences are replaced by the inept execution of smiley faces. All these absences and inadequacies of digital communication mean that the bulk of strategies necessary to negotiate contemporary life cannot be learned from the Internet. Teachers need to encourage the use of multiple resources, recognising that knowledge and communication arch far beyond the Internet.

Teaching — in its best sense — does not focus on an end point. It is not a mechanical routine that involves ticking boxes of accomplishments or marking criteria, but aims to create a life of informed choices. It captures moments that cannot be enfolded in lesson plans. Frequently, students will surpass their learning outcomes and the curriculum directives. Teaching remains an act of interpretation, and the clarification of meaning. Invariably, teachers who attempt to teach too much content create students who learn too little.

If there is a systematic distinction between teachers in universities and those active in primary and secondary schools, it is the relationship between teaching and research. David Kember even suggested that 'Many university academics ... would be quite offended to be called a "teacher"'.[23] What is the role of research within teaching practice? Good teaching does not always stem from good research, and the inverse of that statement is also not inevitable. Lynnette Porter, in a narrow rendering of university routines, argued that 'research, not teaching or training, fosters innovation. Teaching and training typically are conformist activities and too often are repetitive'.[24] Her premise reduces education to content-based considerations. A Doctor of Philosophy, while a significant and worthwhile qualification, does not instruct its holder in pedagogy, assessment protocols or educational administration.[25] Innovation alone cannot be the basis of teaching. Precision and planning are more solid foundations for classroom praxis.

Teachers require systematic information about professional development, and a reflexive attitude towards social justice. Further, teachers must monitor and track their role. The teaching palette is so diverse that the complex function of educators can be forgotten because it is too difficult to mark and describe. In 1969, Morrison and McIntyre believed that particular personal characteristics distinguished the teachers they studied:

> With a fair degree of consistency, those choosing teaching as a career have been found to be more 'people oriented' in their values than most other occupational groups, placing emphasis on personal relationships ... Teachers tend to put correspondingly less value on what is seen as useful, efficient and economic.[26]

Obviously such characteristics lead to a clash of discourses between computer technologies — which sing for their supper through efficiency rhetoric — and the educators' desire for personal connection. That is why the vocational models of personal sacrifice still have credence in economically demoralised educational institutions. We teach, with poor resources, dodgy equipment and unpaid overtime, because we love our occupation. The system needs us to be so forgiving. There is some value in — even occasionally — forgetting our community service model. A focus on professionalism is strategically useful for teachers. It means that attention is placed on pay, social status, power, conditions and management. Teachers are rarely treated as professionals, being predominantly women, belonging to unions and with many members derived from the lower middle class. There is a lack of credibility saturating the field. There is also a bizarre notion that *anyone* can teach. Such a belief undermines the theory and practice of teaching, and the ruthless array of knowledges necessary to make a classroom work. The outcome of teaching — learning — is difficult to measure or grasp. Good teaching is an empowered fiction, an ideal that is almost impossible to define and even more difficult to create.

Professionalism is defined in opposition to the trades. There is a separation of mental and manual labour; theory versus practice. Such divisions serve to underestimate the theoretical and mathematical ability required in such 'trades' as plumbing and carpentry. This mode of demarcation is also found within the teaching field, with a discrediting of early-childhood education and a systematic valuation of calculus over business studies, literature over home economics.

Teachers make judgments about pedagogy, curriculum and interpersonal relationships; judgments that have lasting consequences. It is a self-regulated occupation, whereby teachers on a daily basis make assumptions that have a profound impact on students. The collegiate model of professionalism, emerging from medical practitioners and lawyers, controls the professional/client relationships. The patronage model of professionalism, where a client defines her or his needs and the occupation meets these needs, is found most clearly in accountancy. Teaching is located in the mediated professions, where administrators intervene in determining the needs of 'clients' and how their goals should be met. In this context, the 'professional' is stripped of much power. Other difficulties include a lack of certainty about the nature of a teacher's work, and the precise identity of the 'clients': students, parents, future employers, politicians, bureaucrats or the nation state? The result of this awkward positioning is that teachers are vulnerable and perform an increasing array of tasks in a politically unstable environment.

University academics tend to treat their time in the classroom in a scattergun fashion, a hope-for-the-best kind of affair. With great honesty and clarity, Stephen Brookfield realised that 'my teaching was not necessarily bad or harmful, but it was problematic. By that, I mean that it was shot through with unacknowledged agendas, unpredictable consequences, and unrealized dimensions'.[27] We have all seen lecturers walk into rooms with a few headings pencilled on the back of an envelope. We have all seen lecturers spend three quarters of the lecture trying to get their PowerPoint slides and projector to work. Teachers in primary and high schools do not have this level of luxury. Further, this inexperience, confusion or laziness serves to insult the knowledge system being taught and disrespects the intellectual journey of students.

Teaching is an exercise in qualitative judgment to attain qualitative goals.[28] That is why reflexive teaching is more than an easy cliché of teachers' training colleges. It provides a way to monitor and theorise experiences, to make sense of the educational environment. It is not a process of natural reflection, but actually subverts the taken-for-granted convergence between doing and thinking. Reconstructive reflection is particularly useful for young and isolated teachers. This process takes an event or moment from the teaching day and grants it thought, meaning and context. It reconsiders the hidden assumptions of the classroom, while stitching knowledge into an educational environment. It is a way to reorganise and reconstruct past experiences, ideas and events. When theory and practice are aligned in this way, it creates understandings of a particular class-room, tutorial or web-based discussion forum.

Teaching has an intensely personal component, necessitating deep exploration and application of lived experience. A search for a teaching style requires a hunt through a personal morass of half-remembered lectures, mentoring advice and dark disappointment. Joe Heimlich and Emmalou Norland expressed this journey clearly: 'teaching style comes from "who I am" and therefore must grow from "all I've been" toward "all I could ever be"'.[29] Through self-disclosures, a teacher becomes responsible for knowledge.

My first full-time lecturing experience was as stressful as it could possibly be. I was four years older than most students seated in the hall, and resident in a foreign country. Because it was a short-term appointment to fill in for a lecturer who had attained a year-long research fellowship, there was no funding provided for my teaching materials, or even moving my scattered belongings across a continent. Other staff were not interested in the young blonde woman down the corridor. All they needed was a warm body to 'babysit' the first-years for the short term. I was without family or friends and was 'economically challenged', as my first pay arrived three months late. It was the bland, blind indifference of most experienced staff towards my younger self that shocks me now. I have made it my goal ever since to instruct the young post-graduates in my care with the most overt, precise and honest teacher training that I can give them. I do not want them to be in the same position.

I made a decision after having read David Tripp's *Critical incidents in teaching*[30] that I would not give in to the mediocrity and indifference surrounding me. After describing a demoralising situation confronting a young woman, Tripp stated that 'a diag-nostic understanding would have enabled this teacher to learn from the professional practice and thereby increase her control over it'.[31] I took him at his word. After every teaching and learning experience, I inscribed and transposed the process. What started as an instrumental activity, stressing the *what* and *who*, very quickly developed into a reflexive explosion of the *how* and *why*. Although away from formal educational and teaching instruction, I con-nected theory and practice, knowledge and education. I have a profound memory of no longer being alone in a strange place, but being able to connect my teaching work with this new context. Errors and failures were not end points, but the start of a journalled journey through better practice.[32] My improvement was rapid and my confidence increased. For any young teacher, disrespected or dismissed by the system, I recommend the purchase of an A4 spiral notebook. If the system will not support teacher education, then create a new way of thinking between cream-coloured pages.

To this day, I write to think. At times of crushing and systematic denunciation of education, I mobilise the diagnostic approach, not to knock the institution, but to integrate teaching on my feet with thinking through the pen.

Teaching is indeterminate. Through critical reflection, education can be rendered more formalised and coherent in its applications. Such considered, reflective writing creates a breadcrumbed trail of how wisdom is made. The panic and fear of student teachers can be transformed from questions of discipline and control into an emancipatory intent. The 'what' of teaching crystallises into the 'why' of education.

While teaching clings to a tenuous professionalism, the attitude remains of teaching being a calling or vocation. This notion becomes a way to justify ridiculous staff workloads, and also to validate staff working against their best interests. Teachers expend inordinate effort constructing educational websites that remain a long-term burden. Further, once educators leave the school or university, they lose control of their intellectual property — as they were *paid* to construct these websites (even if the time was volunteered or in excess of their standard duties). That means that their course can be taught years after they leave the institution. These courses feature the words and ideas of teachers, but are not owned by the writer. Such business practices allow educational managers to employ less staff and run institutions more profitably and economically. While universities and schools do not exist for teachers, as a workplace they need to create joy, pleasure and satisfaction, or else staff will leave. Those who remain may disrespect their purpose, creating confusion for students.

Education is not only an economic system competing for consumers. Every citizen is involved in teaching. For communities and societies to exist, knowledge, skills and experiences are circulated, reinforced, discussed and learned. While some citizens are formally trained to be employed as teachers, this is a historically inadequate definition. Knowledge of content does not determine an effective teacher. The best teachers are the best communicators, and the most effective communication requires a concise judgment of context. Teachers, like learners, move between roles, languages and understandings. Experienced educators are able to quarry the disagreements, surprises and disturbing interludes to create new and more advanced modes of learning. But such intellectual swiftness takes time to develop. The teacher teaches him/herself on the feet, and every day. The problems to overcome — crowded classrooms, overstuffed curricula, and too little time to teach too much content — are rarely addressed. Instead, there is a naïve focus on literacy standards, without a sense of history or place. Learning involves a choice, and that choice is dependent on motivation. While teachers can focus effort and energy on creating the best quality materials and a riveting, exciting learning environment, very often the educational decisions are out of their hands. Teaching is not about providing all the answers, but assuming responsibility within conservative management structures. The next section of this chapter will investigate the choices open to students and teachers, particularly through the online environment.

POLITICS 103 OR, IF THIS COMPUTER WAS A HORSE I'D SHOOT IT

The facts of online education are only now being revealed. Few techno-crusaders will admit the scale of failure within digital cyber-classes. For example, Columbia University spent more than US$25 million building a suite of online courses. Unfortunately, it discovered that prospective students were not prepared to pay for the privilege of access. Now, these courses are offered free, as part of Fathom.com, providing 'samples' for 'customers'. Katie Hafner described this as:

> the Morning After phenomenon. In the last few years, prestigious universities rushed to start profit-seeking spinoffs, independent divisions that were going to develop online courses ... Now the grooves of academe are littered with the detritus of failed e-learning start-ups as those same universities struggle with the question of how to embrace online education but not haemorrhage money in the process.[33]

Ponder the amount of money spent by university administrators and technicians to enter digital education. Ponder the waste of talent and time. In 2000, US$483 million was spent on companies building online materials for the educational market. By 2002, this figure was reduced to US$17 million. E-learning has failed through the desire to make money — and quickly. New York University closed NYUonline, its Internet-based learning operation, in 2002. This was after the host university pumped US$25 million into the offerings — courses that only attracted 500 students at its height.[34] The University of Maryland College ceased its online, profit-making courses and wove them back into the conventional curricula. Temple University closed its Virtual Temple at the end of 2001. Through these closures, the point that has not been recognised is that education is *not* a business. Students are *not* consumers. Attaining a degree is not like shopping online. Our students have revealed the farcical misunderstanding by administrators of the university experience. Bulletin boards were built: the customers did not enter them. There has been a confusion of technology with education, and tools with learning. Also, a system that was originally meant to save money through the decline of expensive academic hours has actually cost much more. Professor Tim O'Shea, master of Birkbeck College in London and a major force behind the Blair government's dream of an e-university, has presented his 'supposition ... that you can use information communications technology to improve higher education. I am confident of that — and that it's going to cost us more'.[35] In such statements, there is no discussion of why students choose to complete further learning, or the many reasons why people come together collectively — and physically — to share thoughts, ideas and ideals. The knowledge economy is not one of many standardised arms of the late capitalist body. Students do not behave like shoppers or tourists. Many experts have made much money in selling their wares to the highest bidder, promising cyber-dollars and a smaller teaching staff. The 'best' — or most desirable — education is still based in the Oxbridge system of personal tutors and intense immersion in an intellectually transforming context. Obviously, most students can neither afford nor gain entry to such an establishment. But is the only option to remove their educational experience from the campus? As Janet McCalman has argued, online learners are 'the new tertiary-education proletariat'.[36] Like the horse in *Animal Farm*, they tirelessly work at their courses without the laughter over coffee, the team sports, risk-taking and tutorial arguments that we remember as the most significant part of an education. The cyber-proles assume that universities are simply about completing assignments, courses and modules. They do not have the opportunity to discover another experience, another way of learning and being.

Controversies over teaching and learning are not unique to computer-based education. The special issues of the digital environment show the continuities between non-Internet-based, and Internet-embedded education. But there are distinctions. Although unfashionable to admit, computer technologies operate at their best when handling concrete ideas. They are inappropriate to grasp the abstract, the philosophical and the qualitative. With the nuances of face-to-face communication absent, the immediacy of dialogue and conversation is lost from email. In pondering the rush to the web, teachers need to ask how we have mobilised the other technologies — and the other senses — throughout our careers. Scent and sound, for example, are underplayed cards in the teacher's deck. All the senses and experiences are important, and create conscious scholars.

The primary goal of my teaching is to formulate learning communities, a group of students/citizens who are reflexive about their context, ask difficult questions of themselves and others, and actively care about their region. Intriguingly, many other educators mobilise a similar imperative. James O'Donnell reported that:

> The approach I favor to teaching critical reception of the past might best be called 'teaching the surprises' … So my teaching strategy starts students where they think they are comfortable and then seeks to disorient and defamilarise them so that they actually look at what they are studying. For a teacher who thinks such moments of epiphany vital to education, such a moment is a godsend.[37]

Teaching well is difficult and ruthlessly corrosive of innovation. When teaching, there is nowhere to hide or deflect from view. It is a raw, sweaty, concentrated reality. This work is so rewarding because of the diverse students attending our schools and universities. It is complex to teach students from these different backgrounds, because there are no singular narratives, truths and curricula that can encompass all their histories. My strategy is to use highly integrated mixed media, encasing video, print and audio-based texts, alongside scents and textures. From this basis, a myriad of literacies is hailed. ESL

(English as a Second Language) students gain confidence through print-based triggers. Film and televisual knowledges assist visual learners, and aural texts, such as recorded speeches and popular music, serve to slow the lecture forum and enlarge the affective experiences and public applicability of education. This diversity of media hails a diversity of students. The Internet cannot stand alone as a single mode of delivery in teaching.

While working with plural educational paths, I am disciplined, precise and controlling in the classroom. To many educators, my practices seem draconian. I do not tape lectures, nor do I place my notes on the web or in the library. There is no free access to material through online learning. I have strict deadlines, removing 5 per cent a day for lateness, including weekends. Students obviously try to test the limits of our resolve. Ponder these messages — all sent during one weekend — from a student wanting an extension, and using email to ask for it:

From: ******
To: tbrabazo@central.murdoch.edu.au
Date: Sat, 22 Sep 16:11:43 +0800
X-OriginalArrivalTime: 22 Sep 08:11:44.0053 (UTC) FILE-TIME=[3774F650:01C1433E]

hi Tara

I need an extension?! i'm sorry to ask for it so late; i have just realized that i wont be able to do my "hat trick" and hand in the two assignments dues next week...i've got i right up the ass this time! please let me know what my options are...
be well,

From: ******
To: tbrabazo@central.murdoch.edu.au
Subject: Re: Extension
Date: Mon, 24 Sep 00:22:56 +0800
X-OrignalArrivalTime: 23 Sep 16:22:57.0119 (UTC) FILE-TIME=[012FAEFO:01C1444C]

Hi Tara,

in the eventuality that you did not receive my firs e-mail requesting an extension for the readership expercises i beg you to e-mail me the options that i have left!? i might have miss written your e-mail address ... i shall most probably see you tomorrow.
till then, be well.,

One minute later, the same message was re-sent, either inadvertently or deliberately. This student had obviously assumed that I had Internet access at home and was prepared to handle student queries at 4 pm on a Saturday, and at 12:22 *and* 12:23 on a Monday morning. He became concerned that I did not reply. He *must* have typed the address incorrectly because *everyone* must respond to emails as they arrive ... Obviously, I received all three on Monday morning. I informed him that 5 per cent a day would be removed, as he had had six weeks to complete the allotted assignments. Surprisingly, or perhaps not, he submitted the paper on time.

Besides enforcing deadlines, I also demand attendance and punctuality. If students miss two or more tutorials, I remove a full 10 per cent from their grade. This is the framework in which I teach. I do not make education easy or palatable, and there is a reason for my stroppy structures. My aim is to provide a context in which a learning community is formed. Such a connection and affiliation is powerful and important. Ponder this message, directly responding to this lecturing context:

X-Originating-IP: (144.138.95.132)
From: ******
To: tbrabazo@central.murdoch.edu.au
Subject: Hi Tara
Date: Tue, 18 Sep 19:38:07 +0800
X-OriginalArrivalTime: 18 Sep 11:38:07.0266 (UTS) FILE-TIME=[62C65020:01C14036]

Tara mate

You don't know me, but I do study cultural studies. (And no, i'm not a stalker!). I just thought i'd tell you that I really liked your lecture on monday, and I expecially respected the way you naturally included gay guys when you talked about the group infront of you, as you might guess i'm gay, and that's the first time anyone's ever really acknowledge my presense in a non-derogatory was as been part of a 'team' as you like to say, I actually felt a little 'normal' in that lecture thearte. You know some times even the tutes feel a little implicitly homophobic, and awkward when, you know the topic might be what guys think is attractive in females, and i'm thinking hey what are you looking at me for, but i'm not yet (yet!) the kind of person who can just pronouce to the tute that kind of thing. Anyway i'm mumbling on a bit, but anyway i'm sure you see i'm saying thanks and it would be great to get to know you a bit, but i'm sure you get that all the time.

Seeya Captain

The significance — personally and socially — of such inclusiveness should not be underestimated. Negotitating with cultural differeces is the most demanding and exciting task in education. The diversity of students in terms of age, sexuality, class, race and nationality makes teaching volatile, troubling, but vitally important. A community of self-aware citizens will not be formed if students stay in bed or miss lectures and tutorials. Therefore, I am rigid in demanding attendance, while promising them lively and evocative sessions. They know that I will not waste their time: if they give me an hour of their life each week, they will think differently at the end of each session. In return, I ask that they demonstrate commitment, which they confirm through the discipline of attendance. Through such a process, students display not only respect for me — probably the least significant achievement — but also for fellow students and the powerful material and topics we investigate. Year after year, students reward themselves through the building of scholarly communities, created through a belief in knowledge, and a belief in each other. What starts with my strict framework finishes a semester later with their intellectual rigour, awareness and consciousness. The scholarly journey presents a bill to travellers — of discipline and responsibility — but like the best of investments, it reaps an enormous dividend. The dedication and focus of teaching staff in this intense environment is paramount.

While most teachers spend energy and attention in the development of an educational setting of commitment, challenge and care, money is being spent on computer-mediated education. Without a space for thought, the assumptions — both stated and hidden — of online education are ignored. Whenever instigating education policies or applications, it is wise to be cautious. We are dealing with the intellectual future of too many men and women to rush towards technological imperatives without caution. Universities become like a McDonald's drive-through: pick up your degree, and do you want fries with that?

The online environment has been corn-fed on marketing imperatives and managerialism. Theories of viable and useful knowledge are being stretched and questioned through online educational imperatives. While the sending and receiving of emails is rapid, the transformation of ideas into action, or data into wisdom, is not as swift. Consideration is needed of the distinct world views of senders and receivers. It is not only a question of content, facts and data.

In 1999, I received an email that addressed me as 'Dear Content Provider'. While my initial response was confusion (is this a misdirected email?), my next rejoinder was to laugh. Of all the mainframes in all the terminals in the world, this message had to walk into mine. However, as the weeks progressed, I became very angry. To be addressed as a content provider is to confirm that the many roles for contemporary teachers are being undermined and displaced through the pressures of online education.

I wanted to scream at the screen. I wanted to write one of those nasty emails that we all regret writing but feel profoundly satisfied about when we click the SEND button. What would I say in this diatribe? I am not a content provider; I am a caring teacher who attempts to dialogue with both students and society with the aim of assembling an informed citizenship. Content provision does not begin to articulate my current life, employment or responsibilities. I did not send that email. I am still on their circular, receiving messages with the title 'Dear Content Provider'.

If thinking and teaching have been reduced to questions of content and downloaded data, then how are students to be heard, taught and empowered? The most horrifying story I have discovered through my research on Internet pedagogy was relayed by James Shiveley and Philip Van Fossen. An excited teacher, having just had his classroom wired for the net, tried to integrate it into his work:

> Eager to take advantage of the new opportunity, Thomas asked his students to write their papers on their current unit of study — the Holocaust — that relied on the Internet as the primary source of information. When grading the papers, Thomas's reaction ranged from pleased to disappointed to shocked. The pleased and disappointed he was used to, the shocked he was not. One third of the papers Thomas received presented the Holocaust as a hoax.[38]

Clearly, teachers are much more than content providers. They are arbiters of ideologies, weaving a critical approach to the world and a network of realities. This Holocaust story could be used as the fodder to develop students' analytical skills. However, the time involved in this type of project is simply beyond the reach of most teachers.

It is framed as a great strength of the new online environment that educators work with a team of technicians. As Lynnette Porter dreamingly related, 'now you need to work as part of a team consisting of technicians, who will help set up, maintain, and update the site'.[39] Hollow laughter emerges from such statements. Most of the time, educators are left maintaining an entire system, without acknowledgment of the workload consequences, or institutional and technical support. Having spent my professional life avoiding crisis-prone teaching experiences, more stress has emerged from five years of online teaching than from managing and negotiating hundreds of on-campus students every week. This tension is caused because teachers do not have authority over the delivery process. We assume the responsibility for learning and access, but because of technical 'glitches' beyond our control we are responsible for errors and inefficiencies. Teachers face the students with apologies: technicians can hide behind placating emails.

Through all my ambivalence and concern, online education is surprising. The asynchronous learning network, or discussion forum, is an extraordinarily useful site. However, it is clear that already empowered, confident and bright students — that is, the least in need of teacherly assistance — are the most active participants. Phillip Cartwright was correct:[40] technology is not an antidote for under-prepared university students. It is those who are already enthusiastic, committed and focused who most use the forum. Here are a few samples from the over 400 messages left for one semester's work in H267/H477 Cultural Difference and Diversity's online discussion. I asked students to ponder the process of online study and commentary, and how it could be improved:

Message No. 414
Posted by Tara Brabazon (H267) on Wed, May 23, 12:31
Subject: Pondering the Possible

Greetings Team –

As Leanne is putting the final Xer questions out there, I have something I would like my cybercdders to ponder.
    Just to help me think about the process, I've established this heading so that people can present their point of view about CDD and its relationship with this site.

- Was it worthwhile? * Did it help you? * How did you find the mixing of internal and external students? * What did you get from the web site that the internal or external versions of the course did not provide for you? *

What worked – what didn't?

And all the lurkers who are out there – feel free to leave a
message about the lurking experience …
Just tell me about your semester in and out of the site.
Even a short message will do. It will help me make things
better in the future.

Be well – and thanks for a blast of a time! T.

The responses to this message were fascinating, demonstrating the
breadth of engagement and commitment in the course generally —
and contributing to the collective building of knowledge. The dream
reply for all teachers also arrived in a commentary on the site. The
personal discomfort and uncertainty — which is necessary for any
learning experience — was reflexively recognised by one student, who
appreciated the scale of the intellectual journey:

Message No. 421: (Branch from no. 414)
posted by ****** on Thu, May. 24, 11:24
Subject: Pondering the Possible

i thought the best thing about this discussion list was that people
really played around with the big concepts, and probably had more
time to ponder contributions than in tutes. i am one of those
greedy lurkers, but i really gained a lot from reading how other
people were understanding some of the big issues. Having different input from Leanne and Kylie was very helpful too. i accessed
this site nearly every day, and i'm going to miss it!

on the whole, this unit has at times been very disruptive to virtually my whole life, i have been forced to question myself and my
assumptions and common sense notions about identity etc, more
times than it is reasonable in one semester. i love those units
where you feel a little bit unstable at the end, and its also very
good (very frustrating) when you come out of a unit with many
more questions than answers. in the words of some ancient guy
long passed on, (paraphrase actually) the only thing i know now is
that i know nothing. this is a good thing.

The notion that a university course has been 'very disruptive to
virtually my whole life' may seem like a damning indictment of my
teaching; but to study war, genocide, racism and revolution should
not be a comfortable experience. The instability this student felt at
the end of the course is not only the trigger for further study,

learning and development, but a new way of thinking about the world. Certainly, this is a productive and powerful way to spend a semester.

Remarkably, all the on-campus students who contributed to the online site attained — without exception — distinctions or higher in the course. Correspondence students were also active and did well. Ironically, online students were far less involved in the web-based offerings. That is, the very people who could best gain from the assistance of staff did not use the site. It was those who were on-campus, who were already present for lectures, workshops, tutorials and consultancy appointments, who gained another node of learning. Anthony Smith and Frank Webster described the reasoning for this odd result: 'technologies are more often supplements than substitutes'.[41] To argue that the Internet is an effective mechanism to alleviate the isolation of online education is not addressing accessibility issues. Unfortunately, the funding imperative is online learning. It is assumed that distance education will be absorbed by the Internet. I have found the opposite to be true. While very few students enrol online, the number of correspondence students is increasing. It is important to remember that all learners, but particularly adults, require a variety of learning styles.[42] For students, the ideal teaching environment includes as many nodes of nurturing, reinforcement, discussion and reflection as possible.

The major imperative of my online teaching career is an affirmation that different modes of teaching should utilise distinct methods and assessment protocols. It is important that there are substantial differences between on-campus, distance and online versions of the same course. I have had major problems arguing this case with technical staff. The following email question was raised by my web designer to a net 'expert':

QUESTION Is it possible to restrict access to files in the 'external/study_g' folder to those with enrolment type 'E'[external or correspondence students], and restrict access to the 'online/study_g' folder to those with enrolment type 'O' [online students] at their initial login?

ANSWER They could let other people use their Login IDs, too. How will you stop that. Let's reflect on your assumptions here. What are the reasons for giving different access to different types of users? Is the assessment radically different for each? Does it matter which way the students learn, as long as they **do** learn? Why not provide flexibility to the student? So what if they don't go to lectures. If Tara isn't able to lure them in with the quality of her presentation skills :) then students must have good reasons not to attend. The bottom line is that students learn and engage with the material. Having said all that, I haven't seen your material, so maybe I am pissing in the wind.

Obviously this email is not a strong example of technicians assisting academic staff. I never thought that a colleague would state: 'so what if they don't go to lectures?'. Motherhood statements (Does it matter what way the students learn, as long as they *do* learn?) are politically naïve and educationally retrograde. The notion that some students require discipline and structure — that granting them a chance to not be present at lectures and tutorials might actually hurt their intellectual development — has obviously not entered the 'flexible' mind of this educational administrator.

There are problems in education. There are difficulties confronting teachers on a daily basis. One of these difficulties is how to unravel the belief that the Internet and computer-mediated communication will invariably improve the quality of education. Those who teach real students with valid fears, tears, hopes and desires, rather than imagined digi-scholars, know that nothing can replace the affirming nod, pithy statement or deep commitment that teachers have for those in our care. Anything that decentres teachers from their work in creating better scientists, politicians, social workers, lawyers, philosophers and journalists must be treated with suspicion. The next chapter continues this war of position, entering the ideological wasteland of literacy, generic skills and educational administration.

PART II

SURFING, READING AND THINKING

3

BONFIRE OF THE LITERACIES: :), :(, AND LITERACY IN THE INFORMATION AGE

And so we sit, remote control in hand, a fifty-channel
spectrum to graze, shelves full of videotapes, AM and FM, CD
player, tape deck, phonograph, telephone, FAX machine, waiting for virtual reality, searching for something to remember,
nothing particular to forget.[1]

David Marc

Mnemosyne, the Goddess of Memory and mother of the muses, would weep at the disrespect granted to history in the information age. Such a denial of the past results in literacy issues being discussed in isolation, without recognition of the compromises, threats and decline in funding for the humanities specifically, and the education system more generally. The politicking by 'interest groups' such as politicians, parents or publishers creates scare campaigns over literacy to avoid publicity about other, less popular issues. We need attention focused on the way information is created, stored, accessed, applied and circulated through a culture. For most of its (elitist) history, the humanities-based liberal arts degree was the basis of citizenship, sum-moning a space for critical thinking about significant issues such as truth, democracy, politics, faith and justice. That these ideas and attributes are now framed as non-vocational and generalist, and diffi-cult to tick and measure on a work-based generic skill sheet, is a chill-ing indictment of our time and place. Schools and universities have a responsibility to teach more than what is 'useful' in the short term.

Most weeks, the press is peppered with a desire to return to the 'basics', to stress 'a more balanced curriculum outcome'.[2] Instead of addressing workplace changes or economic shifts, literacy is a code-word to abuse teachers and teaching. After all, word processing and database dexterities are easier skills to attain than attacking the inequalities of the capitalist system. Even acknowledging the (much) smaller issue of computer-based competence, we often forget the hard work — in curriculum development, process drills and professional application — that guides a learner through computer literacy skills. Such development must be contextually sensitive, with the education and library system highly developed, well funded and consciously updated. We all make assumptions about universal reading and writing, most days of our lives. Mark Stefik demonstrates the consequences when inequalities, poverty and hardship are individualised or ignored:

> Literacy is so ubiquitous in the modern world that we look at it without noticing it. Literate people often assume that almost everyone in the world is literate; when they learn otherwise, they do not understand why people lack literacy.[3]

The difficulty with the political catchphrases encircling literacy is that they are empty vessels, filled to the brim with the spin doctoring of pseudo-sages. Debates — about reading, writing, the school, the university, the workplace, the family, popular culture, the digital media and popular memory — all feed into literacy like the slow, disturbing echo of an intravenous drip out of a society's mind and consciousness.

By monitoring literacy with caution and care, a trace is revealed of wider political struggles. Conservative agendas desire a return to the 'basics', while leftist progressives affirm a whole language approach that recognises student-centred learning.[4] Both models have been shaken through the 'revolutions' of Internet-based learning, teaching and research. This chapter does not trail behind this angry fight over reading, writing and arithmetic, but targets a more specific goal: to excavate how literacy is reshaped through the Internet. We commence with a systematic study of why literacy is a political pressure point, followed by an evaluation of the differences between information, knowledge and wisdom. The third section monitors the building of Internet literacy, which is then tethered to Internet-based learning. I show how text-based literacies move between paper and screen.

3 Rs AND A BIG L

We all too frequently accept what we read, and doubt what we hear. The relationship between orality and literacy is politically heated. The binaries of ear and eye, simple and advanced, the emotional versus the rational, serve to create a narrow band of acceptable writing. To stress the written world prioritises sight over the other senses, of sound, touch, taste and smell. For Albert Borgmann, literacy is 'the force that invades and transforms an oral culture'.[5] But I raise another premise: what if *all* senses are considered in terms of literacy? Such an undertaking reclaims non-verbal communication. All discussions of literacy — and evaluations of literacy instruction — must be enmeshed into the experiences and context of the learner.[6] Reading and writing are not confluent: they should be discussed separately.

Good writing, rapid reading and deep comprehension are still valued and validated attributes in the current workplace. For example, Christopher Lucas reported that a 1985 national assessment of literacy levels among 21- to 25-year-olds:

> found that roughly half of the young adults surveyed who had graduated from college with bachelor's degrees could not perform such tasks as summarizing the content of a newspaper article, calculating a ten percent tip for lunch or interpreting a bus schedule.[7]

I understand the desire to stress these skills. Discovering such deficiencies is aggravating, but displays no awareness of the intricate processes involved in attaining these abilities. It is difficult to teach students to read. It is a taxing duty to remind scholars that good writing is not an elective component of a university degree. Sparkling writing is a gift. Sloppy prose, poor referencing and incomprehensible paragraph construction crumble the best ideas off the page.

One of my most remarkable teaching stories concerns a young man who arrived in my first-year course in cultural studies during the late 1990s. He was fresh from a country school in the northwest of Western Australia, a landscape dominated by open cut mines, red dust and beer kegs that never empty. On his arrival in Perth, the capital of this bulging, diverse and sprawling state, he was placed in one of my tutorials. After the submission of the first assignment, I knew we were in trouble. English language proficiency was lacking, he had never heard of referencing, and his research consisted of restating my lecture overheads. After the return of the assignment, we scheduled weekly meetings — and daily in the week approaching submission of the second assignment. I started at the beginning of the writing process: this is a sentence, a phrase, a noun and a verb. I taught him how to spell and widen his vocabulary, then moved to paragraphing and the development of an argument. These sessions gradually built a (relatively) smooth-flowing essay by the end of the semester. After the disastrous first paper, and his much-improved further efforts, he just scraped into a pass mark — 51 per cent. He was disappointed after all his work that his mark did not reflect his efforts. I told him to keep going. In my second-year course, we continued this individual attention, moving to research skills and analytical writing. He became more confident and thoughtful in tutorials, and started to recognise the inconsistencies in his own prose and arguments. He gained a solid credit in this difficult upper-level course. By his final year at the university, he was out of my direct care, but sent me emails and enthusiastically greeted me in the corridor when we saw each other. At the end of his final year, I was walking home to my house, and he shrieked my name. I turned around on the medium strip separating the university from suburbia. This young man bolted across three lanes of traffic and lifted me into the air. The reason for his happiness? In his final semester at university, he had received three consecutive distinctions. I still cry when I tell this story. But it is a tale of persistence and belief that the quality of writing and reading matters. Words on the page have an honesty and integrity that cannot be assessed through multiple-choice tests or timed Internet quizzes. The inked page may be silent, but the energy, enthusiasm and passion that orders those words is a product of a dialogue and dance between student and teacher.

This story reminds me every day why universities are important, and why teachers — although exhausted, overworked and underpaid — need to step up to the intellectual plate and help to transform the lives of our students.

Writing forges relationships between writers and readers, and time and space. The physical and emotional world is squeezed into the overstuffed luggage of language. Cyberspace becomes a writing space — one of many. A truth that has been forgotten through attention to digital literacies, searchable databases and generic competencies is that we learn to write and read by doing it. There is no substitute for daily composition and comprehension. If life offers a lesson, it is that the more time we spend mastering a task, the better we become at it. As a generation of students bullet-point their way through a degree structure, there will be no grasp of the small but significant art of building a finely balanced, memorable sentence. In our textbook culture, chapters are concluded with questions to recall, rather than attack or question. There is little time for revelling in the wash of words, or reading the intricate embrace between style and meaning, ink and eye. The best of books and the best of reading connect word and body, shaking our truths and agitating our irises to trigger a tremulous, affective connection with another world, and another mind.

Language and ideology are locked into a dialectic rumba between literacy and knowledge. All discussions of language require attention to power structures, as dominant groups maintain authority by shifting attention away from anything political, debatable or contestable. Placing time and energy on an Ikea catalogue blocks consciousness of the capitalist ideologies that frame its pages. It is not in the interests of dominant groups to have the working class ask why they are systematically excluded from the spheres of power. Such difficult questions may trigger societal change. Different classes, genders and races speak and write from distinct cultural positions. When individual language users share a social background, much commonality also exists in language use.[8] Theories of literacy are always situated within context and history.

The social function of education is to credential a student for the workforce, but also to maintain the privilege and knowing practices of the dominant. The knowledge taught at schools and universities legitimises for each generation the justifications of those who hold power. The practice of incorporating some subjects, disciplines and ideas while dismissing others as irrelevant or meaningless teaches consensus and commonsense, rather than critical thinking and interpretation. If students use the preferred language of the empowered group, they are rewarded with high marks, university entrance, degrees, awards and a solid job that allows them to serve the system in which they are subjugated.[9] Those who do not use the appropriate modes of writing or do not appreciate this credentialed knowledge have other labels attached to their behaviour, like delinquent, deviant, defiant or even suspended.

Language is not a neutral carrier of meaning. There are competing histories of English, as there are with all languages. A socially-just literacy standard offers more than access to education. We must monitor what is being distributed, and in what context. RW Connell has argued that there should be no arbitrary division of education and social justice, stating that 'it is easier to believe in this separation if you are yourself well-paid and well-educated'.[10] Teaching is therefore not 'about' having good intentions, wearing a well-pressed suit with matching briefcase, or complying with the directives of the Head of Subject or a parent's ambitions. To be a professional teacher is to be reflexive, critical and thoughtful about how knowledge is being taught, used and distributed. We cannot — and must not — avoid or displace a discussion of literacy education.

There remains a caveat to this contract, and a significant one. If teachers do not teach the Master's Discourse, including the knowledge and language of power structures, then those students who are becoming, through education, bilingual in class terms will be denied the chance of mobility. Those from disempowered backgrounds need — perhaps even more than those from advantaged families — the language that can grant them choices, alternatives and options. Literacy theory at its best empowers students to explore, question, critique and gain knowledge. Growing out of the functionalist perspective — where literacy describes a competency in a specific vocabulary and grammar — a critical literacy assembles an evaluative, interpretative matrix around texts. Understanding the content of a book in not enough: questioning why it was written is the intellectual goal. Such a practice is more than restating the poststructuralist mantra — language is socially constructed — but reveals the assumptions of power, value and judgment that saturate our words and world. For disempowered groups, critical literacy conveys to students not only empowered languages and ideas, but an embedded theory to subvert them. The point of education is to create change in students, not to reinforce and replay the truths of their family, friends or a Playstation 2 game of choice.

Indigenous groups in particular have stressed the importance of being taught literacy and mobilising 'traditional' standards. Marti Nakata, for example, reported that:

> Our needs are currently at risk from those who argue that the teaching of English undermines traditional language and culture, without understanding how that has developed in the recent past. The belief that English has relevance only for those Islanders who wish to pursue a life outside the [Torres] Straits or for those in the sector of the marketplace that requires a higher education is quite wrong.[11]

The point is clearly made. To 'protect' traditional languages, the cost must not be the cultural future. Such an argument can be made for many disempowered groups, whether the inequality is based on race, class, gender, sexuality or age. It is a form of meta-racism, meta-classism, meta-sexism and meta-ageism if standards are 'dropped' or students are not instructed in the empowered languages that will grant them movement into the corridors of power. There are obviously unequal outcomes from education. If a student lives in the right suburb, is white, male and fluent in the national language, then success will be easier. This acknowledgment does not mean that working-class students or citizens of colour inevitably read and write with reduced ability or capacity. Class- and race-based prejudices are ground into the fabric of education and the textures of curriculum.

In an environment of vocational training, effective reading and powerful writing require more attention. To read and write well is time-consuming, arduous and requires disciplined, daily practice. Like all 'skills', if (too much) time is spent on other pursuits in the overcrowded curriculum, then students will simply not have the expertise in thinking, reading, planning, writing and drafting. I have taught thousands of students who — after twelve years of high school education — arrive at university unable to construct a sentence, comprehend a question or draft their own work. With care and consideration from teachers, they gain this empowered intellectual capacity. It is time-consuming and difficult, but students appreciate the effort. When teachers demand more, students will raise their expectations. For example, I received this review of my first-year course, H102 Introduction to Cultural Studies:

> Please comment on what you thought were the best aspects of this unit.
>
> Most definately the lecturer, Tara Brabazon. She is the most driven and involved lecturer I have ever had and I wish more lecturers were like her. She was also my tutor and the tutorials were great. Most people really got involved so it was a joy to come to the tutorials. She expects a high standard of work and I believe I have handed in work of a higher standard because of that.

The overwhelming majority of my colleagues have similar testimony to cite. I am not unusual. Teaching standards have not dropped. But — and this is a significant caveat — students must be taught how to read, how to take notes, how to conduct research, how to plan their ideas, how to write well and how to draft. This knowledge cannot be assumed at university level. If we take the time, students appreciate this effort:

> Please comment on what you thought were the best aspects of this unit.
>
> Tara Brabazon's zest and ability to relate to her students well — and despite being a strict marker — which was also excellent coz she impelled us to improve ourselves.

While some students thrive and improve in this environment, others find any critique or questioning of their abilities improper, threatening, or even 'spiteful':

From:
To: "Tara Brabazon" <t.brabazon@murdoch.edu.au>
Subject: Final essay
Date: Sun, 30 June

Dear Tara,
I collected my final essay for Cultural Difference and Diversity on Friday June 28th, and have spent much of the weekend alternating between anger and indignation. My essay was not assesseed; it was given a spitefilled, frenzied attack! I have no idea who ****** is, but the thought of her also assessing my take-home exam is very, very worrying. Had the comments ****** made been true or fair, I would have simply accepted them, but many of them are so

ludicrous as to be unbelievable. I need to take this matter up with someone who can give me a proper assessment of my essay.

This has been a very upsetting conclusion to what was otherwise a most enjoyable unit.

Such an email was a very upsetting start to an otherwise unremarkable Monday morning. As is proper in these cases, I examined the paper and its assessment protocols with some interest, trying to observe the nature and origin of this 'spitefilled attack'. It will come as no surprise to the teachers reading my words, but the marking process conducted by the tutor was reflexive, careful and helpful. Reading the student's script, I observed that it was peppered with spelling errors, referencing flaws, incorrect interpretations of theoretical models and a poorly structured argument. The tutor (rightly) marked all these flaws, alongside acknowledgment of the work completed well. In my re-examination, I found exactly the same errors — and more. What I am yet to understand is how noting spelling, referencing and interpretative mistakes is seen by this student as 'ludicrous'. That is our job as assessors of written work. In this case, the allotted mark has created a spiral of anger inflected outward to staff, rather than inward, to trigger retrospection and learning. No one wins in this situation: the writer assumes that she has been persecuted, and the marker is left amazed that noting spelling and referencing errors is misconstrued as 'frenzied'. I was left stressed and thoughtful, pondering how we reached this state of vitriol and peevishness.

Through the marking and remarking, the complaints and compromises, the appeals and dismissals, the time demands on teachers are great. In this case, I spent three hours re-examining a paper that did not require re-examination, all because one student could not face up to her own faults. It appears some scholars come to university to be lauded for their brilliance, rather than taught how to improve. We need to persist with this critical marking, though, even with the enormous investments of time, emotion and energy. Before we can teach students content —, about cultural studies, chemistry, history, mathematics, economics, politics or the law — they must know how to read and write critically. If teachers do not *intervene* in learning, then student lives will be marked by a parched cultural landscape of bullet points, because they cannot construct a grammatically-correct sentence; and highlighter pens, because colouring in a book is easier than actually reading it. We rarely discuss *intervention* in contemporary teaching. The desire for student-centred learning denies the fact that the scholars in our care occasionally — in fact frequently — need to hear tough words like rigour, discipline, clarity and integrity. They need to know that they are responsible for their work, and that their words and ideas matter. The great difficulty with the loss of leftist critical thinking is that we have misplaced the interrogative, dissenting voice. Consensus, whether skewed left or right, breeds mediocrity and blandness. Our classrooms become as volatile, argumentative and exciting as Oprah's 'Remembering your spirit'. In such an environment, teachers focus on tasks rather than ideas, workplace skills rather than life-long learning, assessment rather than scholarship.

Teachers at our most confident believe that we are changing the world — a person at a time. I always feel this when teaching hegemony theory to 19-year-olds. Hegemony is a theory that explores how (and why) disempowered groups such as women, the working class, youth and people of colour accept inequalities without dissent or comment. Antonio Gramsci becomes the hunchbacked hero of the left, imprisoned for his beliefs. Nicos Poulantzas embodies one of the many crazy, brilliant theorists who changed the mind furniture of the world but could not keep his own life together. Hegemony, when taught as deep, applicable knowledge, shatters the world of young people. They realise that all the consumerable items — the mobile phone, the new shoes and the hair extensions — are actually hegemonic masks that prevent them from seeing the truths of their own lives. Hearing them justify working for $6 an hour in a sandwich shop to pay their Friday night drinking bill — to help them forget that they are working for $6 an hour in a sandwich shop — is a magical moment in teaching and learning. One poignant memory in a hegemony tutorial occurred when one of my bright but ill-prepared students was talking about her job in Target's customer service booth. Six hours a day, agitated customers screamed at her, complained and whined about how a particular top had shrunk, or a toy had broken or chocolates were unpalatable. I then asked her where the pay went. Surprise, concern, stammering — pause — then truth. The money was used to pay for calls on her mobile phone to friends, and to pay her weekly social bill. Hegemony in action. Leisure pursuits and consumerism were being used to mask the conditions of her workplace. Stunned silence. She asked me what she should do. I reminded her that she should stop being a guest star in her own life and make decisions for herself. I did state (and worried about it afterwards) that if students treat university like a hobby then it will get them one. If they treat it like a workplace, it will get them a job. If students are in paid employment thirty hours a week, and slide into university for one day without being prepared for class and with assignments written the night before they are due, then they are not undertaking a university education; they are attending a drop-in centre with an assignment slot.

Before the next week's tutorial, this young woman told me that she had cut her Target hours in half, phoned her friends and said that she would go out once a fortnight rather than twice a week, and handed back her mobile phone. She said it was difficult not going out on a Friday night, but so much better than handling daily, ruthless complaints from customers. She had also completed the entire week's reading and had started the main assignment due in six weeks. By the end of the semester, she gained one of the top marks in the course. She also became the star of her own life.

I am well aware that some students work to survive our current economic system. But they do not need to work forty hours a week to pay for a university education. It is a self-perpetuating cycle: 'a university degree will not get me a job'. But the students spend so little time thinking about that university degree, and so much time focusing on price checks, time checks and drinking tabs that it is remarkable that they even remember the majors in their degree, let alone its significant, specific content and form.

The question is, if these students are arriving at university after completing primary and secondary education with barely-functional academic skills, then how have our understandings of literacy altered? And further, should academics continue to intervene and interrupt the taken-for-granted assumptions of mediocrity, passing grades and falling expectations?[12] David Marc asked scholars to: 'just watch a few dozen hours of TV and you will receive scores of lessons about right and wrong, but very little information about politics, religion, love, or history'.[13] The problem derived from analyses such as Marc's is that to affirm the importance of books and humanities, he attacks and demeans television and popular culture. The hand of Matthew Arnold, that great apologist for high culture and affirmer of 'sweetness and light', shadows his words. The aim for new models of literacy is to grasp the empowering elements of writing and reading, while grafting aural, olfactory, tactile and oral communication onto visual and digital expertise. It is obviously impossible to avoid unspoken value judgments. To refuse a description is to refuse a distinction. The aim is to make the value-based criteria both explicit and precise. Then an argument can be constructed — with political honesty and zeal — that may be persuasive.

Media literacy skills are naturalised. The ephemeral nature of televisual viewing, and the roving eye of hypertext literacies, is under-investigated. If the capacity to comprehend the meaning of images, sounds, scents and textures is claimed as a literacy, then students will be trained to produce a variety of written and visual texts. Every cultural site enfolds many audience interpretations. To read a text is to read power structures. These clashes of social interest are motivated by pleasure and desire: the pleasure of producing meanings that speak to our social experiences, and the desire to avoid the discipline of the power bloc. In this environment, Stephen Petrina is correct: 'literacy and illiteracy are no longer what they used to be'.[14] To explore the characteristics of effective and equitable communication requires an analysis of communication forms in both verbal and non-verbal modes. A critically-reflexive teacher in this environment embeds — in curricula, pedagogy and overt political directives — the many meanings of difference. Frequently, students do not enjoy this complexity. They want a single interpretation that can be regurgitated in a test or essay. I find such an approach boring, but (quietly) amusing.

I recently taught a very large tutorial of twenty-four students in a first-year course. Although almost all students were under twenty years old, they were diversely ordered in terms of physical capacity, gender, ethnicity, and disciplinary and linguistic backgrounds. Such a group is an ideal teaching environment for the volatile, complicated and simply brilliant experience of teaching 'freshers'.

I use a pure Socratic method for these students, presenting a quotation from a featured reading of the week, then a series of questions of increasing difficulty, moving from basic comprehension to deep analysis. Students never notice how their minds are being teased and twisted out of shape as they travel through the questions. I let their debate go, permitting them to slog out their differences. It is a joy to watch — and critical literacy in action.

In this particular tutorial, there was one young woman who came to university after being educated at an elite girls' school, who would always conclude these vocal discussions with a direct question to me: so what's the right answer? On one such occasion, the question was: are textual poachers empowered or disempowered?

The debate and discussion of the preceding fifteen minutes had not impressed this young woman. When I restated the arguments of group members, showing that the answer will depend on the theoretical and political positioning, her cry for the lecturer to give a single reading became shrill. I will always remember her agitated interjection to me: 'Look, I just want an answer to the question that I can put in my notes'. Magnificent teaching moment. My reply? 'Well, if you want a single answer to any question in the world, you are enrolled in the wrong course. Intelligence means seeing all sides — and arguing many positions. That's what I'm teaching you to do. We are not in the business of single answers. We're in the business of asking difficult questions.' Her expression became even more vexed. 'But why do we need so many answers, Tara? Can't you make it easier for us?' She smiled sweetly at me. Again, I avoided the answer she so desperately wanted: 'Life isn't easy, darling. Anybody who makes it easy for you is stopping you thinking. And in this classroom, you are going to think. And your brain is going to hurt. It is a muscle — make it stronger by working it'. She went back to her notes, shaking her head.

The relationship between information, knowledge and wisdom is a pivotal concern for educators. The view being presented of our world in parliament, newspapers and cable news is restricted, narrow and flat. Financially-secure, heterosexual men from a European background — generally presenting in a well-pressed suit — are framed by a camera as speaking a truth. If we can open out the images of normality to include those of differing physical abilities, women, indigenous and ethnic communities, alongside those of sexual or linguistic diversity, then our comprehension of language, context and literacy will shake to its foundation. Only then will communication be more complicated and representative, and therefore prevent particular groups from easily exerting their truths over others. This project is not easy. For teachers, it requires a ruthless attention to details of assessment, required and further reading, the use of overheads and video, and pondering the role of digital technologies. This is pragmatic politics in action, working with what is at hand, and cross-stitching, weaving and unpicking the smooth velvet texture of the dominant culture.

All reading and writing are acts of translation. They are frequently silent and solitary practices. Politics requires more: the explosive fire of sound, the dense texture of touch and the disturbing concoctions of scent. In moving between aural, oral, visual, tactile and olfactory senses, a new, integrated literacy is formed. Isadora Duncan's reminder could be the basis of all critical literacy theory: 'if I could explain it, I wouldn't have to dance it'.[15] If all meanings were squeezed into print, then we would not need to dance or sing, smell or hear. The excess of light, shade and emotion will always spill out from the screen or the page, demanding our urgent attention to other ways of knowing and being.

OPEN THE POD BAY DOORS, HAL: SHORT-CIRCUITING INFORMATION OVERLOAD

Teachers focus critical energy on the pivotal distinction between data, information and knowledge. The buying and selling of information has displaced questions of who has the power to control and manipulate it. There is a need for a theory of information that is able to handle the consequences of digitisation. The control of Internet content — by industry, national governments or religious organisations — is locked into discussions of privacy and (de)regulation. There are many more significant matters to address.

Attendants to the information age are the handmaidens of hype, promise and myth. The Internet has increased the scale, flexibility and circulation of data. There are critics of this explosion of words, ideas and sites. Elizabeth Kirk described the Internet as 'an excellent vehicle for disinformation'.[16] If universities and schools are to be involved in and with the Internet, then there needs to be an urgent application of critical information theories. Most students learn how to use a computer outside the educational system, just as most learn to drive a car without assistance from teachers. Our role is to problematise an unquestioning allegiance to information for its own sake. Too many educators become excited by the mere existence of the Internet in their classrooms: 'Inclusion of the internet into the school curriculum will surely boost educational quality because of the immediate access to information which could be readily incorporated into students' daily education'.[17] Watching soccer does not show us how to play soccer, just as watching someone at the keyboard does not teach us critical use of hypertext. Access to information is not the primary issue for educators. We need to intervene in the blind acceptance of data, to create reflexive interpretation. There are many strategies to slot into this deductive space. Questions of authorial authority, ideological position, credibility of citation, date of uploading and writing, and the original context of the document all assist in determining its knowledge-making potential.[18] Without a rigorous process of refereeing, reviewing and editing, which is a characteristic of the print-based publishing industries, Internet search engines require great care in their use, to determine quality, currency and capability. The Internet is (frequently) a self-published medium, presenting the spurious alongside the serious. The overarching need for users is to be conscious of how information was formed, and why. Cultural studies has been asking these questions for some time, and has inflected the teaching of media studies since the 1970s. Its premise is not only to validate the citizen/student's experience of the media, but to offer an intervention in the assumed truths of a society.[19] Therefore, a cultural studies approach is ideally suited to the strategic movement of information to knowledge.

The human mind interprets data, progressing from information to knowledge to wisdom. Unless this intervention takes place, we lose political struggle and the ability to determine a separation between 'research' and the interests of specific social groups. The more public the information, the more meaningless it is. The most significant personal knowledge is rarely shared. To upload a self onto the world wide web is to share the most irrelevant, public part of identity. We need to work hard to make this manner of information useful. Theorists also need to ask more useful questions, rather than allow applications to lead intentions and aims. For example, who is using this material, and why? The Internet is a sabre that slices through assumptions of acceptable language and behaviour. While the Internet is a wide-ranging social phenomenon, its uses are frequently reduced to email and the most basic of search engines.

With information everywhere, the key problem is determining the best information at a convenient time and appropriate setting. As teachers, students and information professionals become more experienced in the handling of text, sound and image retrieval, diagnostic needs are more pressing. If there is a characteristic of digital media literacies, of which the Internet is a part, then it is a turn to visual representations and an increasing consciousness of multi-modal media competencies. Also, there is a convergence across media formats. A major question is unasked through the smiling acceptance of competence and convergence: how will this new environment work with cultural difference?

Symbols can be disempowering or enabling, allowing some groups to express meaning, while disenfranchising others. Men and women seek out surroundings that are filled with symbols in which they are literate. Those who are poor, old, young or belong to a minority have few resources to express their truths and narratives. While the digital environment makes the reproduction and dissemination of symbols possible, the already empowered gain another site to express their realities. Attention needs to be placed on how emails contribute to, or weather away, literacy. Emails are quick, convenient, asynchronous and framed as informal. Occasionally, they are assumed to lift literacy standards:

> CMC [Computer-Mediated Communication] is student-centred, offers a greater degree of non-threatening interaction than in the classroom and leads to new relationships of ideas and people. They also assert that CMC may help students to improve writing skills, acquire meta-cognitive skills such as self-reflection and relate personal experience to theoretical frameworks.[20]

I am continually shocked at the astonishingly poor standard of literacy revealed in emails. They frequently appear to not even be in English. Writing skills are not improved through email. If anything, it is blunting and undermining the necessity to draft work. It is easily composed, but straightforward to copy and send to hundreds of people, and store for years. I have every student email sent to me in the last three years — stored by year, by course, and by semester. This gives me great power: it demonstrates to employers the consequences of email to the patterns of my work day, but it also means — at the click of mouse — I can show students that they were notified about a meeting, that they did receive detailed help for that assignment, and that — yes — one student did send me 168 emails during twelve weeks of a semester. I spent more time with this student than my own mother. Ironically, though — and students seemingly forget this fact — I can re-send these messages to anyone, at any time. I would not. But I could. Power has not evaporated through digitisation. It is held by those with increasingly-stuffed electronic mailboxes.

Like the agrarian and industrial societies, the information age is configured through the primary commodity of exchange. This will leave few resistive options in the increasingly capitalised and commodified information economy. There is a social impact to digitisation. Representational politics will alter through digital manipulation. The semiotic convergence of film, video, computer-imaging, sound and print-based word processing will — for some time — create a jumbled, contradictory, schizophrenic consciousness. There are consequences when time becomes 'commodified', being framed by 'abstract computational space', while tactility is 'fading'.[21] This disembodiment not only alters citizenship; it auctions off public space.

CUT 'N' PASTE CULTURE

Click … click … click … That's the sound of someone moving through the web. All your efforts. All your hard work. Scanned in the space of a click … click.[22]

Heather Duggan

The Internet and literacy — as two separate terms — are volatile words in isolation; when creating a compound noun — Internet literacy — they are explosive. The greatest difficulty emerging from theorists of the Internet is that scholars focus overtly on the technology 'itself' rather than maintaining a critical approach about its use and application. For example, Todd Taylor and Irene Ward argue that:

instead of being frustrated by the disorientation brought on by such changes, we suggest that teachers and researchers embrace the urgent uncertainty and theoretical disarray as the most reasonable way to negotiate new notions of literacy as they appear on the horizon.[23]

Ponder the consequences of their battle cry: the context for education is disturbing and unstable. The word 'literacy' is being added (ad-hoc) to policy documents with little consideration for the curriculum or political consequences. Teachers, though, are asked to 'embrace the uncertainty'. To enact such a process is not a teaching strategy; it is the commencement of a life-long Valium dependency.

To put it bluntly, education is too important to be based on uncertainty. The tasks that teachers spend their lives performing — writing curricula, planning activities, developing evaluative criteria and marking — cannot be based on hesitation. To improve teaching, teachers require clearly expressed goals. What are we doing today? How does this session fit into the semester's work? What is the point of this topic to these students' lives? Competent teaching is not only conveying big ideas or 'embracing the uncertainty': it is gaining intellectual perspective to transform a learning goal into a successful, teachable moment. Educational institutions are demanding more rigidity, and even more documentation, to catalogue every part of a student's 'progress'. University academics log telephone calls, store emails and file correspondence in case of appeals or complaints from disgruntled students. This culture of complaint and grievance is understandable from the students' point of view, particularly in the model of students as consumers of education. We teach scholars for only one semester, one term, or one year. We do not have the luxury of being 'uncertain', or 'going with the flow', or writing a few lecture headings on the back of a cigarette packet.

The point must be made — stridently — that the quality of education being delivered in universities and schools has never been higher. I am aware that this is a controversial statement, because we have been fed the mantras of decline and crisis for so many years. The training has never been better, the penalties for poor, or even mediocre, teaching have never been more damaging, and the structures of support reasonably functional. Nostalgia for a glorious educational past plays tricks on the mind. Like most of my readers, I have experienced the most startling teachers who have changed the direction of my life during an hour-long lecture. Three remarkable men — and yes, they were all white men in their late forties and fifties, teaching European history — have skewed my judgment of the rest. As for the remaining 'educators', I remember pitiful sessions on poetry, dire lectures on Dada, and morose and muddled presentations about Melville. Most of our teaching experiences are of deep mediocrity at best, and dense banality at worst. A few shining lights in our sepia-toned past have blocked a recognition that the overall quality of education has improved radically in the last decade. To revere a great teacher of the past is to affirm a simpler time.

Lectures are criticised as a mode of teaching, because a physical distance separates lecturer and students. It is also framed as a passive learning experience. These two attacks are easily waylaid. Firstly, any teaching method that masks the power of teachers is not being honest towards students. Also, all modes of learning can be passive if students are not motivated. Aimlessly clicking hypertext links is not an active education. Students do not respond to lectures in a uniform way. Lectures are a multi-literate teaching form, involving sound, vision and gestures. The best of lectures are sheer artistry, and to dislodge their role in the rush to the web is to destroy one of the oldest, most motivational forms of teaching.

Good teaching is not technologically dependent. Only when the needs of the workforce have swamped all other educational goals, has the overarching need become to prepare students for their first job. I am old enough to remember the phrase 'on-the-job training': the notion that employers were responsible for training their own staff in the precise conditions of their workplace. Now, employers have offloaded this 'expense' to the university and school sector. So besides teaching our disciplinary area, we also help students prepare their CVs, teach them about interviewing techniques, show them how to search databases, prepare well-presented and structured reports and ensure that all our assignments produce work that is recognised as 'valuable' by those demanding first employers. This is obviously a bastardisation of the university system. Technology is not the problem here, but it reveals the greater challenge of post-industrialisation: labour surplus. There are simply too many people to fill the available jobs. While our students chase an ever-rising bar of employment, employers demand more qualifications, skills and experience, *because they can*. There are too many extremely bright, well-credentialled, interesting and skilled people. They have been herded by an economic system that has moved from large, Fordist work-places of homogeneity and standardisation to the post-Fordist struc-tures of differentiation, fragmentation, casual and temporary jobs, and niche marketing. This changing economic environment was always going to affect the definition and applications of education. The required skills for the workforce are changing, along with the language used to describe them. Literacy is no longer the traditional three Rs — it is not even the revised version for private boys' schools: rugby, rowing and religion. New spaces are formed for sensational-ism and sermons on the computer screen.

Internet plagiarism has overtaken Jerry Springer in capturing the sensationalised imagination. Becoming a new bogeyman of the acad-emy, plagiarism is treated as if it was suddenly invented through the Internet. What is forgotten is that the Internet, in many cases, actu-ally makes plagiarism easier to find and prove. Also, the countless (unsubstantiated) plagiarism cases that never appeared in the past, where unpublished Honours papers, Masters and Doctoral disserta-tions were used as intellectual cannon fodder in scholarly books, remain a whispered reality of academic life. The mechanism through which to avoid plagiarism in this cut 'n' paste culture is relatively straightforward: it simply requires teachers to be more precise and rigorous in their updating of course materials.

There are three strategies I use to avoid plagiarism, either of other writers' ideas or a quarrying of previous years' papers. Firstly, I ruthlessly update all set questions, essays and assessment tasks each year. In this way, former students can neither sell nor loan their materials to the current cohort. Secondly, I radically change the reading, with at least one third of each year's materi-als being altered. This means that in any three-year period, the complete course changes in its structure, content and intellectu-al imperatives. I knew this system was working when my new PhD student, who I taught in the first-year course four years pre-viously and in which she was now tutoring, said that she went back to her first-year notes and the reading had changed so much that they were useless. My system is working well. The final ele-ment in avoiding plagiarism is to demand a direct, coherent and precise reference to course materials in the assigned written tasks. There is an expectation that unless direct quotations and reference is made of these (endlessly changing) course materials, the student will not pass. I have not — and will not — mobilise a textbook. Life and education and not taught through easily-digestible, bullet-pointed chapters with review questions at the end. As Neil Postman suggested:

> textbooks ... are the enemies of education, instruments for pro-moting dogmatism and trivial learning. They may save the teacher some trouble, but the trouble they inflect on the minds of students is a blight and a curse.[24]

Purchasing an essay on a generic issue of class, gender, race or colonisation is absolutely pointless in my courses. Also, those of us who do not teach in the United States or the United Kingdom hold a distinct advantage. We can — and must — gear our teaching to our region, our writers, our interests. Therefore, using the many 'cheat sheet' sites is pointless for (yearly-changing) topics on Australia, New Zealand or the Asian and Pacific region. Not only is this regional specificity politically important, it allows Antipodean and Pacific Rim academics to regulate the student papers being submitted to us with even greater precision and care.

Even such an integrated system is not flawless, but it forces students to think, read and reference correctly. Certainly they can still pay others to write their paper for them, but such intel-lectual theft has been a characteristic of school and university systems throughout time. My father — to this day an absolute numbers wiz — used to be a very popular seating companion during maths tests in his country school in Northam, Western Australia during the late 1930s and 1940s. Once he realised what was occurring, this enterprising 10-year-old used to com-plete the test quickly, adding one number to all answers — which all the cheaters would religiously copy — and then with two minutes to go would rub out the errors and decode his own ruse. Such a method may seem sneaky, but it is brilliant. Current teachers can learn much from the shrewdness of 10-year-olds. Make assignments so specific, so changeable, and so reliant on the quirky, regionally-specific, supplied reading that cheating becomes more inconvenient, time-consuming and expensive than actually sitting down to write an assignment.

Internet literacy does not require attention to pings and plagiarism, but to problem solving and communication. Literacy not only refers to an ability to use software and determine the difference between packet switching and a pop server, but requires an ethical and social deployment of computers. An Internet literacy at its most effective incorporates spaces for alternative views — to arch beyond the transmission of a message — and explores the function of Internet-based communication systems.

The difficulty with all literacies is that those who hold the expertise often forget how arduous, frightening and complicated it was to attain these abilities in the first place. Such amnesia undermines and silences those who are yet to gain entry into a new literacy and knowledge system. For example, Joyce Kasman Valenza stated that 'information is easy to access and retrieve in a technology-rich environment'.[25] Literacy requires more than access or retrieval. It needs the construction of an intellectual scaffold, a multi-tasking, organic framework that is supple in its application and outward in its inflection. The metaphors of a gateway or interface are therefore not appropriate to capture the requirements of this thinking mode. Cheryl Harris argues that 'the bottom line is that in the foreseeable future, Internet literacy will be rewarded by the marketplace and will be a considerable asset'.[26] If the marketplace is removed from the analysis — and it is becoming increasingly difficult to disengage economic concerns from any discussion on any topic — then it would be useful to research how models of thinking are blooming in response to technological spaces. From this premise, communication and information technologies transform into social relationships, rather than infrastructures. When the Internet is the foundation for a socially-rooted knowledge, then political debate about literacy can emerge.

In this environment, Bill Cope, Mary Kalantzis and a group of literacy specialists met in New London, New Hampshire to form The New London Group, with the aim of formulating an innovative theory of knowledge: multi-literacies. A collective of scholars from Australia, the United States and the United Kingdom pondered how to discuss literacy teaching across diverse national and cultural experiences. While one billion people speak English, there is no longer agreement about the canonical language. Concurrently, the American Standard Code for Information Interchange (ASCII) is the Esperanto code system for PCs. Educational institutions have been squashed into a compliant jelly mould of the workplace:

Our role as teachers is not simply to be technocrats. It is not our job to produce docile, compliant workers. Students need also to develop the capacity to speak up, to negotiate, and to be able to engage critically with the conditions of their working lives.[27]

With the new market logic appearing simultaneously with identity politics, literacy becomes torn between an affirmation of uniform standards and an acknowledgment of diversity. Further, Internet-based literacies are serving to displace and shrink national differences and languages.

Carmen Luke's solution to Internet literacy is for teachers to intervene — and quickly. She believes that:

> unless educators take a lead in developing appropriate pedagogies for these new electronic media and forms of communication, corporate experts will be the ones to determine how people will learn, what they learn and what constitutes literacy.[28]

While her proclamation is correct, this affirmation does not display a strong sense of the threats and difficulties confronting working teachers. I am surrounded by tired academics that battle to answer each day's emails, let alone make sweeping developmental changes to pedagogy. When I speak to primary and high school teachers on their professional development days, they express exhaustion and hostility at the complete consumption of their lives through the classroom. Internet teaching must be developed with compassion and sensitivity. Too many decisions — stark, significant decisions — are formed through crisis management. Taking the lead in Internet education often triggers disappointment, frustration and wasted time. Luke is overestimating the degree of autonomy and power held by teachers at all levels of the system.

Being swept up into this proactive, *inevitably* digital future, some theorists have proclaimed the death of the book and an end of a particular mode of literacy. Actually, new skills — such as touch-typing, file management, database searching and Internet browsing — will be blended with current skills. Too many writers express a desire to erase history and affirm newness rather than continuity. For example, Jay Bolter, in an early history of hypertext, stated:

> The printed book, therefore, seems destined to move to the margin of our literate culture ... This shift from print to the

computer does not mean the end of literacy. What will be lost is not literacy itself, but the literacy of print, for electronic technology offers us a new kind of book and new ways to write and read.[29]

The gee-whiz attitude of technology theorists is neither critical nor historical. The invention of hardware or software does not mean that it has to be, or will be, used. The hypertext link makes the web environment distinctive, dislodging accustomed patterns of reading and writing. The hyperlink blurs the line between gathering information and constructing knowledge. Much of the web is organised around movement, bouncing from statistics to an image, a chart to a fact. Jumping between data streams does not build knowledge: only by interpreting the spaces between the data does it become meaningful. Hypertext is changing the structure of arguments, and what constitutes debate and evidence.[30]

The multiple meanings of Internet literacy confirm that all technology must be cut up, critiqued and evaluated in a context. It is information glowing off a flat surface, but to transform that gleaming façade into a site for meaningful debate requires teachers to intervene in the gap between the click and the content.

EDUCATION AND INTERNET LITERACY

If there are lessons to be learned through educational technology, then there is a need to focus on the continuity of visual literacies, rather than obsessing over each software innovation as the start of a learning revolution. There is a need to place both time and money into teacher training and professional development. Educators cannot be expected to complete their conventional full-time load (which is always an overload) and then develop innovative, provocative and appropriate web-based material. To construct evocative websites takes time as well as huge commitments of skill, design, expertise and knowledge. Further, when the sites are designed, they require constant updating. If schools, universities and colleges demand a commitment to online education, there is no alternative but to reduce the load on existing staff so that these abilities may be developed and nurtured. Technology will not allow a reduction in the number of teachers: it should lead to an increase. Shoddy, ill-prepared websites, with broken links or few hypertexted interventions, are not an appropriate use of the medium. To allow Internet literacies to develop in the classroom requires a major commitment of money, time and energy. To simply expect or assume that websites will be available at an appointed time in the semester will threaten and cajole staff into a Dreamweaver panic. Such a terrorised flurry may generate short-term results, but will not create a thoughtful, reflexive and open strategy of possibilities. Support needs to be overt, formal, long-term and planned. Through my ten years in the academy, I have seen too many promises of 'just-in-time' training, or 'as much help as I need'. These phrases are nonsense and are a way to deny the systematic financing of skill development.

If an environment of crisis, overwork and apprehension is the cause of online education, then the results will betray this origin. The alternative is to place the Internet into multiple teaching and learning techniques. At the moment, the graft between traditional strategies and digital tactics is clunky, obstructive and an awkward extension to a shabby house. Through an emphasis on skills such as problem solving, a pathway is created through the subject matter. Technology in — and of — itself means very little. It becomes useful when situated in educational theory and a context. Therefore, attention is required on the relationship between theory and practice — research and application — in childhood, adolescent and adult education.

While recognising the potential of the aural, the olfactory and tactile — the senses decentred in all modes of education including that offered online — print-based texts remain the basis of delivery systems. Presentational software packages such as PowerPoint can increase the range of visual communication presented in lectures. They also encourage the myth that they 'can shorten your prep time considerably'.[31] This 'innovative' software results in staff not writing lectures, but filling in the gaps between the headings on slides. Also, while computer presentations can be dazzling, hitches and technical incompatibilities can actually make the presentation impossible to run. From overhead transparencies to PowerPoint slides, text-based instructional materials require a careful design, with conscious attention paid to content, context, sequence and mechanisms for revision. The difficulty with print is that it is so familiar as a means of learning that it is taken for granted. Teachers rarely ponder its effectiveness as a teaching and learning medium. Both inside and outside the web — text stands alone as the fount of learning. We must ponder how to collapse the experiential gap between writer and reader. Layout becomes pivotal, transforming text into workable pieces of information with sufficient visual cues to hook into the reader's world, activating a learner's prior knowledge and experience. Integrating the Internet into education requires an acknowledgment of the text-based continuities in the technological palate. Suzanne Silverman quite rightly reminded us that:

> One of the most common mistakes that teachers make in their early attempts to introduce technology is to treat it as something new in the classroom. The fact of the matter is that all of the resources in our classroom were new at one time, but we have fully integrated them into our routines. The same must hold for our technology resources.[32]

To stress the revolutionary nature of the Internet deflects energy, finance and attention away from teachers and students, teaching and learning. We need to watch those who betray an unusually fervent commitment to the apparatus rather than the citizens of education.

Print and media historians have taken to the web with enthusiasm and passion. This fervour is no surprise. Of greater concern is when teachers see the *resources* of the Internet, without any notional trajectories of how they are to be deployed. James O'Donnell, for example, describes an imagined teaching scenario: 'Imagine an online resource where the course lectures are available not in 50 minute chunks, but in 2–5 minute video segments closely matched to a paragraph of the textbook'.[33] There are major consequences for this 'innovation'. Firstly, students lose the ability to concentrate through large quantities of material — surely a significant necessity in the information age. Further, there is something very important in allowing students to move through books and readings in their own way, creating interpretations and making connections. To tether teacherly interpretations this tightly to a textbook crushes student initiative and innovation by reinforcing a single interpretation. For educators, our task is to maximise learning from text, wherever it is located.

Every new technology became the great hope for the future of education: photography, sound recordings, film, television and multimedia.[34] For Stephen Kerr, 'no feature of twentieth-century educational practice has been more puzzling than the gap between what technology has promised and what it has delivered'.[35] Through all my commitment to multi-literacies, I do remain worried about writing and reading. This cyclical unease returns with every new batch of assignments. Students remain unable to see errors on the page. They confess that they never noticed the spelling, grammatical and stylistic flaws. Good writing has longevity. Reducing writing and drafting to endlessly shifting text on a screen, or a quick spelling check before submission of an essay ignores the life of a word through space, time and an audience. There is a sizeable leap between button-pressing and the virtual landscape of education.

The desire for flexibility and constant revision serves the purpose of a capitalist system requiring an unstable workforce and continual consumer turnover. Such vocational directives have done a disservice to universities and the society they serve. Neil Postman expresses this disrespect, at his argumentative, confrontational best:

> Specialized competence can come only through a more generalized competence, which is to say that economic utility is a by-product of a good education. Any education that is mainly about economic utility is far too limited to be useful, and, in any case, so diminishes the world that it mocks one's humanity. At the very least, it diminishes the idea of what a good learner is.[36]

To create questioning, independent thinkers is antithetical to the imperatives of vocational training. Armani is no replacement for Gramsci.

Internet literacy holds a major promise and threat to teachers. Both the Internet and literacy — as words — carry (too) much ideological baggage to the online learning table. In an environment where languages of the marketplace and education dialogue with uncomfortable frequency, words like literacy and empowerment are emptied of their inflective for social change. Literacy is not only a capacity to read words on a page. It is the ability to understand ideas, and promote alternatives. But further, literacy necessitates grasping the world of the text, the notes of a melody or the kaleidoscope of colours that form a television programme.

All of us are multi-literate: we possess aural, visual, tactile, olfactory and written skills. Some literacies and texts are framed as more significant than others. Empowered groups, such as teachers, parents, journalists and politicians, tend to have their meanings believed.

They promote the status quo. There are always multiple renderings and readings of every text and historical event that circulates in a place and time. Within education, we are always in a political situation; always questioning and struggling to form a cultural literacy that allows us to understand our life and the lives of those around us. We are not born with a gene marked 'Shakespeare good/Britney Spears bad'. We are taught how to rank and judge — to be literate — in valuable and important cultural institutions such as schools and universities. Such knowledge greatly influences the stature and role of libraries, which is the topic of the next chapter. Tussles — over curricula, learning strategies, assessment protocols and pedagogy — are sandpapering the rigors and passions of education. We must reclaim cultural and political complexity, and the importance of struggles and stipulations, negotiation and negation.

4

DOUBLE FOLD OR DOUBLE TAKE? BOOK MEMORY AND THE ADMINISTRATION OF INFORMATION

PROLOGUE

My garage spells of naphthalene. Because I hang washing out to dry in the conjoined garage, my frocks smell of naphthalene. Because the car lives there, it smells of naphthalene. This piquant odour requires the telling of a story.

One of the joys of teaching hundreds of students every year is that I have the chance to meet thousands of family members and friends. By the time an academic has lived in a city for ten years, it is impossible to attend an aerobics class or go grocery shopping without meeting a former student, or their mother, girlfriend, boyfriend, spouse, partner, significant other, son, daughter, or other (blended) family members.

It is known by my friends and students that I am obsessed by both books and the 1980s. Books on the 1980s are special favourites. The son of one of my favourite cultural studies students — he attended lectures with his mother during school holidays and 'sick days' from high school — has also become a friend and followed his mother's footsteps into cultural studies. To pay for his education, he works at one of Western Australia's libraries as the jack-the-lad lifter, stacker, shifter and gopher. One day, his mother informed me that this library was disposing of — or 'chucking out' in Australian English — the entire collection of *The West Australian*, the longest surviving state-based newspaper. Her son was responsible for putting these elegant volumes into the dumpster. However, if I desired, he would preserve a range of the 1980s collection for me, after he 'put them in the dumpster' (not). Within weeks, carloads of 1980s magic started to stockpile in my lounge room, making it difficult to move around the house. Delicate and remarkable tomes from the world wars, twenties and thirties were also added to the collection. The rest of *The West Australian*'s run was simply destroyed.

Then a new problem befell me, and everyone who wanted to move through my home. How was I to store this material? I have a large house, and lived alone at the time. This may appear the solution to my problem. Because of my prior collecting habits, however, the house was — well — full of groaning bookshelves featuring past hits of postcolonial theory, critical pedagogy, Marxist historiography, cultural studies, gender studies and Internet theory. The appropriated *West Australian*s had no place in my house. The garage was a concern — would it preserve the materials?

The advantage of being in the first generation of family members to attend university is that I have parents who can accomplish useful, quantifiable tasks, such as building, renovating, painting and fixing things. So a shelf was constructed, airtight boxes bought and naphthalene peppered throughout the structure. My father's cataloguing, while owing nothing to Anglo-American Cataloguing Rules (AACR2) or the Library of Congress Subject Headings (LCSH), is appropriate for the oasis of the 1980s that now frames the garage.

This is not an ideal situation, for my social life or for the newspapers. The librarians reading my words are probably cringing into their coffee. But I smile every time I walk into the garage and smell the naphthalene. I hold something special — a vast collection of 1980s *West Australian*s. As a shrine to big hair, Bond and Black Monday, it conveys a textured reading of the past not possible through microfilm. The information may be on those ghastly reels, but there is something magical about feeling the paper, being branded by newsprint and — yes — inhaling that naphthalene.

ASSAULT AND BATTERY

This chapter revels in the controversial place of libraries in education, so clearly revealed through the publication of Nicholson Baker's *Double Fold: Libraries and the assault on paper*. The book unleashed a barrage of commentary, critique and hand-wringing within library journals and 'quality' newspapers. Such a furore is useful: libraries are a forgotten part of the educational experience, being sidelined as an inelegant appendage — rather than the throbbing, bubbling cranium — of schools, universities and civic life. Building on the literacy debates, this chapter directly confronts and questions the role and place of libraries in education and learning broadly defined. Firstly, Baker's argument is monitored, revealing the profoundly contradictory imperatives confronting librarians, as either information professionals or knowledge managers. The second section excavates the long-term political controversies that have punctuated the histories of the book, with emphasis on how this history impacts on libraries. The third part ponders the notion of information 'access' rather than 'preservation', with the final component sketching the potentials and problems of digitisation for assembling popular memory.

Nicholson Baker's work has always offered challenges; it is difficult to situate in fiction or non-fiction, and subverts overt, classifiable genre-based categories. He is a fine writer, swimming through language with a precision and purpose usually only seen in paid political announcements. His topics are rarely *significant* or *important*: his gaze is drawn to the banal, the negligible and the overlooked. He discovers beauty, pattern and purpose in the minutia of the age. There is detail, intensity and enforced solitude in his writings. He remains interested in how words appear on the page:

> The footnote is the poor man's hypertext. It is not fancy … You don't need any software at all. All it takes is a little number, a little asterisk, and smaller type. It's great. You can choose. Do you want to go into the subroutine of the footnote and follow it out and move back, or do you want to skip it? … I was very proud of one of my footnotes that went on for four pages with only three lines at the top.[1]

This fickleness is very attractive in our era of tepid textbooks and predictable prose. His words massage the contradictions of the age. From *Vox*'s phone-sex marathon to *Fermata*'s office-worker protagonist who can stop the clock and undress women during the stasis, Baker demonstrates what Laura Miller has termed 'a passionate enthusiasm for the neglected flotsam and jetsam of every day life'.[2] *Double Fold* is therefore unusual, creating an anger far beyond his earlier attention to toenail clippers.

Nicholson Baker is an activist by accident. He was infuriated by the actions of the San Francisco Public Library when it placed hundreds of thousands of books into landfill. The rationale for this destruction varies from chemical — the acidic infirmity of paper —

through to issues of the physical space occupied by the collection. Baker argues that throughout microfilming history, newspapers and then books have been destroyed through the guillotining of their spines to quicken the filming process. This 'destroying to preserve' ethos has been a trait of successive Librarians of Congress, particularly the incumbent, James Billington:

> There's always a trade-off. The happiness and satisfaction of seeing the whole thing in the original is a short-lived privilege for today's audience. It's likely to be, in the real world, at the expense of the variety and richness of what future generations will be able to see in the microfilm version.[3]

The language of economic rationalism — of efficiency, productivity and the real world — necessitates the reduction of primary source materials to questions of content. Efficiency has been the lubricant of bureaucracy throughout the 19th century (at least), but tethering to the market has added a more destructive orientation. While the encyclopaedia is the (fallible) representation of the perfectability of human knowledge, microfilm is also part of this desire, even though microfilm is unable to capture colour printing or even greyscale photography. The dismantling of library collections, particularly originally-bound newspapers and 'brittle books' to create microform editions, is a destruction of both print and paper history. It also ignores the weaknesses of microfilm, with the polyester-based films permeable by fungal attack and silver-halide flaws. Baker argues through attention to the infamous Double Fold test[4] that the degradation of books has been overstated. A more accurate judgment of value would be a focus on legibility.

Significantly, *Double Fold* is not a damning treaty against digitisation. Actually, Baker argues that such a process has value for access and preservation. He recognises that there is yet to be a standard resolution for the scanning of newspapers,[5] and — at this stage — more research is needed on the migration of data. Archives require the stable storage of information, which may not be accessed for many years. Refreshment, migration and software revision renders such archival practices unpredictable in their feasibility. Digitisation and convergent media are not his target. Baker attacks microfilming, believing that this process has prevented the effective presentation of the archival past through the Internet. Poor quality digital scanning results from the migration of reels to bits and bytes.[6] As he states, 'you can't digitize something that has been sold off piecemeal or thrown away, after all'.[7] He is not against technology, but remains resolutely passionate about reading. Looking through the viewfinder is no replacement for flicking through the pages of the past. Between 1968 and 1984, the Library of Congress destroyed 300 000 books, worth approximately US$10 million.[8] Those who critique this practice have been described by Billington as 'luddites'.[9] This is an easy judgment. Those who problematise the directives of the powerful are invariably ridiculed as blocking progress. Baker's critiques describe Billington as being part of a 'cultural holocaust'.[10] Ironically, this Librarian of Congress not only headed the move to digitisation, but also started the American memory project to provide 'the memory for an inherently memory-less society'.[11] He obviously saw no contradiction in his policies.

Microfilming has altered the way history is researched and written. To read a newspaper is to gain a breadth and texture of daily events. As Malcolm Jones affirms, 'when it comes to books and especially newspapers, nothing beats the original. Historians know this. Librarians, who are the curators of physical objects, ought to'.[12] The subtle development of ideas and attitudes is difficult to track. To read microfilm is to look up only a specific citation or page, as there is little pleasure to be discovered in the blinking parchness of reading from the reels.[13] Indeed, in an Ontario Archive, a microfilm reader had an air-sickness bag appended to it.[14]

Baker has reminded us that books are both 'physical artifacts' and 'bowls of ideas'.[15] There are so many debates about the book because there is no agreed notion of how its value is determined. Are the words all that matter? How significant is the cover, the grade of paper, or the illustrations? Is the book an object of art, or a site of popular memory? To prioritise access — a common librarian catcall — is to reduce the multiple meanings of the book. There is a chill factor, a sinewy tissue that connects readers to old books. As Maggie McDonald reported, 'not long ago I bought a book, slightly damaged, for 30p. It had been printed in 1674 in England. Books are survivors'.[16] Through holding and pondering such texts, readers learn about deep time and lasting ideas.

Double Fold propels a powerful, percussive narrative, provoking discussion and controversy. Baker thumps the lectern and dials a diatribe. He speaks from a position of passion, not as a professional

librarian or archivist. What makes Baker's argument so convincing —
even through its excesses and hyperbole — is that he is not only
eccentric, but prepared to put his money where his madness is. He
actually bought — with his own greenbacks — 4700 volumes of
newspapers being sold and/or destroyed by the British Library. He
formed the American Newspaper Repository in 1999.[17] Obviously,
not every textual trace of a culture can be preserved, catalogued and
made available indefinitely. To achieve this state would be the
extreme resolution of Baker's position. Richard Cox asks the pivotal
questions of Baker:

> Should we also save all old buildings, old books, and printed
> ephemera? Should everything always be saved in the original
> form? Or, is this a misunderstanding of just what the responsibil-
> ity of librarians and archivists represent?[18]

Cox should recognise that only by preserving the comic, the feminine and the fan, will we see how the serious, masculine and intellectual have dominated our history. Through ephemera, there is a
negotiation with the elasticity of time and memory. Popular cultural
fans reinscribe and reframe the material that is trashed as trivial and
worthless by the powerful. Without this ephemera being preserved,
the fervent and everyday questions of power structures remain hidden. Even while presenting these caveats, Baker's case is controversial but well made. Invariably, librarians were going to answer Baker's
charges with aggression and pricked professional consciousness.

One of the most aggressive attackers — and one lacking courage
or conviction — signed their details as 'b.q.'. Asking: 'Can we get rid
of him? Will he just go away?',[19] the unnamed critic revealed their link
with the hyper-conservative Rand Corporation. No surprise that
Baker — the guerrilla librarian — had rattled this person's neoliberal
cage. Ironically, considering this background, the critic argued that
'librarians serve people', affirming the saturating trope of access above
all other concerns. 'Content matters, not format. Format only matters
when it affects the endurance and transmission of content.'[20]
Destruction of books and popular culture does not ensure access; it
only inhibits flexibility. Similar arguments are made about Internet
teaching. The content of the course is the imperative. The form of lectures is inconvenient, rigid or inefficient. The world wide web
becomes a way to present the content of a course at the convenience

of the student. There is little sense of the integral role of format, tone, texture and context in the learning experience. To emphasise content above form is to suggest that format is not actually part of the meaning structure. As the most basic of semiotics informs us, the signifier (form) and the signified (content) are inseparable. Both make up the sign. Both shape meaning. Carl Sessions Stepp contends that:

> ... newspapers are living originals. They have unique tactile intimacy, an exotic scent, a singular drawing-power keyed as much to their shape and feel as to their content. They are tangible artifacts, with innate historical and literary value. Neither microfilm nor digitization, for all their archival benefit, can re-create the bond of touch to text.[21]

The difficulty in (over)stressing access is that librarians are not fortune-tellers. It is impossible to determine what material from the present will be pivotal to the interpretation of a time and place in the future. *Use it or lose it* is not the basis for librarianship.[22] That is why maintenance of materials must be a node of consideration, rather than the unbridled trope of access overcoming other concerns. The book is an artifact and text, not a container of words.

EVELYN WAUGH'S WAR

> Books are the best of things, well used; abused, among
> the worst. What is the right use? ... They are for nothing
> but to inspire ... The one thing in the world, of value,
> is the active soul.[23]

Ralph Waldo Emerson

One of my favourite stories about book-lovers is taken from Evelyn Waugh. During the Second World War, he ordered that his books be taken to the country, to be protected from the London Blitz. He told his son to remain in London. Books are a serious business. One of the most famous scholarly suicides is that of Brian Courthorpe Hunt, who shot himself while in the London Library. Hunt was dismayed by the fact that the second volume of the book he was reading was not available.[24] Anyone who believes this story to be ridiculous does not do enough reading. As Geoffrey O'Brien, in the wickedly strange *The Browser's Ecstasy*, recognised, 'the book isn't single and solid: it's a permeated field, a pool'.[25] Therefore, to claim it as a static object does not recognise how ideas and energy fly from its pages.

As disclosed in the last chapter, there has been much cheese-board chattering about literacy. Those who do read books, as Hamilton realised, 'care profoundly. What they lack in numbers they make up for in passion'.[26] A study conducted in the 1980s demonstrated that while only half the American population had read a book in the six-month period prior to the survey, of those 'readers', one third read a book a week.[27] For these people, books dominate and filter living space. Books encase a history of introverted meditation. For example, there is a book in an Oxford library with the inscription:

> This book belongs to the monastery of St. Mark of Robert's Bridge, whosoever shall steal it, sell it or in any way alienate it from this house, or mutilate it, let him be forever cursed. Amen.[28]

Besides leading to eternal damnation, books are also codex photographs of past lives, interests and ignorance. For writers, pursuing the most solitary of activities, books are constant companions and helpmates to the cause.

The only difficulty with owning thousands of books is that moving house is hard work. But there is something enjoyable about leaving one set of bookshelves, touching and reconnecting with previously loved books, and transferring them to a new home. When I moved into my current house — which was actually bought for the wall space — I felt dislocated in a small room while the house (and bookshelves) were being painted. I was propped on one of those ridiculous fold-up beds, making me terminally uncomfortable, with my hips and ribcage connecting at awkward angles. But to make me feel more at home in a space that was not yet one, I removed a few old history books from their carefully labelled cartons. Having these around me and hearing the sigh of the spines made the space warmer and more hospitable. Home is where the books are.

Social needs are serviced by the book. The pleasures of reading are rarely discussed or presented. Instead, the speed of InfoTrac and ProQuest database searches and the clicking movements of hypertext, have overshadowed the introverted imaginings of reading. Rarely do we remember, write about or recognise how our lives have been shaped and changed by these solitary sorties of the mind, eye, page and ink. Books are objects to be pondered, discussed — and are the seed of critical thought.

I arrived at university at eighteen having come from a house with few books. The university library was a church, temple and retreat for me. The bookshop was breathtaking. The first book I bought in the weeks preceding that first semester was *The Making of the English Working Class*, by EP Thompson. I devoured it, ravished by the dense description, tightly enmeshed footnotes, humour and energy of the drumming narrative. History's losers were finally victorious via their greatest benefactor/historian. I read it — and kept on reading it — in baffled wonderment about how magisterial and enchanting good writing could be. I still own and read this tatty paperback book — spine intact and a survivor of the Double Fold test. I will die with it in my possession. It is far more than content or words on a page to be accessed or stored in a database to be downloaded at will. It is a codex memory of my development into a better, more socially-just person.

Earlier this year, I completed the entire EP Thompson collection with the purchase of *The Essential Thompson*. Leather bound, gold edged and delicately printed, it is the finest, most beautiful book I will ever own. Most weeks I wander into my library and pull it out, to touch its sand-coloured pages and textured cover, and open it randomly to a page, to an essay, that I have loved well.

If this obsession is romantic or gothic in its intensity, then so be it. Books are objects of devotion because they not only contain ideas, but they perform knowledge and capture the spark of imagination and context. I understand Baker's passion: 'leave the books alone, I say, leave them alone, leave them alone'.[29]

Through the long arch of historical continuity, there have been transformations of the book. Baker has a tendency to forget that it has a history of (slow) change and alterations. Through the last 5000 years, there have been four renovations to the book:

BOOK HISTORY: THE TRANSFORMATIONS

2500BC–AD700	Clay tablet inscribed with stylus
2000BC–AD700	Papyrus roll written with brush or pen
AD100–	Codex, originally inscribed with a pen
AD1990–	Electronic book

What such a table demonstrates is the profound stability of clay tablets and papyrus rolls, which existed for 2500 years, and codex, which has maintained its dominance for 2000 years. But books contain many non-linear trajectories rarely incorporated in such a tabled chronology: cowrie shells, message sticks and wampum are all read and circulated. Books have changed very little through time, which means that rapid change in the reading discourse creates panic and dislocation, such as witnessed in the Baker controversy. Such a historical moment also emerged in AD4, when the Roman Imperial Library commenced the conversion from papyrus rolls to vellum codices. Decisions were made about which texts were worthy of the time and expense for transcription. Writing was a mechanism to codify and reinforce linear language modes.

There remains a tight embrace between the graphic expression of ideas and the material on which these written signs are inscribed. In some ways, following on from Socrates, writing is an artificial memory. Ironically, Socrates' interpretation of writing has only survived through Plato's inscribed recollections. Socrates remained concerned with what would happen to the human mind through the act of writing:

> If men learn this, it will implant forgetfulness in their souls; they will cease to exercise memory because they rely on that which is written, calling things to remembrance no longer from within themselves, but by means of external marks: what you discovered is a recipe not for memory, but for reminder ... telling them of many things without teaching them you will make them seem to know much, while for the most part they know nothing.[30]

While we may know nothing about Socrates, his highly mediated written 'voice' via Plato both confirms and critiques his own argument. He was worried about the commitment to knowledge and the loss of speculative thought encouraged through reading and writing. Quite significantly, though, Henri-Jean Martin reminded readers that 'writing is nothing by itself'.[31] It must be placed into wider debates of interpretation, memory, literacy and politics. An obvious site for such a study is the education system.

Universities are bookish cultures. Those who read and write well at high school succeed in the exams that facilitate university entrance. Similarly, academics fill journals and write books while drawing a university salary. Doctoral programmes require the completion of a dissertation, not the passing of a teaching competency grading. So much of intellectual writing requires the goodwill of academic staff. Sixty per cent of scholarly journals do not pay their authors.[32] There is even a journal that demands a US$10 'submission fee' (with cheques payable to the University of Illinois), for the 'privilege' of offering an article, for which there is no payment even if it is published.[33]

Writing and reading at universities have reached a point of stasis, provoking a crisis of purpose. Textbooks have replaced the wide reading that was a characteristic of the Oxford tutorial. With the expansion of higher degree recipients, the demands on university libraries and librarians are increasing. Through the widening of the curriculum, everything becomes of potential value. Quite significantly, some university libraries have claimed special interest collections, such as the university in Bowling Green, Ohio, which has established one of the world's best popular cultural studies collections.

There is a major argument to be made — which is verified through the work of cultural studies practitioners — that an emphasis on books is elitist, narrow and politically problematic. We forget the history of the chained book, where reading matter was studied where it sat — on the lectern.[34] This is not a bizarre phenomenon from the Middle Ages. Fresh chains were purchased at the Bodleian in 1751, and others survived at the Magdalene College in Oxford until 1799. The fight over lectern space displays stark similarities to the current scramble over computer terminals.[35] Since this time, schools, libraries and lives have become more open to a plurality of interpretations, attitudes and texts. If we lose the ability to read words on a page, what else may evaporate? Fred Lerner declared that

reading and writing are 'the ways in which men and women collected and organized the records of the human experience'.[36] The purchase of books requires disposable wealth. Such a recognition only
increases the significance of the publicly-accessible library. Besides
the wealth required to own a library, there is also the necessity for a
leisure-based reading time that few double-shift, change-fatigued,
post-Fordist workers now possess. Reading is 'opportunistic';[37] an
activity of comfort, meditation and breathing space.

'Star Trek', in all its televisual series, has always conveyed a commitment to the book. Through all the technology — warp drives,
transporter beams and phasers — the book is read, discussed and
seen. In the last season of 'Voyager', Captain Janeway was interrupted by another Seven of Nine emotional crisis. The Captain
looked comfortable in her easy chair, devouring a well-worn
leather-covered volume. She was irritated at being disturbed from
the solitary nature of her leisure-time reading. If science fiction
— the present stories we tell about the future — can display a
pledge to reading in both form and content, then surely library
discourses can do the same.

   The traditional book has been with us for the last millennium
because it is a functional way to convey both the sharing of content and the passionate solitariness of the reading experience.
Janeway knew that. She was not reading a Rocket e-book. She
knew they looked like an etch-a-sketch on steroids.

The history of books is a tale about the propagation of print and
script. It is an intensely tangled study of the social, economic and
cultural. Therefore, the book will not die, or be replaced by digitisation, because there is an emotional investment in text contained
on cream pages encased in stiff covers. There is a physical link
between seeker and sought, reader and book. A particular mode of
reading is encouraged through the intense concentration on the
page. For example, Gertrude Himmelfarb offers a reflexive interpretation of her reading practices:

With the physical volume in our hand, we are necessarily aware of
the substantiality, the reality of the work, the text is, as Milton or
Rousseau wrote it and meant us to read it ... Moreover, each

page of the book — in the case of a difficult work, each line of the page — has a distinctness, a hard reality of its own. Holding the book in hand, open at that page, it is easy to concentrate the mind upon it, to linger over it, mull over it, take as long as necessary to try to understand and appreciate it.[38]

An irony that few scholars of the book have recognised is that the medium is versatile and portable. The computer screen holds much in common with the scroll, permitting only an awkward reading of the document, being difficult to transport and based on an unstable media platform. What Himmelfarb is suggesting here is not the stability and flexibility of the medium, but a desire to maintain elitist cultural values, rather than a way of reading. Debates about the book need to be ideologically sieved, so that a troubling elitism does not link a particular medium with a specific class. Divergent media encourage particular methods of accessing information. A book can be flicked through, just as a hypertext link can be jumped, but electronic information encourages a smash-and-grab style of reading, rather than a smoother, more reflexive meditation. The key for teachers and the library profession is to show students and the public how to use divergent modes of reading and research. I want my students to click on to the New Zealand government's website. I want my students to use databases and print out PDF documents that they would be unlikely to find on shelves of an Australian library. But I also want them to read, chew, spit out and re-ingest the monographs of Spivak, Bhabha and Balibar. This sort of tight, challenging reading is very difficult to accomplish on the screen, even before considering the various copyright and licensing issues involved if such large-scale retrospective digital reproduction was possible. With dense historical description and high theory, the reading is slow, drifting along with the sensuality for the words, so that detailed and intense meanings may emerge.

The materiality of searching — the evocative potential of exploring an exciting array of potential sources — is still a significant part of an intellectual journey. Particular cultural practices have been lost through the electronic age: flicking through a card catalogue, dialling a telephone or winding down a car window. Everyday life has changed, desensitising corporeality and tearing the sensual surfaces off a textured life. Work has become more efficient, but the banal and mundane have been lost. The sensuality of reading, searching and thinking links the corporeal with the intellectual. That is why this chapter is infused with stories of books, and a passionate connection with ideas, their context and order.

Research is changing. Databases are organsing reading material in new ways. It is profoundly convenient to search the Gale Group's InfoTrac or Bell and Howell's ProQuest databases. They are searchable by keyword, date, author and document type. There are consequences for the commercial development of digital media and research. For those of us residing south of the equator, it is magnificent to have access to thousands of journals we would never ordinarily see. But there is a major price to pay. Not every journal, newspaper or magazine is being digitised.[39] This is no surprise, considering the cost. What is being scanned is overwhelmingly in English, and sourced from the United States and the United Kingdom. Colonisation by digitisation is enacted through the shrinking library budgets and the money needed to pay for these extravagantly-priced databases. These factors mean that fewer monographs and journals are bought for our region, our specificities, our histories. Students enjoy exploring a knowledge appropriate to their context, rather than being instructed in pseudo-universal (trans-Atlantic) truths. Ponder this message left on one of my discussion forums by an external student who conducted his education while working on a ship for the semester. He stressed the importance of understanding our region:

Message No. 423: (Branch from no. 414)
Posted by ****** on Fri, May 25, 19:07
Subject: Pondering the Possible

Dear Tara, I loved the whole concept of a webct the BB was great, I only wish I could have contributed more. My computer access has been limited this semester, but I found catching up with it very interesting. CDD is awash with so many possibilities and concepts and the readings were great. It was good to see coherent intelligent writing without too much academic obfuscation, not to mention the Aust/NZ content. Thanks very much

---

Claiming the regional and specific is still significant. Library budgets have not kept pace with the demands of the new technology and the expanding demands and expectations that these technologies reveal. Only a few years ago, an undergraduate student would not become upset or frustrated by the fact that a university library did not have access to an obscure journal with poor distribution. Now, because of specialist databases, information is provided about articles well beyond the scope of even the world's largest libraries. The expectations of users have grown exponentially. While database searchers know about more, they believe they have access to less. So the work that we write can rarely convey the depth of source material from the Asian and Pacific region.[40]

The difficulty with e-journals is that they require major purchasing decisions. A package of journals and documents must be bought, with some strong titles and many others that merely fill out the 'package'. Aggregators and publishers determine what is added, excluded or dropped, and negotiate short-term licensing agreements that provide temporary 'access', but no archival ownership. This is particularly concerning when collection managers are required by either budgetary or off-campus access concerns to make difficult decisions about the maintenance of print-based/archival collections. Print subscriptions are often sacrificed if access can be gained through aggregators like the company Bell and Howell. The arrangements that aggregators make with journal publishers are never permanent, and titles move between companies. If print subscriptions are cancelled, based on the notion that a journal is available electronically via an aggregator, then that library loses archival access to those issues once the title moves to a new company. This creates gaps in collections more rapidly than irregular distribution or vandalism. The transfer of the license to the electronic version of the *Harvard Business Review* from a Bell and Howell to an Ebsco database in 2001 is an obvious example. Premium titles are often acquired by aggregators in competition with one another. The continuity of library collections and serial runs is sacrificed in this competitive environment.

Stories of reading, thinking, researching and being are not acts of nostalgia or self-absorption. Instead, they offer a reminder of the ardent connection between the bodies of readers and bodies of knowledge. All present technology — particularly when it is being described through metaphor — is an extension of past technology. It is a way to increase the comprehension of discussions. How do we establish the equivalences between journals and e-journals, lectures and e-lectures? If we celebrate the movement from script to digitised text, then a far more engaging, convincing history is lost, which encases manuscripts, book, printing and popular culture. The role and function of communication through print has altered radically through the post-war years, but the book has not died and libraries are surviving. If the structures for presenting information are breaking down, then what will replace them? As information gains a more overt commercial value — to be bought, sold and traded — brokers will earn their living through its exchange. Companies will be devoted to the creation and distribution of resources, not knowledge.

The division between the information rich and the information poor necessitates a discussion of how a socially-just agenda is attached to a celebration of the information age. In such an environment, a library becomes central. Therefore, the next part of this chapter addresses how libraries in particular manage the trope of access.

DUMPSTER DISCOURSE

The net is like a huge vandalized library. Someone has destroyed the catalog and removed the front matter, indexes, etc., from hundreds of thousands of books and torn and scattered what remains ... 'Surfing' is the process of sifting through this disorganized mess in the hope of coming across some useful fragments of text and images that can be related to other fragments. The net is even worse than a vandalized library because thousands of additional unorganized fragments are added daily by the myriad cranks, sages, and persons with time on their hands who launch their unfiltered messages into cyberspace.[41]

Michael Gorman

Libraries are one of the outstanding institutions of the last millennium. They are a site of reassuring continuity. Libraries once stored papyrus scrolls: librarians now assist users to scroll across computer screens. Nicholson Baker's prosecutorial thrust has raised serious questions about the function of the institution. Obviously this function is tethered to the history of reading, writing, communication and education. Libraries also provide a context and venue for the development of social relationships.

Higher education in Ancient Greece arrived through Plato's Academy, circa 387BC, and through Aristotle's Lyceum in 335BC.

It was Aristotle who made reading the pivotal marker of education. It was part of a social history of community and collectivity. The Library of Alexandria is a testament to the power and tragedy of libraries.[42] The library was set up by Ptolemy I in 300BC as a temple to the Muses (*Museion*, which became 'museum'); the scholars in this library aimed to advance the arts and sciences, while distancing themselves from the mundane concerns of life. Through this cultural site, a community of writers, translators, editors, historians, geographers and mathematicians deliberated the problems of the age. The first librarian, Zenodotus of Ephesus, formed the authoritative text of both *The Iliad* and *The Odyssey*. Books were carefully catalogued and bibliographic details established. But a tragedy adds a sting to this magisterial library tale. Although the fire of 48BC destroyed 400 000 rolls, it did not gut the library. The library ended through neglect of what was left. This great institution simply faded from influence and impact through a lack of use. Libraries contain memories, but both can so easily be lost.

The libraries of antiquity were for the benefit and use of kings. In medieval Europe, libraries were shared by king, pope and monastery. After industrialisation, a new master was summoned: the economic foreman of work. The 19th century, besides being the era of explosive but uneven development, was also the period of the municipal library. Emerging in the United States and Britain by the middle of the century, the practice then moved to France. Being supported through taxation, books were loaned without cost to the user. The public libraries of Manchester (1852) and Boston (1854) opened as the embodiment of this principle. The concern with equity was significant. Frederick Kilgour confirmed that 'the vast majority of the library users who borrowed these million volumes yearly were unable themselves to purchase the books they used'.[43] Clearly, the standards used to select the books to be read remained elitist and narrow.[44] The public library movement, formed through the establishment of schools of arts and mechanics' institutes, was a way for working-class citizens to 'improve themselves'. It also added value to the workplace, creating a skilled worker. Marion Wilson recognised that:

> Libraries supplied worthy texts and moral tracts, designed to make people better fit the world as the Victorian ruling classes wanted it to be. People were to better themselves, but only within their class distinction.[45]

Similarly, the current focus on Internet-based information is a political mechanism to block a critical reflection on the changes to education and knowledge, along with a discussion of those socially excluded from the electronic revolution.

Different libraries have precise uses, from the corporate and academic to the public. There is be a specificity to the collection, determining its usefulness. The Library of Congress, founded in 1800, held a distinct purpose. Formed after a revolution and moulded by the Enlightenment values of reason, progress and knowledge, it was established to assist Congress with research to make laws. Popular culture was excluded from the collections of most of these early libraries. Therefore, as newspapers became cheaper through the 19th century, their place and function in libraries became significant in presenting an alternative view of politics, pleasure and power.

By the 20th century, library management became a science and the catalogue a commodity to be sold.[46] Throughout history, librarians have been situated at the margins of the society and discourse they serve. From the medieval monastery (where the needs of prayer dominated) through to the university sector with the stress on credentialling, librarians are not central to any institution. Libraries are the ideological bedrock that allows other discourses to be formed and naturalised.[47] Centring libraries is difficult, because they are necessary accoutrements of other institutions of power. That is why such wide-ranging interpretations circle, vulture-like, around their buildings and collections. Baker's *Double Fold* caused librarians to respond defensively and present their political rationale with overarching simplicity. For example, ponder this editorial, written by Francine Fialkoff from the *Library Journal*:

> Nicholson Baker doesn't get it. He didn't get it when he sensationalized libraries that were 'dumping' books along with the garbage. He didn't get it when he wrote about the conversion for card catalogs to OPACs. Now, he doesn't get it when he writes about the destruction of newspapers and books in the name of microfilming in his latest book, *Double Fold* … However admirable his efforts to preserve newspapers and books and to ensure that original copies of every publication be retained, he doesn't understand — and perhaps never will — that the purpose of libraries is access … Libraries aren't museums. Baker still doesn't get it.[48]

Unfortunately, Fialkoff does not get it either. The ancient history of libraries and museums is tethered to the Library of Alexandria — the temple for the muses. Preservation was part of the agenda. Also for most of their history, libraries have been exclusive institutions, carefully defending a static knowledge system through the ages. Even through the 19th century, the aims of the library were not access, but a civilising imperative for 'the masses'. Access cannot be a primary directive, because there is always the significant follow-up question: access to what? Therefore, assuming that students have 'access' to the Internet is both naïve and disrespectful of library history. Students — particularly those studying through distance modes — affirm that the Internet resolves the difficulty of isolation:

Message No. 322: (Branch from no. 320)
Posted by ****** on Tue, Oct 23, 09:04
Subject: Fun on the Net

Hi all,
For my first assignment for this course, all my extra research was done on the web. The internet for me has had a huge impact on the way I study and do research.. though I was told by Kylie (my tutor) that I should be careful of doing research solely from the internet. I will say that it's so much easier to find information on the internet: articles etc. than it is for me to do in a library (where, in my situation I have only a little while to visit a library, and also here in Cairns the pickings are slim in terms of information for Cultural Studies). I have requested books from Murdoch Library, but what these books contain is often a lot different from what I thought they would (or could) contain given their descriptions on the library internet resources. There's no substitute for being there and flicking through a book, or looking at the books which are near the book you thought you wanted, and finding something else even more appropriate in another book.

External study is ideal for me; I don't mind it at all, though I guess I do 'miss' face-to-face contact in a certain way, but I also think that I am more removed from the pedagogy of internal study, in terms of feeling its immediacy (such as the feeling one gets when one walks into a lecture theatre, sits down in a tutorial): I don't have those concerns. Sure, I have to 'censor' what I say here on the discussion boards, but when it comes down to it, I do think that I am much 'freer' in terms of allowing for the validity of my analyses than I possibly could be in an internal study situation, given that time has to be allowed for other things than for analysis by students in these situations.

Also, when it boils down to it, I probably wouldn't be studying at all (in a university course sense) if external study wasn't available to me, so I can be happy about what I have got, or complain about what I haven't got.

Not surprisingly, on-campus students affirmed the significance of non-digital sites and the importance of interpretation:

Message No. 331 (Branch from no. 320)
Posted by ****** on Wed, Oct 24, 23:12
Subject: Fun on the Net

I suppose if you're researching your assignment exclusively through the web you wouldn't be gaining great research skills or interacting with subjects.
I think if you're getting information from the web there's also a greater tendency to simply copy it and not cite it because you think you've got a good chance of getting away with it. And since it is more hands-on when you're looking for information in books, journals, other non-web resources etc, you're probably more likely to hold on to the subject matter you're investigating and connect ideas you've gathered.

Problems of interpretation and inequality are not only issues for students or the library, but for all institutions negotiating our challenging economic and political environment. Information that is expansive in its social origins and carefully structured is necessary to ensure social justice. While the political function of data, information and knowledge has never been greater, librarianship as a profession is facing what Herbert Schiller described as a 'thorough privatization of the information function'.[49] In this context, technology camouflages the socially-regressive nature of education and democracy. Further, there is a profound necessity for librarians to focus their energies and training on the hardware, software and programming of information. The social nature of the profession, the crafting and grafting of an integrated palette of specialties, specificities and representations, has been deflected. The skills of professional librarians are remarkable, and frequently underestimated and undermined. This situation is made worse through the emphasis of technical skills over intellectual abilities. (Un)fortunately, the consumer's requirements of libraries are narrow. In a 1998 survey conducted by the American Library Association to discover what people wanted from a library, 81 per cent of those appraised stated that they simply wanted to borrow books.[50]

Ignoring such findings, librarians are reinventing themselves as information resource centres, and myriad other banal phrases. Michael Dirda believed that 'it was a dark day for book lovers when libraries started calling themselves media learning centers'.[51] Acquisition budgets are decreasing and more money is being swallowed to maintain database subscriptions.[52] Through all these challenges, the creation of networked services is not a sufficient goal for the library. 'Information' is derived from the Latin *informare*, meaning the imposition of a form. The role of the powerful in the information age becomes clearer when recognising this origin. The expertise of librarians can support new modes of reading, writing and communication, integrating and connecting discovery, searches, navigation and use of diverse resources. In this way, libraries remain institutions of the public sphere, an integral core to any conceptualisation of citizenship, civilization, knowledge and social justice. The earlier roles of the library are appended to the new convergences of publishing, cataloguing and information aggregation. This is not a hybrid (digital and analogue) library: it is an integrated approach to print and electronic resources that does not instigate an ungainly graft onto 19th century models of space, time and information. It is a meta-library, an institution that reflexively ponders its aims, goals and purpose.

The expansion of the information economy — of librarians, archivists and information professionals — means that a map of information industries is being constructed and corrected by many hands. Just as the 1980s and the 1990s were times of culture wars — politicised discussions about the nature of culture — Edward Shreeves discerns that the conflicts on university campuses about the place of print and digital resources in the library are 'acquisitions culture wars'.[53] The attendant debates about the function of computers and books in the information age provide a shrill, emotive edge to such discussions. Such debates revolve around notions of cultural value, and where the decreasing budget should be allocated: to digital or book-based knowledge systems. Obviously, this either/or option is highly inflammatory, and is avoided through Nicholson Baker's *Double Fold*. He holds no difficulty with digitisation, but believes that a book or bound original should *also* be held.

The Baker controversy raises questions about the role of libraries, particularly research libraries, in public discourse. A good library is determined as much by what it excludes as by what is incorporated into its collection. The history of a library is always a narrative of those knowledges that transcend it. The point of the institution is to make available the sights, sounds and textures of an earlier age for the purposes of the current reader. It is on this issue that Christine Cody believes 'the libraries failed us'.[54] They are not archives, with the task to preserve a corporate or societal memory focused on a very precise period, topic or organisation. Libraries provide a record of a far wider information landscape They hold not only content, but provide a context for information. While libraries are not archives, if material is not preserved, then it cannot be read. Further, how is the citizenry to be encouraged to read the collection? Libraries must not end up like neglected cemeteries.

As yet, there is little agreement about the nature of the digital library: it may refer to document delivery, research training, database instruction, computer support, or network-based reference queries.[55] In academic libraries, reference services are handling a mixed clientele, some with highly-advanced technological proficiencies and others with more pressing training needs. If a digital library is a motif of the age, then it needs to be filled with content far beyond technical expediency. Social, intellectual and political issues need to attend the party. Certainly, there are technical challenges. To develop an integrated systems of documents, with standardised means of classification and the use of meaningful metadata, is a challenge. Without standard metadata, there is no way to ascertain the value and relationship between diverse documents.

The Internet is a convenient, less time-consuming way to conduct research, if the user possesses the necessary equipment and literacies. The copying and distributing of digital information is fast, and the issues associated with the storage of library holdings seem to be solved. However, the surprises of research — the unexpected reference, the book next to the book on the shelf that we were retrieving — are far less common. The Internet is not a library: this is a dangerous metaphor. The characteristic of a library — the organisation of knowledge into preservable categories — has hardly left a trace on the Internet.[56] Cataloguing systems are not simply a collection of numbers, but a sequence of ideas. While such structures may appear a relic of the analogue age, they hold a social function — to enable users to search, gather and assess information. While the web may appear to remove the physicality of information, we are yet to make this leap conceptually. The main question to be confronted is how the information is to be deployed with responsibility.

THE LURE OF THE LONG NOW

*Who was I, after all, before I started reading? Does it
matter, since from the moment I started on that path
I became the creature of these pages.*[57]

Geoffrey O'Brien

The final part of this chapter conducts epistemological spadework to
determine the cultural politics of information and its preservation.
There are far-reaching consequences for the information explosion.
Baker's anger was directed at what he saw as the destructive treat-
ment of books and newspapers by librarians, those entrusted with
their safekeeping. I want to stress that the situation is even more serious than he suggested. It is in the realm of digital materials that the
greatest cultural losses will be sustained.

Digital documents are much more difficult to preserve than
paper. While the digital realm has created an explosion of information, sites and voices, it also possesses its own attendant, destructive
silencer and destroyer: self-obsolescence. Every new piece of software
and hardware steps over the broken bodies of files, images, peripherals and ideas that — with ruthless precision — have been lost and
destroyed, rather than migrated or moved. Programming languages,
storage formats and operating systems are made redundant alongside
the documents, images and words written through the platforms.
What language do we choose for preservation purposes: HTML,
XML, SGML or CGI scripting? Every new Microsoft upgrade burns
a digital Library of Alexandria. We accept the losses, the tragedies, as
the nature of working in our long now. Brand showed that 'science
historians can read Galileo's technical correspondence from the
1590s but not Marvin Minsky's from the 1960s'.[58] The replacement
of hardware and the upgrades of software show that the maintenance
of a digital database, let alone an archive, will be very expensive.
Most websites have the lifespan of an open bag of M&Ms, and are
treated with about as much social significance. Such a statement is
not technological determinism: the Internet did not increase the
sense of speed, just as the printing press did not cause the
Reformation. Critics want to find rupture, discontinuity and difference. It is timely to recognise the political and ideological conflu-
ences between the analogue and digital, alongside the specific
difficulties evoked through the maintenance of digital data.

The difficulties and problems confronting librarians and archivists who wish to preserve digital information are revealed in the Australian government's PADI (Preserving Access to Digital Information) site:

> Compared with an object in a museum which may lay undis-
> turbed for years in a storeroom, or a book on a shelf, or even
> Egyptian hieroglyphics carved on the wall of a tomb, digital
> information requires much more active maintenance. If we want
> access to digital information in the future, we must plan and act
> now.[59]

Much information, particularly in governmental and university settings, is currently being generated only in a digital form. If this material is lost, then much 'documentary heritage'[60] will be absent from the historical record. To stay up to date in our time will cost our past. We are losing popular memory. That is the price for prioritising the present over the past. The speed of digitisation means that responsibility for preserving information increases the pressure facing information professionals. Major structural problems confront the archivist and the librarian. Inadvertent destruction of, or tampering with, data is matched with little systematic tracking of change. Digital storage is a straightforward process. To be able to actually read and use this data is exceedingly difficult.

Digital migration obviously solves these problems. It involves the transfer of files from one computer platform to another. The complexity is that an integrated sequence of migration must be maintained. For example, documents written on the pre-Windows Word 5 could be used in Office 97, but not Office 2000. Without the migration chain, the documents are lost. Ironically, digital archivists' task is similar to those masterful scholars in the Library of Alexandria, possessing a responsibility to copy and translate. The future of memory is in their keyboarding hands. This is fractal preservation, during an era of heavily-centralised economic power.

Pessimism dominates historians of library preservation. Lerner moaned that 'the preservation of the literary artifact is an impossibility. The best that can be hoped for is to protect the information contained within the artifact'.[61] Only particular archives will be significant enough to store digitally. Samuel Florman stated that 'in the digital age nothing need be lost; do we face the prospect of

drowning in trivia as the generations succeed each other?'.[62] The trivia of academics is the fodder (and pleasure) of everyday life. Digitised
preservation, like analogue preservation, can never 'represent' plural
paths through the past. There is always a limit, boundary and border
to what is acceptable obsolescence. The loss of cultural texts through
digitisation will further erode the status, role and place of disempowered groups.

The profound uncertainties derived from the maintenance of digital documents are undermining the enormous potential that digitisation offers for disseminating data. Textual, numeric, pictorial,
video, audio, multimedia and simulation necessitate divergent preservation tactics. While the ASCII character sets allow standardised
character mapping, there are documents where these codes are not
representative, such as those involving formulae or multiple languages. Once more, an (over)emphasis on English is serving to
reduce the presence of other languages in the archived and preserved
digital environment.

Popular cultural information will suffer most from the blind spots
of digital archivists. While libraries rarely preserve the ephemera of a
time, many homes (including mine) preserve the 'trash' of a culture.
A lightsaber, toy dalek, Duran Duran poster and a talking
Undertaker are all traces of past obsessions. Passion evaporates, and
interests morph into new trends. These objects remain in attics,
under beds, in boxes and sheds throughout the world. Digital documents necessitate a larger project of preservation, with great financial
(and spatial) commitments of technology, software and staff maintenance. Libraries rarely preserve the ephemera — the texture and light
— of the analogue world. That task is left to popular cultural
experts/fans. While the fan experience is based on gleaning knowledge, the intellectual imperative is to control knowledge, not just to
collect it. The popular cultural intellectual faces particular challenges
working in and through librarian preservation practices. Moving
through scholastic and fan spheres, different knowledges and traditions are hailed. These dual identifications create bipolar discursive
disorders, and schizophrenic literacies. The digital era reduces the
number of tactile, fan-based archives. Subsequently forfeited is the
spectrum of interests and ideologies that construct the popular memory of a culture. The tactility of popular cultural sources is already
lacking from the historian's database of the last century. This absence
will be exacerbated through digitisation. Even a scanned colour

image of a talking Jedi knight is not an adequate — or perhaps even meaningful — representation of the three-dimensional cultural figure. Ephemeral material, by definition, is transitory. Digital ephemera is merely an enhancement of that principle.

The metonymy of this process is William Gibson's story *Agrippa: The book of the dead*. Only thirty-five copies were 'printed', with the script programmed to only scroll once, therefore permitting only one projection. To enact this reading, it was encoded using a RSA algorithm. These algorithms in the United States are classified as weapons of war. The threat of obsolescence — of disappearing data — is a munition of the powerful. Institutions always validate particular information. Archivists and librarians have always made these decisions. Currently, the timeframe in which these choices are being enacted in the digital environment is shortening. The media's instability through technological obsolescence adds a time imperative that is absent from other archival discussions. The scale of preservation is also far more encompassing. If a hypertext document is preserved, then the links also must be maintained, granting interactivity, context and affectivity of the site. A digital document without hyperlinks does not present the capacity of the medium. A far more profound question concerns who has the responsibility for preserving digital information. Without refreshing or migrating the data, digital information can only be displayed and used through hardware that is continually tumbling into obsolescence. Therefore, the creators/preservers of these texts would also need to establish a collection of archaic computer systems, to 'guarantee' the survival of documents created on them. It is hardware obsolescence that is a primary problem facing archivists. Electronic information is watermarked by a tension between permanence and the ephemeral. Electronic texts require a mediator — a translator. Frequently, this process also needs an appropriate computer. Relevant hardware and software must also be preserved. Librarians are confronting these changes in literacy standards and readership strategies unrehearsed and under-prepared. A commitment to mediate information is desperately required.

When considering the future of memory, digital or otherwise, I remember a comment made by my seventy-something mother. She rarely travels on airplanes, and I am terrified of heights, but in one of our few flights together she made a remarkable statement. While I sat perched on an aisle seat, with gaze averted from the view and attention placed on anything except my disgruntled stomach, she happily watched the clouds jutting past the window. Her thoughts were drawn to the past as much as to the future. Half way through the journey from Perth to Sydney, and after looking out the window for about three hours, she said: 'You know, Tara, people have to die, or else the changes would kill them'. Perhaps that is the greatest fear of digitisation. Will the mind of the analogue age 'die'? Are the changes — or the rhetoric of change — killing the passion, humour and affectivity of our time? While revelling in the play of progress and technophilia, we must monitor the digital future of the popular cultural past.

PART III

TEACHERS AND TEACHING, STUDENTS AND LEARNING

5

RECLAIMING THE TEACHER'S BODY

It is a tough era for a teacher with a body. The corporeal form of educators has been stripped of the cane, de-gowned and threatened with claims of sexual impropriety. These three necessary legislative and social interventions in teaching behaviour and practice have transformed the teacher's body into a dangerous, scrutinised cultural formation. We all have stories — gossiped whispers in the corridor — detailing sexual impropriety between students and staff. As we titter into our long black coffee, teachers become ever more conscious of limiting their bodily gestures, repressing enthusiasm for ideas, people and places, and always leaving their office door open for all to see the banal routines of education. The landscapes of sex and desire are shorn from the terrain of learning, creating a disembodied self that is judged, regulated and scrutinised. Through such self-monitoring, we are hiding from our identities, emotions and responsibilities as teachers and scholars, denying what makes education important and memorable. In such an environment, web-based education offers an obvious medication to the dangerous passions of the classroom and desires lurking in the corridor.

This chapter reclaims the teacher's body, arguing that one of the major reasons it has been so easy to celebrate online education is because we have neither theorised nor admitted how flesh, blood and bone function in our classrooms. In the startling white glare of an overhead, I write of my body as a teacher. When the body is rethought, so are societal frameworks. Through leaking corporeality, a radical remaking of politics and embodiment are sketched. Using David Tripp's model for critical incidents in teaching,[1] I align theory and practice to imagine new possibilities for bodies in teaching, and bodies of knowledge. These 'thinking strategies'[2] allow the formation of alternatives that widen the parameters of effective education. There is much of my teaching and students in this chapter. It must be this way, so that biographies of the self are integrated into the projects of the body. Before becoming wired professors, we need to mourn the losses of the cyber-classroom. Teachers who are happy to be replaced by computers — should be. For the rest of us, we draw the jurisdiction and rationale for our bodily fight.

There is another reason why there are some personal insights in this chapter. We live in an era where teachers are criticised, undermined, assessed, judged and ridiculed. The teaching conducted at universities is not given the credit or attention it deserves. Politicians and educational administrators talk a great deal about teaching, without detailed knowledge of current educational contexts. Those of us who teach are locked in isolated classrooms, lecture theatres and tutorial spaces. We rarely share our concerns, fears or expertise. The experiences of joy, sadness and frustration we confront every day never make it into government reports or press releases. With the intense demands on academic life, collegiality and group discussions about best practices are rare. I therefore welcome readers into my teaching life and my troubled thoughts about bodies and education. In committing to the page some tremulous moments of teaching, I summon all the great educators who it has been my pleasure to know, meet and watch. Invariably, we teach as we have been taught. There is little remarkable about me, my teaching or my students. All teaching is part of a system, and has a context and a history. This chapter offers a reminder of the remarkable effort that all teachers are conducting every day, without having the time, energy or inclination to commit the bright, stark, but transitory educational revelations to print.

My words take shape and direction from the brave, forthright work of bell hooks. Through her writing, she has stressed the erotic in her classrooms:

> Individuals enter the classroom to teach as though only the mind is present and not the body. To call attention to the body is to betray the legacy of repression and denial that has been handed down to us by our professorial elders, who have usually been white and male ... No one talked about the body in relation to

teaching. What did one do with the body in the classroom? Trying to remember the bodies of my professors, I find myself unable to recall them. I hear voices, remember fragmented details but very few whole bodies.[3]

The first time I read her descriptions of the love she felt for students in her classroom, I recoiled from the page, eyes turned away in fearful confusion, believing that such forthright body knowledge in education is an unforgivable intervention. Yet the point of education is to move teachers and students out of their comfortable mind furniture, a task at which bell hooks excels. Feminist pedagogy is a significant corrective to debates about web education. By corroding the mind/body divide, academics become textured identities, rather than disembodied texts. This is a culture of resistance that challenges normative education and academic master narratives. Therefore, the imperative of Internet teaching can be read as another way to discredit feminist imperatives.[4] Because the body in teaching is rarely researched, we are all eager to erase our flesh with phosphorous luminosity. To offer a suicidal metaphor, teachers' bodies are where the rubber meets the road. We feel the pain, disappointment, sweat, anger and passion. Our corporeality creates an affective, transformational space.

Throughout my career, students have expressed happiness and enjoyment in my classes, and also regret at the conclusion of a semester. The place of desire in my lecture theatre is also a site of great humour.

I used to teach in a tough town in Central Queensland, where men are men and women laugh at them. I was a young female lecturer at the time, teaching a big first-year course. I always used to wonder why my male students would be waiting outside the front of my lecture theatre and then race in to dominate a particular section of the room, always sitting in the identical chairs. I thought they were expressing their enthusiasm for cultural studies. Thankfully — at the *end* of the course — one of my female students explained the male students' great enthusiasm and commitment to specific seating arrangements. They sat in that position every week so they could get a quick look at my cleavage every time I bent over to change the overhead transparency.

They did not teach me about a breasted pedagogy when I was in teachers' training.

This trend has continued through my teaching life. Invariably, the semester commences with the last five rows filled with young men, arms crossed over tatty Metallica T-shirts, shades flexed, beanies on, and ready for a quick exit. Slowly during the semester they move forward through the rows until by the last sessions, the first five rows are filled with young men who arrive at the lecture theatre early, with shades off and beanies removed, chatting with all their new friends about the course, or at least about what I am wearing that day.

I am not worried that students watch my physicality. It is one way — and a powerful way — to teach a body of knowledge. While lecturers and teachers have a responsibility for the learning environment, students have a responsibility to be present, aware and prepared for learning. We provide the frame: they create the landscape. If students miss lectures, they have simply stepped outside the frame. To get students into the lecture theatre, awake and interested, I will use anything, especially my body. Ponder this message left in an open discussion forum on a course website:

Message No. 44:
Posted by ****** on Tue, July 31, 15:44
Subject: Hi

Hi Tara, I just got on to Webct today, and thought i'd just tell you what a change your lectures are compared to my past experiences which just encouraged us not to turn up and yes I am one of those students who has actually fallen asleep in a lecture. I think for sure the best aspects of the first lectures were the slides of Kylie minogues ass, and that freeken hamster, I even talked about those jokes and the hole lecture to some friends (and believe me I would never vouluntary talk about a lecture). And one last thing ahs anybody told you you remind them of a cross between Edina from absolutely Fabulous, Gina Riley from Fast Forward (one o the best shows created by us Aussies) and Bridget Bardot the resemblance is scaring me.

Obviously, one of my hopes is that this young man learned how to spell during the semester. He is what our system would term an at-risk student: missing lectures, falling asleep, more committed to friends than to an education. At least my strategies to invoke multiple literacies from popular culture seem to be working. He has yet to miss a lecture I have delivered. Some educational managers may be somewhat concerned that a young man is seeing any similarity between Bridget Bardot and a university lecturer. I cannot see it myself. This student is obviously watching my body, perhaps a bit too closely for comfort, but through this bodily attention, knowledge is revealed and an expertise developed that would not occur if he did not attend this lecture. Adult education is meant to be tempered by the self-directed seeking of both knowledge and understanding. Students in this environment are goal- and learning-oriented. Well, that is the premise. This student is not a good candidate for an online course. He lacks the self-starter discipline and motivation required for the successful completion of a virtual education. Instead, he requires the enthusiasm and energy of a lecture theatre to assist his learning. Lecturing is not a performance. It is public speaking at its most precise and advanced. The body creates an interest in the content: it is the medium for conveying this content. Through gestures, hand movements and eye contact, a lecture pitch can be varied, along with the volume and inflection of the voice.

Communication arches between written and oral modes. It is important that clothes, gestures and grain of voice become an integral and reflexive part of teaching. As with all non-verbal communication, meaning is ambiguous and negotiated. There is little control over how bodily behaviour is read and understood. There are major cultural differences negotiated through the use of space.[5] Teaching philosophies are marked by a personal vision and a compilation of values and attitudes. Education triggers a response that is of the mind, body, intellect and emotion. As bell hooks reminded us, though, 'rarely is such passion institutionally affirmed'.[6]

I have always filled the five minutes before the commencement of a lecture with loud pulsating music that has resonance with the week's teaching. Sometimes it is a joke track (Ace of Base 'The Sign' to start — you guessed it — the semiotics lecture). Pulp's 'Common People' is used to teach class. But I have a poignant, sensory memory of my first lecture as a full-time staff member, delivered in New Zealand. I was the foreigner — I was the one that spoke oddly, not them. I started this first lecture for a survey course of European history from 1830–1992 with Blackbox's 'Ride on Time'. Besides being a brilliant song with a powerful backbeat and screeching female vocals, it seemed an ideal way to orient students into thinking about time, movement and history. At the end of the song, one of my new students turned to his friend and said: 'What about Blackbox's "Ride on time"? Do you think we are going to be examined on this?'.

And, in a strange way, he was.

Education is a struggle with powerful ideas and a fight over meaning. I remain deeply moved by bell hooks' realisation that 'even when students are desperately yearning to be touched by knowledge, professors ... allow their worries about losing control to override their desires to teach'.[7] It is the desperate yearning to *feel more*, live differently and activate an alternative way of being that is the point of education. The invidious, seething anger of the current political environment — which our students bark back to us — is based on the cool, clear realisation that the market is not going to save us, and a shareholding citizenry offers few entrees into social justice. Through this despair, our responsibility as educators is to do nothing less than change the world, via each of our students.

The body is the repository and vehicle for social injustice and disciplinary action. Lives are written through facial lines, swollen hands, roughened feet and scarred knees. The future — an imagining of what could be — is written in our students' bodies with shoulders back, eyes forward and head up. There is a knowledge enfolded in the skin that is not always placated or bent by conservative politics or national histories. To avoid teachers becoming lost to the system, we ponder on a daily basis how our consciousness and mental abilities are translated through the body. Female teachers in particular must not waste their bodies, as they have been the vehicle for our oppression. We turn the site of disempowerment and struggle into a display of survival, confidence, joy, energy and enthusiasm. Sherry Shapiro's realisation is a significant one: 'What is rarely found in such work is a pedagogy where the body/subject as a lived medium becomes part of the curriculum'.[8] Consciousness emerges through the sensory experiences of the everyday. Life has a taste, touch and smell that is part of our teaching. Through this practice, relevant, living truths can emerge, provoking questioning, activism and writing.

Education is a passionate formation, triggering deep, lasting change. It involves being committed to more than the next meal. Classrooms are sites of challenge, confusion, and passionate dialogues about ideas. Considering the feminine domination of the profession, it is surprising that much of the fear and concern about sex in education is aimed at the men who hold power in schools and universities: the headmasters and professors. This fear does have some currency and appropriateness. William Kerrigan, Professor of English at the University of Massachusetts, acknowledged his sexual conquests with some pride:

> I have been the subject of advances from male and female students for twenty-five years. I've had them come at me right and left. I've had people take their clothes off in my office. And there is a particular kind of student I have responded to ... I'm talking about a female student who, for one reason or another, has unnaturally prolonged her virginity ... There have been times when this virginity has been presented to me as something that I, not quite like another man, half an authority figure, can handle ... these relationships between adults can be quite beautiful and genuinely transforming. It's very powerful sexually and psychologically, and because of that power, one can touch a student in a positive way.[9]

I shiver when reading such words. I was one of those Catholic-school-educated female students who 'unnaturally prolonged her virginity' through my university years. I remember being frightened by my own body most of the time. If the men who I respected so deeply had 'touched me', then my mental health and capacity to trust would have been severely damaged. Such behaviour from empowered scholars is appalling and needs to be structurally and institutionally reprimanded. Teachers are not the equal of students, and friendships can only be formed much later, not in the educational oven of tutorials and lectures. The reason for this distance is that teachers require a demonstrated credibility in their field. If students trust us as teachers, then they will follow us anywhere. But the excesses of Kerrigan's fantasy life raise myriad questions about power, authority, education and sex. Is the only solution for such unforgivable actions to withdraw the body completely and retract to the corseted self of the keyboard, bulletin board and chat room? It is a safe mode of teaching, but is education — in its best sense — ever safe? The line between modelling intellectual leadership and mentoring student change is never as cleanly drawn as we may hope. A teacher's interest in ideas can be read as an invitation for a different type of intimacy. While I have never had students remove clothing in my office — perhaps because I leave my door open and they may become either cold and/or embarrassed — they become agitated, emotional and obsessive on a daily basis. It would be very easy to take advantage of the power that we as teachers hold. To do so would be not only unprofessional, but destructive of the potential we have to channel that passion and commitment for educational imperatives. Through our bodies and voices, students construct knowledge in an educationally-relevant way. By granting attention to teachers' bodies, a critical rupture cuts through the teacher–knowledge–student relationship.

One of the *advantages* of multimedia is that students can receive *training*, *just-in-time* and *flexibly*, slotting into their timetable, and based on their *individual needs*.[10] This nonsensical language is sold so pervasively and so often that we no longer balk at the harm and damage such words enact on education. When I encounter a new idea or way of thinking, my hand shakes, my mind cartwheels and normal, everyday activities like housecleaning become a low priority. 'Individual needs' are an insular and narrow base on which to build an education system. It is forgotten that *Universitas* refers to formal associations of like-minded people; it is not based on individual achievement. Halal and Liebowitz attacked the traditions of education, commenting that 'today's typical college classroom is archaic: the only thing that distinguishes it from the classroom of the medieval university is an overhead projector'.[11] It obviously did not occur to these writers that a system that has survived through war, depression and genocide perhaps has some strengths and advantages. The excessive droning for change has hampered an affirmation of the functional continuities of the system, most precisely the role of the teacher's body. Meeting customer/student needs only serves the interests of those who believe that the workplace should determine the limits and expanses of self and identity.

SENSUAL SOFTWARE

Teaching operates across the boundaries of nation, class, justice and desire. It is therefore not surprising that interdisciplinary approaches from cultural studies and critical pedagogy work well in summoning this history of possibilities. There is a strong argument — verified by precise review of the scholarship — that cultural studies was built through teaching. While the canonical texts rarely summoned the politics of pedagogy,[12] the references and beliefs are revealed after considered evaluation. Lawrence Grossberg remembered that:

> All of the founding figures of cultural studies (including Richard Hoggart, Raymond Williams, E.P. Thompson, and Stuart Hall) started their careers, and their intellectual projects, in the field of education, outside the university, in extramural departments and adult working-class courses.[13]

My work in this book is part of this critical tradition of cultural studies in/and education, reigniting the pilot light and political fire of this early work. It is Internet teaching that requires a cultural studies skewer to pierce the pomposity. There is a dignity and importance in Stuart Hall's affirmation that:

> I am convinced that no intellectual worth his or her salt, and no university that wants to hold up its head in the face of the twenty-first century, can afford to turn dispassionate eyes away from the problems ... that beset our world.[14]

The aim, therefore, is to use theory and practice to probe and disturb commonsensical, heavily-funded and institutionally-applauded structures and truths. The role and place of the Internet in such a directive remains ambivalent. Students know about the vocabulary and grammar of the Internet, but we need to teach them what these structures and signs mean — who is left out, and what is to be gained and lost.

The idea that multimedia programs supplement or replace the teacher has been increasing in frequency. Significant follow-up questions need to be asked, though: is this change motivated by cost savings or a commitment to improved learning and teaching? The mobilisation of educational resources in this fashion privileges some learners over others, prioritising hardware over peopleware.

To celebrate the individual freedoms of technology is to block a systematic evaluation of the intangibilities of learning: the feedback, reinforcement or praise. To assess educational technologies requires a language of resources, efficiency, cost and interactive delivery. Too often, human resource questions are absent from this model. This dearth is completely understandable. As Daniel Chandler laughingly reminded us, 'the world is divided into those who divide people into two types, and those who don't'.[15] Human history becomes concisely simplified by the discovery of a determinant, such as the DNA cluster or the locomotive. To avoid analytical ambiguity, there is an intellectual desire to codify, classify and order. Focusing on multimedia displaces discussions of power and societal struggles by stressing a new array of 'basic skills'. Not all modes of teaching and learning require content-based drills. Not all difficulties or challenges in life can be solved by a multiple choice test or short answer quiz.

BODIES AT A DISTANCE

Importantly, the problems and advantages of distance learning can be considered in bodily terms. Distance — emotional, intellectual, social and physical — is a profound barrier to an education. The key is to select the right media for non-campus-based learning. Distance education demands that teachers place disciplined attention on methodology and materials, so that their knowledge is conveyed appropriately and carefully for students already studying in difficult circumstances. We search for a way to replicate the intimacy of face-to-face discussions — to move the body through space. (A)synchronous web discussions can rarely capture the energy and immediacy of fiery debate in a classroom. While there can be compensation for a loss of the physicality from the web, students still need to move conceptually. A robust web platform may not be enough to shift learners' expectations.

Distance, correspondence and external education create specific challenges. These students obviously have succinct needs to be nurtured, as they are completing education under arduous conditions. I worry about my distance-education students, and the main reason I persist with the online environment is to assist these scholars in overcoming isolation. I often worry that on-campus students dominate discussion forums to the detriment of other modes of study:

Message No. 428 (Branch from 426)
Posted by Tara Brabazon (H267) on Tue, May. 29, 08:10
Subject: Pondering the Possible
Thanks

I agree with you. I got the feeling that discussions were growing
organically from what happened in the lectures and tutorials. My
only fear was – and this is the question for my externals – did you
feel excluded from conversations, or more involved?

My aim was to try to bring all the different modes of the course
together – so that we could share the discussion. I don't think
we've got the mix right yet, but it is getting there :)

Thanks for the support darling – I guess we'll keep the site going
for 2002 :)
Be well, T.

My external students answered the call with the clarity and
passion that I expect of them:

Message No. 434: (Branch from no. 414)
Posted by ****** on Wed, May.30, 16:09

Subject: Pondering the Possible

go away to NY for a few days and i miss out on too much
–where to start?! (the big apple was delicious!) anyway to
tatra's questions:

* Was it worthwhile? * Did it help you? * How did you find
the mixing of internal and external students? * What did
you get from the web site that the internal or external
versions of the course did into provide for you? * What
worked – what didn't?

in all honesty this is the best course i have done at murdoch-
the level of involvement i experienced was far higher than
anything to date. being external, isolation can be a real prob-
lem- this course allowed me to hear what was. going on at uni
and in other students heads. while yes, there were a few
times i felt left out because i wasn't internal in the end it
didn't matter too much as i gained so much from being able to
pasively listen. also Tar, Leanne and Kylie – you are the BEST.
the support you gave to everyone was brilliant- you never
made anyone feel like an idiot rather you encouraged,
prompted and congratulated- this is a real bonus to our self
esteem especially when we doubt ourselves. thank you for

such a rewarding course- a suggestion would be a site where we externals can go and see what you guys look like- all semester you have been but typed words and not faces- this is weird. anyway that's all from me.

Even when separated by antipodal distances, teachers' bodies matter. Whenever I ponder removing the online options and facilities from my courses, I read this message and recognise that the Internet has occupied an educational niche for students isolated from a campus. However, it is important to remember that there are other ways to embody education.

In the history of teaching and learning, it is off-campus students who have first experienced the advances that technology provides to lessen their disadvantage and improve their learning environment. From paper, to video, audio-tape, telephone, audio-conferencing, voicemail, email, file transfer protocols and the world wide web, distance education has been a testing ground, an experimental litmus paper. The Internet offers an opportunity to resolve a lack of communication options for off-campus students. The technology for teaching is judged by the home and school environment, not the most advanced university-based software. Costs to students are the pervasive consideration in decision-making. There are effective and cheaper methods for embodying education for off-campus students. Aural technologies in particular have been under-discussed in the teaching literature.

The sensualities and senses of our bodies can be used with care, compassion and thought. The mechanisms of teacher training and teaching support often lack attention to audio technologies and aural education. The Open University has always been a leader in the field. Bates demonstrated that:

Audio cassettes are low cost; all students already have facilities at home; they are easy for academics to produce, and cheap and simple to distribute; students find them convenient to use; and, when designed properly, they encourage student activity. (UK OU audio-cassettes are rarely lectures.)[16]

Well-designed audio cassettes, in combination with print, are extremely cost-effective. They also allow the grain of voice to be transported to distance learners. They add sensuality and texture to education. The choices of technology must always be determined by learning goals, not through technological directives.

Sound is an underplayed part of education. It projects the corporeal sensations of laughter, memory, movement and meaning. I like my classrooms buzzing with music, rhythms, backbeats and basslines. I want my students to hear Dr Martin Luther King or Betty Friedan; to hear the resonance and feel the passion. To write and teach for the ear is an under-developed — and very undertaught — skill. Voicing for the ear is also an imperative for audio cassettes, teleconferencing, conference calls and one-to-one telephone consultations. These are blind media, where visible data is not available for us to gain sensory information. One of my greatest agitations is the taping of lectures for distribution and replaying by students. For me, this is a ridiculous act and a mockery of lectures as a tactile, aural, visual, sensory explosion of possibilities. Once more, education is reduced to content. It is far more difficult, yet more satisfactory, to create purpose-built audio technologies that are not 'lectures', but more amenable to the aural realm. Writing for the ear is completely different to writing for a visual, gestured delivery, with the accompanying props, sweat and energy. To formulate effective audio texts requires a personality and voice to be squeezed through the microphone, making the print live beyond the eye and the brain, but passing through the mouth and dancing around the listener's ear. Voices push the body through space.

It is easy in the era of real audio and real video players to claim that audio-only methods are superseded. Yet their cost to students and educational institutions will guarantee their currency for some time. Meacham and Butler affirmed that:

> For almost all subjects the audio-cassette can be a practical and inexpensive means of personalizing material, providing variety and interest, and presenting information whilst the eyes are occupied elsewhere, or merely resting.[17]

It is a highly empowering and significant realisation that the eyes can be 'elsewhere' while aural media present material in an innovative fashion. The speed of listening to a tape is far slower than reading words on a page, so for specific topics requiring reflection and contemplation, audio texts are ideal, and distinct from the point, click, aural, visual and motor stimulation of the web. The skills necessary to create this special learning environment — in accent, pronunciation and inflection — are rarely taught. The voice is a technology that needs to be trained, moderated and improved. While convergence is allowing the voice to pass through digital modes, there are still verbal techniques to be learned, compensating for the lack of body language. As a blind medium, audio technologies refocus teachers on the strategic nature of words in communication and education.

There are some brave online educators. There is so little recorded in the professional literature about the difficulties, confusions and paranoia that result from teaching, learning and writing online. With so much funding thrown at online development, it takes courage to affirm non-digital alternatives. Too often there is an easy celebration of the online environment as magically creating student-centred learning. Jack Kenny, for example, applauded that 'Pupils will be able to take more control of how they learn'.[18] It never occurred to him to ask how students attain the skills to monitor, control and evaluate their own learning. We do not emerge from the womb with either a library card or a modem. Ellen Cronan Rose has a strong dose of pluck in her review of women's studies courses via distance education. She had believed the maxim that technologies can enhance a collaborative learning formation, which is so appropriate to all classrooms, particularly those inflected by feminism. Her results were more patchy than she had hoped:

> On balance, computer-mediated communication in this course did not result in the 'enhanced discussion' ... Of the eight students in WOM 301, only three regularly posted messages. Most did not have modems at home and hence could gain access to e-mail only in campus computer labs, a problem for students who work from twenty to forty hours a week in the paid labor force ... And at least three were just plain terrified of the technology. So nothing like a 'full discussion' of various issues occurred.[19]

All the best intentions and design innovation cannot guarantee student learning, regardless of whether the course is offered on-campus, online or through distance modes. In such an environment of student responsibility, students actually blame teachers for their failures and inadequacies.

Rose's disappointment has been accompanied by serious disquiet from other educators. Angela Benson and Elizabeth Wright unleashed a serious warning to wired educators:

> The potential and drawbacks of online learning are so great that the widespread move to digitize courses needs to be accompanied by a broad-based discussion about the social implications of this trend.[20]

But what of teachers? Internet-based educational theory focuses on students, rather than on the slogging work necessary to make the frames function and keep the hypertext links current. While it may have been assumed that online education was a way to teach more students more cheaply, that neoliberal mirage has not crystallised. Michelle Vachris traced the expenses required for this learning mode:

> The development costs associated with an online course do not disappear after the first semester. Instead of developing a set of lectures that need only minor updating each semester, as in a classroom setting, the online instructor must carefully devise new assignments each semester through which the students discover the concepts for themselves.[21]

Obviously Vachris has exaggerated the argument to make a point: a poor teacher allows on-campus lectures to go unchanged from year to year, just as an inadequate online educator allows broken links to go uncorrected. She shows that online education is not an easy option for educators or students. Vachris also wished to conduct 'an analysis of the high online withdrawal rates'.[22] I have observed a similar tendency in my classrooms. In an environment that requires teachers to instruct larger classes and be more entrepreneurial in our marketing directives, it obviously does not suit universities to publicise the fact that the online-mode scholars are poorly disciplined, even when working in well-developed sites. The best of web education is ineffective if students do not switch on their computers. Their bodies are absent from the classroom, and their minds vacated from knowledge.

NICE FROCK AND THE COURSE
WASN'T BAD EITHER

It is remarkable that in this era of the low credibility of teaching, students are being asked to evaluate teachers' expertise. Bill Readings attacked this system, believing that 'it immediately asks us to consider whether student pleasure is the absolute criterion of value; after all, learning may be a painful experience'.[23] He is absolutely correct in his assessment. To assume that students are the best qualified to assess teaching or a course is to create a 'customer satisfaction' model. A popularity contest is not the basis of either scholarship or learning. Having argued that, I am always amazed by my student evaluations, but their usefulness is rarely explicit. How does a teacher utilise this manner of feedback?

Please comment on what you thought were the best aspects of this unit.

Everything – the variety of topics and the vibrancy of our lecturer!

What do you think needs to be changed?

Nothing – I think all round it's a really good subject and very informative.

How would you go about changing it?

I wouldn't.

This type of assessment is not useful, and does not assist me in the revision of course content or methods. Such evaluations rarely serve a function, beyond proving popularity for promotion committees. Teaching is being institutionalised, ranked, graded, averaged and assessed. Surveys rarely measure teaching and learning quality, with students ranking some courses highly because they can absentee without consequence. Certainly these surveys provide feedback, and useful comments are made at times, but I always feel faintly voyeuristic reading the students' words, a verification of Zygmunt Bauman's maxim: 'I am talked about, therefore I am'.[24] So following on from the bravery of bell hooks and others, let me invite you into my pedagogic parlor ...

Too rarely do we consider the significance of the first classroom encounters between teachers and students. A learning environment is created, and a new future summoned. I am an expert in such life-shattering encounters.

It was assumed through most of my high school years that I would become a lawyer. Such an occupation seemed an obvious vocation for an Australian woman with a big mouth. I was not so sure. I had no real notion of what a university was or what being at a university actually meant. Also, my parents — who never attended a university — wanted their children ensconced in a real job for the real world. They could not predict what was about to happen on the first day of my university career.

Monday morning arrives on my first day of university. I am carrying an enormous bag, overstuffed with seven history books, three files, a drink bottle, diary, make-up, deodorant, cheap perfume and a packed lunch. Earlier in the day, I had tried on my entire wardrobe to make an impression for the first lecture. I need not have worried. I was one of 300 students packed into a lecture theatre. One shining face of many. Then a man entered the lecture theatre to a Goon Show soundtrack and blew the room apart. He — like me — had just arrived at the university. His name was Professor Richard Bosworth, and that title certainly suggested that he was important. The passion that he conveyed for history, teaching and students in that first lecture changed my life forever. On *that day*, I decided to be a historian. I did not really know what a historian was, but if being one contained 10 per cent of the excitement I felt in that lecture, then it was enough for a lifetime. Ironically, that judgment by my younger self was absolutely correct. Our 18-year-old selves always know truths that we must hear, remember and activate. I remember going home that first day and looking up qualifications in the university handbook, about which I knew nothing. I decided to complete a Masters degree in history. Obviously, I had no idea what this qualification involved, but to be a Master of something sounded like a worthwhile goal. Unbelievably — only a few years later — I completed that task.

It took my father years to forgive me for not becoming a lawyer. When he found out that I was not moving to the law school, he did not speak to me. He thought I was wasting my life. Breakfast times were appalling. Only last year, he told me that he was proud of my gutsy decision, and I have ended up far more successful, contented and happy than (his) legal career would have allowed.

Teaching at its passionate best gives students courage to be different and think differently. Richard Bosworth gave a girl, fresh out of a conservative, restrictive Catholic school, courage to mark out a terrain beyond the expectations of her family and friends. For some reason, I do not think that a website for this course would have possessed a similar impact. But on that day, in that lecture theatre, my life changed.

Bodies allow the connection of ideas with people. Richard Bosworth has always used sound, particularly radio, very effectively in lecture theatres.[25] Because of my cultural studies training and belief in multi-literacies, I use more diverse popular culture, from music video to perfume, from food to fashion. It seems appropriate to use popular culture to teach it. However, this directive is also in keeping with the teaching maxim of my life: talk to students *where they are*, rather than *where I want them to be*. Such a truth is also confirmed by Henry Giroux and Roger Simon:

> By ignoring the cultural and social forms that are authorized by youth and simultaneously empower or disempower them, educators risk complicitly silencing and negating their students ... Educators who refuse to acknowledge popular culture as a significant basis of knowledge often devalue students by refusing to work with the knowledge that students actually have and so eliminate the possibility of developing a pedagogy that links school knowledge to the differing subject relations that help to constitute their everyday lives.[26]

As the borders and structures of societal differences overlap and loop, culture becomes the pivotal site of battle. Popular culture in particular offers challenges for teachers. To over-emphasise web-based learning removes the sensual, textured, weathered surfaces of popular culture. We lose the taste, smell and texture of texts, and the roughened, grainy skin of life. By stressing the flexibility of the Internet, we squander the passion of the popular. Our enthusiasms are rarely expedient. When we love a song, a star, a television programme, a book or a dress, it is rarely opportune. It is a truth of life that at the point we can least afford a new frock, we find one staring at us from a window. We know that we will be unable to live with ourselves if we leave it there. But when we actually have money, even shiny shoes with a diamante buckle cannot sustain our interest. The delights of life are not convenient. Why should the passions of education be any different? The enthusiasm and excitement of the classroom disrupts lives, promoting ruthless debates between partners, friends and parents. It should be exciting, distracting and highly inopportune. I have never — in my life — seen a fervent, agitated, angry, volatile involvement with PowerPoint slides. Play Barry Manilow in a lecture theatre: watch the difference.

Please comment on what you thought were the best aspects of this unit.

The energy and passion that Tara brought into the unit.

While students feed off energy and passion, the battle cry of student evaluations has, over the last few years, been to demand that lecturers place their notes on the web. One reading of these conscientious students is that they wish to increase their learning and emergence in the subject. However, David Newlands and Melanie Ward found distinct results:

Students in our experience accessed the Web materials at various times, of day and night. The vast majority felt that the quality of the Web materials was at least as good as their own notes from traditional lectures. These results would seem to confirm the benefits of using the Web in allowing students to work at their own pace and in providing richer learning materials. Closer analysis of student behaviour however yields some less positive results. Forty per cent of the students printed out notes without reading them and only one quarter used the hypertext links provided or went in search of additional information themselves ... It appeared that the students were reluctant to explore the Web and take charge of their own learning and were instead more concerned with producing a paper copy of the Web materials.[27]

I do not place my notes on the web, because I am teaching the students a bigger lesson. My lectures are one-shot deals. If they miss one then it is gone forever. What I am actually teaching them is punctuality, intellectual discipline, community loyalty and personal responsibility. To place my overheads or cue cards on the web actively blocks students from attaining these meta-lessons. Further, in Newlands and Ward's study, 75 per cent of the students felt that electronic lectures — deposited on the web — should only be used as a 'back up' to traditional lectures. Teachers possess a role not only in management, but in leadership. There is much staff time being wasted on such a 'back up'. Teachers have more important tasks to accomplish than medicating the conscience of students unable to spare an hour a week from their schedules to attend a lecture.

Education is politically worrying and personally shattering. It is a highly affective, agitated environment. There remains a justifiable concern that for students to learn, they require intellectual distance from their own culture. Teaching students about their own culture can create complacency. Such a premise is probably true. Yet did the question ever arise for teachers that they may be unable to distance themselves from their intellectual culture, their education? We assume values of culture, quality and standards, whereas these values are continually negotiated. This statement does not mean that we accept popular culture uncritically. In fact, my positioning affirms the exact opposite. By questioning *all* cultural formations, inquiries may be activated into the very nature of education. Why are you here? Why am I here? Why are we talking about these issues? What are you going to do about it?

Education is not predictable or efficient. It is the unproductive searches, the confusions, difficulties and frustrations that allow students to learn and make significant connections. The point of a great teacher is to grant meaning and context to the hard work, drudgery, disappointment and repetition that is required of scholarship. Body knowledges are messy: they leak, are squashed into (metaphorically) too-tight trousers, fashion disasters and bad hair days. This type of consciousness is outside university strategic plans and educational goals of consumerism, productivity and marking criteria. Instead, students frame 'real teaching' as distinct from that in the online environment:

Message No. 315 [Branch from no. 313]
Posted by ****** on Mon, Oct 22, 16:30

Subject: Fun on the Net

I think using the web for education sux! I'm doing Introduction
to Multimedia and the Internet this semester and most of the
contact is done on-line (even tough it's not specifically an online unit as such). I've complained about this before. I think it
can be useful, but I think it just doesn't work when you try to
replace real teaching with teaching on-line.

You need face-to-face contact (I think on-line teaching is being
introduced because it saves money, and also some teachers are
lazy so they want it). I'm very cynical about on-line teachiong
after my experiences with it. While it would be beneficial, when
it replaces face-to-face contact it can destroy real education.

Technology is not the solution to poor teaching. If we are committed to improving education, then we must increase our knowledge
and reflexive deployment of our bodies in the classroom, before they
morph into cyberspace. The managerial boa constrictors are strangling
the teaching corpse, crushing (and digitising) the passion of cultural
life. Whenever money is granted to technological improvements, there
is a financial siphoning from the education system, either into terms
of pay and conditions for staff, or the funding of places for students.

FORGOTTEN SOMETHING?

There is an increasing database of material that focuses on the potential for plural identities and conscious selves to emerge through the
Internet. Zygmunt Bauman's corrective is a significant intervention
in this debate: 'one thinks of identity whenever one is not sure of
where one belongs'.[28] The endless discussion of identity — from
Oprah to Posh & Becks — has transformed the performance of an
articulate and empowered self into a social necessity. The Internet is
part of the trend Bauman discusses, serving to both reinforce and
destabilise an awareness of self-identity. An 'I' at the keyboard is not
an authentic expression of self, but a performed construction of written highlights, awkwardly aligned with corporeal selves. The self,
through print history, has been moulded socially and institutionally
through writing.

The Internet does shift how we think about the self, the 'I'. The information that we convey to others alters, as does our understanding of personal and group responsibilitiy. Stephen Talbott was fearful of a 'scattered self', pulled between Net-centred idealism and profit-motivated corporations. He believed that 'the knowing self has disappeared into a vague sort of insupportable subjectivity ... which forces a superficial, abstract, associational reading of disjoined texts'.[29] This flighty 'I' does not serve the purposes of education, which requires commitment and deep interchange with ideas.

The determination of real life — its limits, potentials and tragedies — slides through our fingers like sand. The desire to be someone else online is an act of denial, as well as empowerment. Through that denial, there is a decentring of responsibilities, history and consequences. Sherry Turkle has termed this contradiction 'Life on the Screen or in the screen'.[30] Perhaps Howard Rheingold's questions are even more disturbing, particularly for educators:

> What does it mean to have millions of people online, living through at least a couple of identities each, scattered over the entire world. More and more of us divide our attention into windows, then turn on the stereo and groove with it. How is this affecting the way we think?[31]

Perhaps the most obvious answer to Rheingold's inquiry is that we are distracted, tired, stretched, pulled and socially frayed. Obviously, there have always been competing narratives of identity, community, exclusion and marginality. The passage of ideas, bodies and performances through the Internet invokes an unstable trafficking of signs and sighs, codes and caresses. All modes of writing and communication require a puffing out of the self, through print, telephone cables, automatic teller machines and emails. Theodore Roosevelt's radio-based 'fireside chats' pushed an identity and community through the wireless. The current change to such initiatives is the scale and breadth of the interface. In virtual systems, the relationship between self and corporeality problematises the structure of both. Stone has reminded, though, that:

> forgetting about the body is an old Cartesian trick, one that has unpleasant consequences for those bodies whose speech is silenced by the act of our forgetting; that is to say, those upon whose labour the act of forgetting the body is founded — usually women and minorities.[32]

Such a statement renders the gender-swapping of the multi-user domains far more than playing with possibilities or a bubbling 'identity workshop'.[33]

There is a significant argument that computer-mediated communication allows a critique of prejudice because the body is masked and blinded.[34] Similarly, without the 'problems' of bodies, men and women can communicate with greater equality. As Gladys We disclosed:

> communication between women and men has always been problematic, to say the least. Simply put, women and men don't communicate well with each other, even though they may both be speaking English ... Most people answered that men and women are able to communicate far more easily online than face to face.[35]

This mode of communication does not actually change the economic and social differentials of power. How is social equity being addressed for the differently-abled, minorities and women if — to attain a more equalising communicative modality — they leave behind their bodies? The hierarchies continue: the male dominance is perpetuated. Online, women write like men so that they will be taken seriously. Lisa King asks the pivotal question: 'Should women learn to adapt to the prevailing style of discourse online?'.[36] When women lose our bodies online, we enable, embed, perform and accomplish the final act in the misogynist project.

REMEMBERING THE BODY

To open the intimate spaces between students and teachers is to ask questions about the sinewy tissue between the classroom and the 'society' it serves. Only then may we theorise, interrogate and politicise the space between education and culture. The difficulty in creating a speaking position on education is made more difficult through the systematic denial of teachers' and students' bodies.

Please comment on what you thought were the best aspects of this unit.

The unit covers a wide range of issues which are of relevance to everyday's life. It helps me to think more critically about dominant ideologies within our society!

While these corporeal manifestations hold distinct positions and values, it is important to hear the voices of students, rather than placing them in the position written for them by the educational discourse. That is why this chapter has intentionally mobilised students' words. There is a more lasting record of the transitory comments left on web discussion forums or in anonymous teaching reports.

While students are rarely granted a voice, teachers must assume responsibility for the power of their knowledge. Grossberg affirmed the contradictions of this position:

> The elitism for intellectuals comes, not merely from our assumption that we already know the answers, but even more from our assumption that we already know the questions. It would, however, be too easy to assume that we simply need to ask our students what the questions are. We need to use our authority, mobilised through a pedagogy of risk and experimentation, to discover what questions can be in the everyday lives in our students, and what political possibilities such questions open up.[37]

Teachers interested in social justice and change need to focus on teaching alternatives, opportunities, risks and chances. The body is the basis for resistance and opposition, and a way to — overtly and clearly — create distributive justice.[38] A smiley face is not an adequate way to embody technology. Bodies possess an honesty, a stand-and-deliver energy that can be lost from our educational system if not protected. If I have one criticism of our present school and university sector, it is that we do not feel enough, we do not allow the well of sorrow, the ache of grief and the dark disappointment to drip through our bodies. The best of teachers and teaching should make us cry, feel anger or outrage — but make us be active, make us *be more*.

George O'Brien asked: 'why are books on higher education so boring?'.[39] The reason is that few are prepared to commit the tired muscles, the pen-inked wrist, the tissues wet with student tears or the post-lecture exhaustion to the page. We have denied teachers' bodies for too long. The claims of sexual harassment and impropriety have resulted in a denial of the flesh and sweat of teaching. The cap and gown are corporeally filled. Because we have not stressed the role and place of the body in our teaching work, it has been traded for the new models of leadership, plug-ins and peripherals. Only by re-entering the teaching body can we assess the costs and consequences of

Internet-based teaching. In 1969, an education textbook reported that 'for all our general or professional involvement as teachers, we still have difficulty in describing and analyzing what it is we are doing and what influences we are having'.[40] I was born in the year that this book was published, and I still agree with this early analysis. Maybe that is the point. There is a tissue of continuity and commitment that connects teachers, from Socrates to the present. It is that community that we should nurture and recognise. Teachers have bodies that matter. We teach bodies (of knowledge) that matter. Only through claiming our long-term contribution to history can we critique and discredit those wish to jack-in our skills.

6

POINT, CLICK AND GRADUATE: STUDENT MOTIVATION IN THE INFORMATION AGE

Jumping into light speed is not like dusting crops, boy.

Han Solo, *Star Wars*[1]

Han Solo, alongside the trusting, carpeted companion Chewbacca, reminded his cocky, confident, but inexperienced passenger Luke Skywalker that the difficult tasks in life take time, effort and knowledge. Self-belief and the Force rarely provide the skills necessary to run a combine harvester, let alone enter hyperspace. The development of knowledge takes years of planning, failure, boredom and motivation to allow the accomplishment of the most difficult tasks.

While Han Solo understood this life lesson, few teachers and fewer students have grasped the message. This chapter presents the stance of my book at its most aggressive and robust. While most of my writing is (intentionally) focused on teachers and teaching, knowledge and knowing, this current section is bewitched by the current behaviour and framing of students. The motifs of student-centred learning and flexible, just-in-time delivery, which have been used to justify the movement into the online environment, are highly ambiguous. These maxims demonstrate no awareness of how learning is actually accomplished or of the role of motivation in education. It cannot be assumed that upon arrival at school or university students know what is in their best interests, how to structure their time, or their responsibility to themselves, their family, their community and their nation. They need to be socialised into the space. Education is the greatest endowment citizens can give themselves. It is not convenient. It cannot be sandwiched around work or drinking games. It demands precision, determination and discipline. Such language — of course — is no longer fashionable, and is rarely heard in the beanbagged lounges of teacher education. It is unfashionable because it is not in keeping with psychological models of surface and deep learning. But teachers know — and students know — that we are all being cheated and cheapened in this game of generic skills, marking criteria, open-book exams and bullet-pointed textbooks. This is a simulacra education, for a hyperbolic age. This chapter therefore displays the 'problem' of increasing student numbers, the 'solution' of computer-mediated education, and then addresses the two words that require reclamation in our education system: motivation and discipline.

SAGE ON THE STAGE OR A MUSE ON THE LOOSE?

Through the earliest histories of teaching, distinct roles were created for the teacher and learner: one party would impart knowledge, and the other would partake of the feast. These assigned roles also attributed responsibility. Through the 1960s, the progressive educational movement created more collaborative models for learning. Teachers gained a name change — facilitators — and their calling was no longer to knowledge, but to the creation of a positive learning environment. A top-down model of education was critiqued, creating 'partners in constructing knowledge'.[2] Through the 1980s and 1990s, facilitators transformed into managers of a learning environment, with students becoming collaborators in their own learning process. Perhaps it is my history training, but I am reminded of what happened to collaborators with the Vichy Regime after the Second World War.

The creation of a whole learning environment transforms the teacher into a co-learner. Such a model seems ideal, equitable, joyous — and completely disengaged from the actual process of scholarship. Planning, learning and teaching are the three tenets of an education. Learning does not magically erupt from the energetic space between co-learners. Teaching is hard work, and effective learning requires a disciplined attention to planning and curriculum development. To transform teachers into co-learners and facilitators is also to forget the myriad roles held by educators through history: mentor, model, counsellor, manager, parent, judge, referee, ego-booster and library. These roles do not necessitate student compliance and passivity.

Planning for learning creates tangible and explicit outcomes: lesson plans, weekly programmes, semester outlines and exit points for certificates or degrees. The more a teacher plans, the more likely that the lesson or instructional environment will create a learning moment. Planning is not only — or even mainly — a question of content. It is the placing of knowledge in a wider context: of exams, the workplace, degrees and the codification of credentials. Such a procedure involves decisions that require skill and judgment from the teacher, with the aim to balance diverse educational, social and political imperatives. Planning makes teaching more predictable, and ensures the formulation of instructional objectives and the practical stages necessary to move from concrete to operational and abstract ideas. Do not confuse predictability with boredom. To hide behind student-centred learning — let us all get into groups now and talk about it — is wallpaper for a lack of planning. As a proactive and reactive process, educational planning provides a way to mentally and physically prepare for a learning experience, and to structure evaluative protocols at the conclusion of the educational encounter.

The relationship between teaching and learning is an intricate, intense dance. It is based on assumptions — experiential knowledges and impressions — about the social baggage that students carry into their first year of university. The emotional investment brought to the classroom is based on prior experience with education. This manner of familiarity can be a disadvantage, particularly in a university setting. Alan Rogers realised that 'a number of our student participants assume that adult education will be like school. They expect to be taught everything by a teacher who "knows everything"'.[3] Mature-aged students, who are also frequently studying part-time, balance education with the other demands of life such as employment, families and social lives. This will alter the pace of learning, and the commitment to educational objectives. The educational orientation of students is difficult to fathom, and is not lessened through the online environment. To transform students into scholars requires a series of intentional interventions.[4] Compare these strategic intercessions with what Entwistle believed were student expectations:

Students see good teaching as involving pitching lectures at the right level, presenting material at a sensible pace within a learning structure, providing lively and striking explanations in an enthusiastic manner, and showing empathy with students' difficulties.[5]

These rudimentary, practical issues and pastoral care concerns are not, alone, an education. The interactions between students and teacher are distinct from all other relationships that exist outside an educational environment. It is an artificial, monitored and constructed dialogue, and all the ideological masks of facilitation and co-learning do not decentre the power held by a teacher. Also, there are many — and increasing — positions and roles situated between students and teachers. An array of paraprofessionals, technicians and administrators also hold a teaching function. These roles have increased with the proliferation of online education.

The thoughtful linking of curriculum with pedagogy and educational technologies remains a challenge. New information is grafted onto an already-existing world view, producing meaning and knowledge through a negotiation between lived experience and new consciousness. There is a continual pattern to learning, grasping some material, misunderstanding other sources, but formulating a long-term consciousness of change. All education is interactive. Lee Alley affirmed that 'as long as I held on to the traditional "sage-on-a-stage" style of teaching, I would keep reinventing ways for the students to be a passive audience'.[6] Why does shifting media initiate a transference from passivity to activity? All audiences — whether responding to popular music, television, film or a lecturer — negotiate and graft a teaching/cultural experience to their lives in an active, engaged fashion. Lectures are not the problem: bad lecturers are. The computer, as muse, is not an effective replacement for the sage. Neither model is explaining the role and place of student motivation in powerful, productive learning. Jorgen Bang realised that 'during the last 5 years a lot has happened in the field of educational technologies … But within theoretical thinking on learning almost nothing has happened'.[7] The key is not technical interactivity: the aim is to gain intellectual interactivity, with the student situating information in a political matrix and experience. Unfortunately, too many apologists for the Internet confuse the implementation of new software with learning.

There are three significant modes of technology for education.[8] The first — technologies for presentation — incorporates word processing, print and scanning. The second mode — technologies of interaction — encases media presentational packages including PowerPoint. These systems are based on fascination or contemplation, and initiate the building and testing of hypotheses. These modes of presentation are not end points, and this is frequently where Internet-based educators lose their students. The third stage is crucial. The most significant mode is 'technologies for communication';[9] that is, a mechanism for dialogue and feedback, allowing information to be transformed into knowledge. Through communication technologies, there is a negotiation between text and audience, and a movement in the power relationship between teachers and students. Unless all three modes of technology are activated, learning will not result. That is why PowerPoint is such a disappointment. Even though slides may be placed on the web, they are not able to create the third stage of learning. All the investments in technology are pointless unless there is a shift to this third stage of communication technology.

Regardless of the media, active, problem-based learning is the starting point of social change. The profound difficulty of mixing information, sociality and cognition creates enormous challenges in building a learning community through the Internet. Such an imperative has particular attractions in our current system. We teach through turmoil, disappointment and chaos.

THE PROBLEM

The many economic and social problems in life — unstable employment, fraying family structures, hyper-individualism and poorly-funded health and housing sectors — have necessitated that education be both a cause and solution for societal difficulties. The 20th century was the era of growth in access to education.[10] Such an expansion is interpreted in many ways: as a building block for democracy, a necessary component of social justice or the means to prepare a workforce for the changeable rigors of industry. Not surprisingly, quantitative questions about student numbers have raised more qualitative concerns. In the United Kingdom, the solution has been to lock education into the needs of the market. Nick Small realised that:

> The focus for the Conservative government was administrative and structural reform in schools. The present Labour government has continued changes, more concerned with pupil performance, and the school as a preparation for employment in a society undergoing fundamental economic change. Changes are based on assumptions of the work-force not staying in the same job on a long-term basis.[11]

The multiplicity of educational aims has been culled to one: workplace training. The goal is to create a compliant, competent and skilled workforce that is quietly accepting of the need to be frequently retrenched and retrained. While there are consequences for such an imperative in primary and secondary education, the brunt of this ideology has been faced by universities.

Probably the greatest difficulty facing university educators is the teaching of large classes. There is a continual struggle for a methodology to enhance and improve learning, but little governmental discussion about how class size impacts on self-esteem and the attitudes of students. The challenges boiling in the gladiator pit of large lectures unify students and teachers with a desire to create a passionate learning community. Teaching large groups has three characteristics that arch beyond nations and subject disciplines: they are lecture-based, and face scarce resources and absenting students. The primary binary that structures this mode of teaching is flexibility versus discipline. In this environment, teachers resort to the web as an easier mechanism of crowd control.

As the salvation for the challenges of enormous classes, the web bounces between being a communication tool and a learning strategy. The web not only allows the handling of large student numbers, but decentres infrastructure questions such as the building of more lecture theatres. I was a participant in a large research project in Australia that gathered the best teachers in the country to solve many of these problems. The results of this session, while exhilarating and empowering, were also depressing. There was a desire to prioritise form over content, asserting that a tyranny of content creates a cramming, examination culture. However, to create a tyranny of form (over content) is not a solution, as it formulates banal, basic web-based platforms. The energy of educators is focused on the *relationship* between signifier and signified, context and content, media and meaning.

While much talk focuses on the potential of the web for student-centred learning, most consideration should still be placed on lectures, as they remain the cheapest, best-organised means to convey ideas and interpretations to students. In the space of one hour, students are guided through a journey that has taken responsible scholars many hours to formulate. Students still appreciate and acknowledge a teacher's role in motivation.

> Please comment on what you thought were the best aspects of this unit.
>
> **The lectures were made interesting. It made me want to be here.**

Preparation time is spent not only in the research and writing of the lecture, but the integration of overheads, PowerPoint slides, video and audio into a dynamic package that slots neatly into an hour. This session certainly is exhausting for the lecturer: my clothes are generally soaked after a session. Again, students are reflexive and conscious of this effort.

> Please comment on what you thought were the best aspects of this unit.
>
> **Tara was extremely well prepared for lectures & made them entertaining.**

Good lectures are sites of energy and enthusiasm, not passivity and boredom. They provide an ideal venue for the translation of knowledge and the building of Socratic method — from description to high-level analysis. Lectures — and the best lecturers — are also far more lithe than a technologically-determinist framework would suggest. Pace and content is adjusted, and enthusiasm for content is revealed.

Large classes are not the problem. Resourcing for large classes is the snag. Libraries are under-funded and non-technical support staff are being reduced in numbers, necessitating an even higher administrative burden on teaching staff. This creates a survival of the quickest mentality, where the demand for resources — both material and human — is stretched. The pressures on the curriculum, to decrease the number of subjects and specialty, serve to increase the student numbers in already bulging courses. In large classes, every aspect of teaching is more complex: administration, architecture and the assessment protocols of diverse student backgrounds. These problems frequently emerge at first-year level, where the largest pool of students is located. The world wide web has been the response to these structural problems. As a result, the students least aware of the university environment, the least knowing of the hidden curriculum of higher education, are being taught in the most emotionally barren and hyper-individualised mode. At the moment that universities had to handle increasing numbers of students, the resources declined. Instead of admitting and resisting this reduction, teachers use the web as a tight tourniquet.

When students are challenged by the subject material and ask the pivotal questions about who they are and why they decided to attend university, the banal structure and predictable quizzing of WebCT cannot address their queries. At first-year level, students do not have the experience to place a bad mark or a difficult reading into a more overarching context. Teaching first-year students is like working in the triage unit of a hospital. Every day, we have an emotional bleeder or are confronted with a metaphoric gunshot wound to the head. What is needed is not more funding placed on and in computer-mediated education. Instead, what is required is a remaking and rebuilding of the first-year experience. The most significant intellectual moments of my life have taken place in lectures. The three most powerful, earth-shattering revelations have erupted from history lectures at undergraduate level. The wit and swiftness of these lectures changed the way I thought about time, space, self and history. That is not a bad way to pass an hour of the day. None of these inspirations would have happened through the web. They were about a tone of voice, the feeling and energy of the room, and the passion and gusto for ideas. Clicking 'Next Thread' does not have the same impact. The ineffective use of technology, the removal of tutorials, or dumping printed materials on the web simply to overcome the problem of large classes will destroy everything that represents the best of university teaching.

Those of us who care about the student experience of university must not back away from the threats and attacks. Teachers are giving up on scholarly standards because they are too difficult to maintain. Alex Cowan, for example, suggested to teachers that 'it is clear that anyone planning a history curriculum afresh would be unwise to rely on most of the old assumptions about the skills and experiences of potential students'.[12] Cowan does not resolve his presented imponderable: do curriculum standards then (inevitably) drop? The aim of an education is to unsettle assumed dominant ideologies and initiate cross-cultural communicational skills and meta-learning. The foundation of this process is the lecture system. To rebuild the lecture experience requires a recognition that both the

staff and student body are now culturally and socially heteroge-
neous. There also needs to be an institutional recognition that
teaching first-year students is the most difficult of tasks, because
the pitch is moderated almost constantly. To handle this scholarly
gymnastics requires the deployment of multiple and diverse writing
and thinking styles. Teaching smaller classes is easier for staff and
better for students. McKeachie realised that:

> Large lectures are not generally inferior to smaller lectures ...
> [when] tests are used as criterion. When other objectives are mea-
> sured, large lectures are on shakier ground. Goals of higher level
> thinking, application, motivation and attitudinal change are most
> likely to be achieved in small classes.[13]

Performance in content-based disciplines is not minimised through
large classes, but theoretical, social justice work and critical writing
through essays are harmed.

Good teachers — and there are plenty of them — are overcoming structural problems, declining funding, scarce resources and
technological disasters on a daily basis. Being an effective teacher of
students means having the capacity to manage change, to acknowledge that education is a journey, not a map. The fact that students
are not even aware of the strain facing their educators is a credit to
a beaten and battered profession. Technology must not be judged
against the efficiency of other technologies. There is an outside to
this discourse, and it is called the history of education.

The collegial tradition has always been changeable, but the three
Ms — 'massification, managerialism and marketisation'[14] — have
presented its most overt challenges. Quite rightly, educating the
best and brightest is no longer the aim of higher education. The
class-based bias of universities is no longer acceptable. But there is a
need to remember the elite universities' contribution to pedagogy:
the college tutorial. This small-group-teaching encourages proce-
dural and structural flexibility. Such an environment tests and
probes students, as it is both challenging and competitive. Without
recognising the high standards and dense challenges of this system
— where a student prepares a well written, well referenced paper
and then presents it to a tutor for questioning and critique — we
will too quickly move to the web, or accept uncritically the bulging
lecture theatre.

THE SOLUTION

I worry that there are some students who are so put off
by the entire concept of online classes that they won't even
try them, believing that they are being cheated somehow
because of what they perceive as a lack of contact. Many
students here are traditional to the point of being
hidebound, and will NOT cooperate, preferring instead
to take face-to-face sections of the course or enrolling for
other elective courses when available. Unfortunately also,
there are quite a few faculty who believe that any method
other than what they use (unchanged for decades, as you
might guess) is somehow less rigorous, requires less work
by the professor, cheats the students, and so forth. These
professors are not above intimating to students that online
courses are less worthwhile than traditional courses.
Academic turf wars reign supreme![15]

Respondent to Zane Berge

Education is conservative. It must be. The fate of thousands of students and their futures rests in the hands of academics and the curricula that they create. The traditional model of lectures and tutorials can appear rigid.[16] The nature of how students learn through virtual universities and e-learning is under-researched and therefore risky. Zane Berge believes that there are five major concerns with online education: quality, change, accountability, productivity and access.[17] Different problems are also revealed at different educational levels. Primary teaching has different requirements to the higher education environment. What is clear is that flexible learning and web-based teaching have developed in tandem, with little care for the many students who require more organisation, motivation and cajoling.

To create a learning environment necessitates a concise evaluation of the characteristics, behaviours and skills that the students possess *before* they begin instruction. Once these have been assessed, remedial work, particularly in terms of reading, writing, note-taking and interpretative skills, is woven into the content of the course. Very little can be taken for granted. For example, I produce a series of checklists and sheets that list the abilities needed to read an article, write a paragraph and utilise a quotation. Five years ago, it could be assumed that students possessed this knowledge; now that is no longer the case.

In 1994 Barbara Means stated that the aim of computer-based education is to 'center instruction on *authentic, challenging tasks*'.[18] She favoured a radical model that changed the language and directives of education.

COMPARISON OF CONVENTIONAL AND REFORMED APPROACHES TO INSTRUCTION

Conventional instruction	Reformed instruction
Teacher directs	Students explore
Instruction is didactic	Instruction is interactive
Students work individually	Students work collaboratively
Teacher as knowledge dispenser	Teacher as facilitator

SOURCE Barbara Means, *Technology and Education Reform*, Jossey-Bass, San Francisco, 1994, pp 5–9.

Means is proposing nothing less than a reinvention of the school and university. But in the decade since her work was published, some unusual results have surfaced from the use of technology. The individualism of education through technology has increased, withstanding the discussion forums of the most popular instructional software. The use of email has amplified the dependence of student on staff member, *increasing* the role of teacher as knowledge dispenser rather than facilitator. Students are not discussing possible solutions with fellow scholars. They send staff an email to quickly solve their problems — and we answer hundreds each day.[19] There has also been an increased emphasis on content and marking criteria — didactic information exchange rather than interactive exploration of knowledge. For example, students — without hesitation — send me pre-submission copies of their essays as an emailed attachment. They expect me to read and draft this work before submission, only to peruse it again, this time for marking. I refuse to open these attachments, and instruct my tutors to do the same. Instead, I ask the students to come and see me, and I will teach them how to draft. If I make the corrections, then they have learned nothing about the process of proofing, and have given themselves an unfair advantage over the hundreds of other students in the course.

Obviously, web surfing is an action of active exploration, but without attention and resources placed behind developing web abilities, students will not be searching with ability, direction and interpretation. Putting two keywords into Yahoo is not an academic search; it is the equivalent of flicking through a *Cosmopolitan* to find detailed, accurate information on women's health. To celebrate student exploration — without preparation, guidance or responsibility — is short-sighted and destructive of education. Ken Feldt offers a great corrective to Means' directives. In 2001 he recognised that:

> now that the tech press is full of articles asking about the 'next big thing', I humbly suggest that when it comes to e-learning and e-teaching, many students and teachers are still waiting for the first big thing to show up.[20]

There are so many barriers to teacher–student interfaces: not only questions of design and the encoding of text, but also gulfs of social literacies. For mathematics, chemistry and music students in particular, the web causes major problems. How do we 'represent' a natural logarithm or phrase of music through email? Once more, this is an example of form — software design — being emphasised over content concerns. There are distinct technological needs for different courses, levels and students. Foundation and first-year courses require a different mix of media from upper level. The Internet is an instructional environment that requires sizeable interventions from staff to actually work effectively. The most difficult and important part of creating an online community is ensuring that the set-up messages from teachers establish an appropriate frame. I always ensure that another staff member is the webmaster or webmistress of my online courses. As I deliver all the lectures and tutorials, and am also the course controller, students require alternative voices and views. Therefore, my discussion forums feature the words of both a webmistress/master and distance-education tutor. The aim is to assemble a tone of friendliness and helpfulness. Importantly, because of the tight and reflexive relationship between the teachers, the web is far more than a site of chat and gossip. Consider this web forum 'boot up' procedure. The site commences with my first message:

Message No. 1: posted by Tara Brabazon (H267) on Mon, Feb. 19, 07:48
Greetings to all my CDDers

Welcome to the Discussion Forum! Well done on getting through the login details and passwords... Everything will be much more exciting from now.

To everyone cruising through the site, leave a message here –
and tell us something about yourself!
O.K. I'll start ... ;)

My name is Tara (unfortunately pronounced TAWA after a
few drinks...) I love dance music (Particularly the prop.heads
decksanddrums and ... the legends who are PSB). I'm also a
sports nut. I love wrestling so much. Big fan of Chyna and
The Undertaker. I also do aerobics every morning – 6am. See
ya there ba-bee.

O.K. that is enough of my dim dark secrets. Tell me about
you.

Lots of love people – have a great semester...
T.

A non-threatening atmosphere has been set. Students then are able
to commence the course *where they are* — on their own terms. The
external tutor then intervened, hailing distance students specifically:

Message No. 2: [Branch from no. 1] posted by Kylie Murphy (murphy) on Wed, Feb. 21, 08:11

Hello everybody,
My name is Kylie and I am the external tutor for CDD this semester. So a special little hello to all the external students :). I am
sure you will find this forum particularly useful, especially with
the marvelous Leanne McRae mistressing it for you all.

I'm just entering the final year of my Ph.D. which ahs the nice and
confronting working title of 'Bitch: the politics of Angry Women.'
I'm telling you this so if you ever see it on the shelf at a book-
store your curiosity will overcome you, and you will have to part
with your hard earned cash and buy a copy!

My obsessions include: my cat, his name is jack and he is way cute
even with stitches in the side of his head (due to an abscess).
Buffy: the Vampire Slayer, and to a lesser extent Angel (How
Heathers was that diary writing by Dawn last night? I am sure the
soundtrack to it was a direct rip off/tribute to Heathers???). And
I am quite partial to food, both the cooking and the eating of it.

Anyway ... here's to a kiss ass semester

Kylie Murphy

The establishment of an alternative voice also demonstrates
that external students are central to the course, not ignored or

marginalised members of the community. Most importantly, though, the webmistress then built on the foundations of the other two staff members, and channelled personal information into wide-ranging discussions of identity, thereby knitting a self into the curriculum:

Message No. 5: posted by Leanne McRae (mcrae) on Thur, Feb. 22, 09:41

OK.

You've managed...somehow...to get yourself onto the site. Well done. You've read through the introductory messages and you've gained some sense of how this site works. Now, where to start...Let's start with an easy question?

Who the hell are you? How do you categorize/construct your-self? Does this vary in different contexts?

I am Leanne McRae. I am one of Tara's PhD students. My the-sis explores notions of popular cult. This means I wish to explore what people mean when they say something is a 'cult' film or TV show or whatever. How does this term circulate within popular culture and how does it apply to different texts. I am supposed to be about half way through my disser-tation, which is freaking me out because its way to close to finishing for me. My God I still have sooo much to do. I am definitely a Buffy fan, though I try very hard not to let it obsess me too much. I really like Spike. I am also into Henry Rollins, Dogma (the film), and Hong Kong Action Cinema. I do not have a cat, though I do love animals. Well, I do not loooove animals, I just think they are cool. OK. I think that's definintely enough about me. Let's hear about you? Who the hell are you?
L.

This is an outstanding teacherly moment. She was able to estab-lish control of the modality and move the discussion forward into the tasks of the course: the arc of identity politics. Obviously, between these three messages, students are provided with a frame-work in which to weave their attitudes, ideas and answers. They even expressed their reflexive awareness of the distinct nature of this teaching experience:

Message No. 110 [Branch from no. 24] posted by **** on Fri, Mar. 9 05:40**

Hello all- what a shock to the system. i am so used to being isolated that i'm not sure how i will cope with all this attention- i have done basically all of my studies (since 1995) not only externally but also in sunny-NOT-switzerland...! my other hobbies include two ratbags under 4, ESL, and planning the long waited return to Oz at the end of the year (after a 6 year stint os). i hope to finish the last two units of my course on my return. until that day i will enjoy my only course for the year- 'CDD. ps i think i've been in this country too long as the 'managers' of this course seem a bit...ummm...different from what i've experienced so far.... :o)

My reply was an obvious one, signifying both similarity and difference:

Message No. 116: [Branch from no. 110] posted by Tara Brabazon (H267) on Fri, Mar. 9, 15:43

So lovely to hear from you. I was hoping that you'd pop on to the site. Well, you now have a team of people to interact with for the semester.

By the way – as one of the 'managers' of the course :) (my father would be so proud), I wish I could live up to your expectations. I'm just a tired old academic like any other. I do like frocks, though :)

Be well – anything we can do or help with – let us know.
T.

Researchers have claimed that students facing communication difficulties in tutorials or seminars are assisted through web-based discussions.[21] Few recognise that many students require a higher level of discipline than that provided through an Internet-based curriculum. Frequently forgotten is the fact that the bulk of communications on the web take place through the written word — invariably only in the English language. Therefore, students possessing literacy difficulties are again blocked from teaching assistance. Their language concerns are on display through emails and discussion lists. I aim, through my Internet teaching, to alleviate student stress and increase their confidence with ideas. We do not rely on students to ask any question in any order. If students choose the content, then there will be sizeable gaps in the knowledge constructed.

Therefore, in my educational discussion forums, web controllers structure the discussion overtly, with two questions posted each week. Student responses are then monitored and addressed each day.

Online education is celebrated for its flexibility — students can be educated in their own home, in their own time. But distance education, using the most conventional of print-based, audio and visual texts, accomplished this inclusive goal decades before the world wide web. The groups that have taken advantage of distance and correspondence education are frequently unable to be part of synchronous 'chats' — that is why they are not on-campus for lectures and tutorials. The flexibility of online education is lost, by needing to be in a particular space, with a computer, and at a particular time.

Although the problems in our educational system are vast, such difficulties cannot be rectified through a single medium, even the Internet. The digital opiate is not working. The final two parts of this chapter address the most under-discussed (and unfashionable) words in our student-centred environment: motivation and discipline.

MOTIVATION

What we have to learn to do, we learn by doing.

Aristotle

The aim of an education is to transform students into scholars, and create critical, interpretative thinking. Although unpopular with the political leaders of the day, this is a teaching of activism and subversion, instructing students how to probe and poke the foundations of the political system. All courses in schools and universities should be a theory of knowledge, removing 'big ideas' from their pedestal and walking around with them in everyday life. In this way, knowledge is alive, and every student, at every campus, in every era, builds it anew.

It is no wonder educators become either bemused or disgusted by the question, 'But will this course get me a job?'.[22] We write our curricula to help students change the world, not only to gain employment. The role of education is to create an environment of research and development that arches beyond current needs. There is little use in training students with technocratic skills that, by the time they complete a three-year degree, are redundant.

To learn, students require motivation. Through this motivation, students are able to connect their lives with the subjects of a course.

Some students cope well with the freedoms of university; others do not. That is the point of assessment: to provide sufficient checks in the system so that contact is maintained. As Pithers and Mason suggested:

> it may well be that the cognitively able student is able to switch or adapt their learning style whereas the student with poorer cognitive ability may be less able to adapt.[23]

The student with minimal experience in a learning environment will have an inability to move between diverse learning styles. The goal is to increase the match and range of a teacher's teaching modalities and the learner's most effective mode of learning. I support constructivist approaches to learning, the assumption that learners build their own knowledge. But no learner is autonomous. We are all social beings, and are socialised into our reality. Students cannot be dropped in the midst of a digital desert and assume that they will build a hotel, spa and sauna to make themselves more comfortable.

Students — particularly in the early undergraduate years — cannot solely regulate their own learning. While it is important to mark out new roles for teachers and students, there are some students who need to be dragged into their learning lives. The alternative to this pushy pedagogy is that they drop out of university. David Presti is concerned that 'removing the social aspect of the physical classroom and requiring students to motivate themselves to attend virtual lectures has obvious drawbacks'.[24] With the signal-to-noise ratio of information so high on the web, and with it appearing an easy option for research, inexperienced students do not possess either the conceptual tools or theoretical framework to moderate the material.

Ask teachers about the greatest difficulty they have with their students and most would reply: attendance. The problem remains one of motivation. Whether studying on-campus or online, students must commit to the idea of study and be methodical in the application of ideas, energy and obligations. Ponder the following student survey, reproduced on the web:

> What did you enjoy/find useful about studying in units with Internet-based learning?
> * the ease of going back to a missed lecture
> * didn't have to talk to a teacher if I didn't like him/her
> * the lecturer was 'reachable'. He was able to respond quickly and no phone messages and waiting were required[25]

Three answers to a simple question. These responses demonstrate laziness, poor social skills and hyper-dependence on the teacher. This survey is not a glowing endorsement for self-sufficiency in the current student body. Similarly, a follow-up question asked:

What have you gained from studying units with Internet-based learning that you have not gained from more traditional approaches?
- flexibility — can work from home; can fill in breaks; effectively can overload on units
- more freedom to do other things; it doesn't seem as time consuming

After reading these comments, we need to ponder whether we want ideas, histories and politics to become *flexible*, allowing course overloads, contracted degrees and freedom to accomplish other tasks. This is an education put together with duct tape. At times, course co-ordinators receive bizarre emails, raising questions about why students enrol for a university course at all:

Subject: Intro to Cultural Studies
X-MimeOLE: Produced By Microsoft Exchange V6.0.4712.0
Date: Mon, 22 Jul 12:55:42 +0800
From: ******
To: <tbrabazo@central.murdoch.edu.au>

Hi Tara,
I am enrolled to do Intro to Cultural Studies this semester but as I have an appointment with an oral surgeon this afternoon, I am going to miss the first lecture. I am hoping that you will be able to help me - I have been advised that you are the coordinator for this unit. I assume I will need a unit outline, and to enrol in a tutorial time. I am especially concerned about the tutorial time - I work full time, so I don't want to miss out on a tutorial time that doesn't interfere too much with my work. Could you please tell me what I need to do to get into a tutorial, and also where to get the unit outline?

Thank you very much

This email is startling and troubling in equal measure. It does reveal the wide-ranging responsibilities that staff are now managing because students no longer treat education as a priority. This student had just completed a six-week mid-year break, but chose the first day of semester to see an oral surgeon. My course has only two contact hours a week. It is remarkable that this student seems unable to manage even this moderate commitment. She could not even come into the university to sign up for a tutorial. My question, which is yet to be answered, is why she did not enrol as a distance education student, or in an online mode? Her desire to attend a university that 'doesn't interfere too much with my work' makes very clear the irrelevance of scholarly discipline, further reading and the deep exploration of complex ideas.

I am not nostalgic about older modes of scholarship and learning; they were arduous, emotionally debilitating and intellectually challenging. But I would not trade one day of my education, reading, thinking and writing to gain more 'freedom to do other things'. Even at its worst moments, education *was* 'the thing' — the central moment in a journey through life.

I always remember my Honours year in history at an Australian university. The work was so hard, many nights I returned to my family home, collapsed into the lounge suite and sobbed. I was at the library when it opened at 8 am and the last to leave when the library was closing at 9:55 pm. I lived in the same spot on the third floor of this old sandstone building: reading, writing, thinking and being frightened. It was the fear of failure, the terrorising confusion of creating scholarship, which was — and is — the most horrifying component of the Honours experience. I hated it. I (privately) abused my (remarkable, brilliant) teachers to the heavens, and became frustrated and angry with myself.

By the end of the year, I had survived, but I had to ascertain my mark. This university — in the great Oxbridge tradition — placed the surname and the grade on a public building at an allotted time and day. All the frightened Honours students, with eyes like a kangaroo's transfixed by headlights, quietly edged towards the long wall of results. I followed them, shaking, legs buckling under my body. Then I saw two blocks of ink:

Brabazon   I

The first class Honours I had dreamed of receiving had actually happened. The success I attained later in my professional life never meant as much as this horrifying moment. All of the emotionally drained, disappointed or elated students then withdrew from the wall, like grazing cattle, to collapse on the grassed field, with tears of exhaustion, happiness, disappointment or fear. I simply sat on the lawn cross-legged, looking at the wall with tears streaming down my face.

This is education. It is not pleasant. It is not flexible. It is not something I look back on with nostalgia and warmth at the good old days. But I learned something. Discipline, fear and hard work are brutal but effective mistresses.

Participation in adult education is voluntary. No one is forced to attend university or sites of further education. External factors may sometimes trigger it: economic downturn, parental pressure, job loss, divorce or bereavement. Because of its voluntary nature, when students express laziness or anger or apathy it is a surprise. Adults should possess high learning motivation: they have *chosen* to be in this lecture theatre, at this time. Teachers cannot be blamed for students' choices, or their marks. While students require motivation for this personal journey, they need to show a desire to move beyond the self and reflect upon the nature of the activity.[26] Once they realise that their life, hopes, passions and prejudices are provisional and relative, then learning can take place. At its best, the teaching-as-facilitation model creates what Brookfield described as 'self-directed, empowered adults'.[27] Learning is not a stable, predictable narrative. Teachers never possess the complete knowledge of an individual's past or motivation. But this unpredictability makes education exciting and volatile. Schools and universities are social environments, and — at their best — provoke a negotiation of meaning. Too often, though, post-compulsory educators confront 'mental absenteeism'.[28] Such behaviour raises significant issues about the elusive nature of learning, and exactly why students want to attain an education at all.

Students are not Pavlov's dogs, requiring endless external stimulation to create behavioural change. Behavioural approaches to motivation set up a linear relationship between particular actions and pleasant consequences. The cognitive revolution suggested that an individual's thoughts about the self create motivated behaviour. Intrinsic motivation ensures that a student remains on-task and learning.

Challenge and curiosity are the most common triggers for intrinsic motivation, stimulated by a surprising event, idea or connection. Teachers have a role in modelling this mode of motivation, by being enthusiastic, interested and curious.[29]

I spend most days of my life working on lectures and tutorials. They are finely honed, carefully scripted, well researched and carefully punctuated by multiple aural, oral, visual, tactile and olfactory sources. Attendance is high in my lectures and the pass rates are excellent. But the consequences of that success mean that preparation dominates my life. All my private, waking hours revolve around the teaching experience. Research is conducted early in the morning and late at night. I hold impossibly high standards for my tutors and make their lives miserable as well. I certainly do not blame any teacher for not exhibiting this level of commitment. The work is too hard, too caustic of the self. That is the cost for gaining high attendance from students who should be motivated to gather a learning moment wherever they may find it. What of our students, our co-partners in learning?

Michelle Vachris celebrates the great progress made in education through the information age. She asserts that 'students can complete their general education required courses online and can earn four-year undergraduate degrees without ever coming to campus'.[30] Whose interests are being served here? The desire for self-paced learning, independent learning, individualised learning and self-instruction seem an ideal way to devolve teaching from the teachers and encourage students to educate themselves. The economic tone of such celebrations of the online future is worrying. Obviously, for some students, gaining physical entry to a university campus is a problem. But correspondence courses and distance-education programmes allow non-standard learners to attain a university degree. Materials are specifically geared for their use, and many distance education students still come on to campus when work or family responsibilities permit.

Some students enjoy the electronic learning environment, while others will be alienated. The goal for the critical professional is to dance delicately between these modes, to access the many experiences and ideas that are present in our classrooms. While there is much desire to reassess the role of teachers and students, we are already seeing the consequences of this shift. Without intellectual leadership — a tour guide on the journey through education —

students are absent, bored and boring. It is interest and curiosity that creates learning, and makes a scholar. To learn, we need to be extrinsically and intrinsically motivated, and these desires and expectations must be brought to the teaching moment. Interest and attention is required, not flexibility and freedom.

Motivation can be built. If teachers embed study skills and write authentic and significant assessments, then active and avid learning may result. Assessment is a means of learning, not an educational end point. Such praxis requires leadership from teachers, not the mask of facilitation. If the word 'teacher' is creating too much concern, then mobilise the rapporteur: the weaver of ideas. But like the craft on which this metaphor is based, it requires dexterity, skill, knowledge, confidence and discipline.

DISCIPLINE

There is no singular theory of learning, and no single medication to overcome the 'problems' of education. The most difficult part of teaching is not relaying content, but attempting to create an active context for the students, which encourages heuristics. To forge a link between old and new information is a day-to-day challenge. All these complex preparations and initiatives are meaningless if students miss classes, ignore assessment deadlines or do not prepare adequately for tutorials.

If a teacher teaches and the students do not learn, then teaching has not happened. The question is how teachers handle the students in post-compulsory education who want the freedoms of a university timetable and the status of being a university student, without actually realising that they must contribute to the discourse. Obviously, learners' orientations are not stable, and are strongly inflected by teaching and assessment. But excuses are being made for ill-disciplined students who really need to get a life before they attain an education. There is much talk of the part-time work conducted by our students, and the cost of an education. Invariably though, the best students in our classes are the busiest: those working full-time or who are full-time carers for parents and/or children. Mature-aged students are far more effective at cognitive activities such as planning and the negotiation of deadlines and timetables. In this environment, educational technology is a bandaid to deflect from the sticky issues of personal discipline and commitment in the student body. There are students in our system who do not know why they are at university and lack motivation or interest in knowledge, reading, writing or thinking:

Message no. 23
posted by ****** on Tue Jul 30, 10:39

Subject hey there everybody

hi, my name's ****** and I just kinda ended up at uni this year after doing better then I expected in my TEE results. I'm still confused as to what it is that I'm going to do, right now I'm in 1st yr for a journalism course but who knows, I may become a sales rep or a real estate agent tomorrow! Hopefully I can get my head around this course, it's a bit mind boggling right now but I'm sure i'll cope! oh yeah, I played drums and guitar a while ago but I'm just too busy now so I'm a bit rusty, I played polocrosse for about 6 years but also too busy now! cya guys next lect!!!

This message was left on an open web forum. The lack of commitment, motivation and direction displayed is of incredible concern, particularly for its impact on other students. While good teachers can turn these students into scholars, the effort from educators is enormous, and requires the modelling of different behaviour. I replied to this message, trying to give her some care and understanding, realising later that no one can give another person focus in their own lives:

Message no. 35 [Branch from no. 23]
posted by Tara Brabazon (H102s2) on Wed Jul 31, 07:47
Subject: hey there everybody

Hi
Great to hear from you. University is a weird thing, eh? The key about the 'first year experience' is that you discover things that you never thought about. I've always been a big enthusiast of an education, universities and learning. I would be absolutely nothing without the wonderful universities I've gone to. They have really made me as a person. I hope you find you education to be the same!

Remember - you can be a sales rep for the next 50 years. But the chance to do a degree for three years is really the chance of a lifetime. It is mythic - exciting - life changing. Don't worry - I'll look after ya.

And don't be a stranger either – come and say hi.
Be well
T.

This response probably will not work. It leaves me saddened and agitated that this young woman has been given an opportunity, but is unable to see either its value or its importance.

The way students see and frame their educational environment impacts on how they regulate the learning processes. Learners do have control over their learning processes, but the web and email is encouraging students to relinquish responsibility and to be more dependent on a teacher. Good teaching embeds higher cognitive skills — of planning, goal-setting and intellectual responsibility — into the curricula. This process will assist students in the major question that only they can answer for themselves: what do they want from an education? Through all the problems that students are facing, either self-caused or through inadequacies in the system, I often ponder how Socrates would handle it. Zane Berge asserted that:

> should Socrates live today, the educational establishment might not go so far as to require him to drink hemlock because his teaching methods have so changed the tradition of learning that they are perceived as corrupting students. On the other hand, he might not be granted tenure.[31]

How would Socrates view our students? How would he assess their level of commitment to knowledge, belief in big ideas and the capacity to challenge the self?

The Internet possesses a great opportunity for the keen, committed students in our schools and universities, as they have an opportunity to further the discussion and explore terms and approaches in greater depth. However, this 'advantage' can be overstated. These students do not need the help; it is merely an expensive 'add on'. The students that it could help — the less able — have neither the motivation nor the inclination to use it. The least dedicated students want web-based notes, to substitute for reading they have not conducted, and will send a panicked email for assistance from teachers the day before an assignment is due. Computer-mediated communication encourages the ill-organised students to infect as many people as possible in their problems and lack of planning. At a meta-pedagogic level, web-based teaching and learning has changed the very notion of education: it must be convenient and fit into a 'lifestyle'. Education is not like browsing through a grocer, picking up the cheap, the delicious and the colourful. It is life-changing — and tough. By displacing this struggle, Internet learning has, so far, been a tragedy for education. It is a relaxed, ill-focused environment for the students who can least manage this pedagogic plasticity.

There is a reason for the strong, committed tone of this chapter. I am a practical educator, and summon theory on my feet. Teaching is exhausting — mentally and physically. For those of us who actually teach — rather than just talk about it — we need to ponder practical strategies for education. All our students, whatever their ability and background, deserve our efforts and care. We must respect their journey, rather that allow them to complete a second-rate qualification because they lack leadership or direction. Teachers and students do matter. Time must be spent pondering how to improve the experience of our tutorials, lecture theatres and classrooms. It is time to reclaim commitment and responsibility.

PART IV

WHO IS THE TARGET MARKET?

7

HOW IMAGINED ARE
VIRTUAL COMMUNITIES?

No educational trend better reflects the growing convergence between new classrooms and new businesses than the
current focus on 'communities of practice.' Communities of
practice are 'in,' both in new workplaces and in new schools.
In communities of practice, the romantic nostalgia associated
with 'community' is recruited, while the primacy for
sociotechnical engineering is masked.[1]

James Paul Gee

I have few intellectual rubs with contemporary cultural theory. I do,
however, become a volatile, vulgar pedant when seeing carefully configured scholarly works cut up and clichéd without any sense of context or history. EP Thompson,[2] Germaine Greer[3] and Gayatri Spivak[4]
have been among the most quarried. Varied societal formations
become 'made, not born', the eunuch limbers through anti-feminist
tirades, and subalterns descend from their pyre to represent an array
of nameless, voiceless social forces. As the Internet and world wide
web have entered everyday language, new intellectual clichés have
been poached, most obviously the phrase 'imagined communities'.
This provocative title has been excised from Benedict Anderson's
most famous book to become a description of the virtual communities formed in and through the Internet.

This chapter — and the next — offers an intervention in debates
about the supposedly global village infusing around and through the
Internet. Too often, multiculturalism, diversity, difference and community are words trotted out by advertisers and politicians to justify

tax concessions for multinational companies and international investors. The problem is that as the world becomes globalised, it is increasingly homogenised around American values such as individualism, deregulation and big business. It is a challenge for all businesses and organisations, including universities, to manage diversity in a positive, proactive fashion. I want to ensure that diversity refers to more than minorities, women, and people of colour. If the Internet is to offer opportunities, as much as access, to social mobility, then attention needs to be focused on those who use the digital environment, and why. This short chapter therefore lays out a series of theories about race, nation and language, which are then applied in the following section.

I demonstrate how the Internet has grafted onto the pathways and shipping routes of the colonising nations, narrowing the values and validations of knowledge and history. Benedict Anderson's subtle attention to race and nationalism in the remarkable *Imagined Communities* provides a corrective to the broad brushstrokes of educational theories of community. I aim to displace the binary of real and virtual communities. Particularly, I focus on race-based questions, asking if virtual communities trigger colonisation by other means. The notion of an e-democracy promotes a denial of differences outside the Internet, allowing for the proliferation of middle-class, white, male and American values. While unravelling 'virtual communities' — the most popular description for the web's users — I show where power is held, and who is excluded from the globalising mantra.

IMAGINING THE LIMITS

Benedict Anderson's *Imagined Communities* is more than an evocative title. He defines the nation as a constructed political formation. The nation is not natural, or emerging organically from the landscape. That word — imagined — triggers thought about the self, identity and collectivity. It signifies for Anderson that the nation is 'both inherently limited and sovereign'.[5] He particularly wanted to show that the globalising and localising forces have not overtaken this most potent of social constructions:

> the reality is quite plain: the 'end of the era of nationalism' so long prophesied, is not remotely in sight. Indeed, nationness is the most universally legitimate value in the political life of our time.[6]

It did not take the destruction of New York's twin towers to demonstrate that we are not post-nationalism. Anderson's point is clear: we are not born with a particular nationality tattooed to the forehead. A nation is a form of both consciousness and self-consciousness: citizens consent to their nationality.[7]

Schools, universities and family networks construct notions of who we are, and what we consider others to be; these notions are summoned out of our definitions of words like nation, culture, society, citizen and individual. This manner of division can be socially damaging, culturally narrow and oppressive. Functional national ideologies enact closure, ensuring that few questions are asked of those who are excluded or under-represented in symbols such as flags, anthems and pledges. As the great Subaltern historian Partha Chatterjee remembered:

> the two greatest wars of the twentieth century, engulfing as they did virtually every part of the globe, were brought about by Europe's failure to manage its own ethnic affairs.[8]

Frequently, discussions of race are seen to apply only to people of colour. Evaluations of gender are framed as only relevant to women. Colonisation refers only to nations outside Europe. Actually, to manage diversity in the workplace, school or university requires all members of the organisation to become critical, empowered players in a team. Participants in culture bring their differences to work and school not to be judged, but to offer new ways of thinking and communicating.

Conflict is created when race and nation rub rather than overlap. The aim of immigration policies and citizenship rituals is to simplify the relationship between race and nation, to render them synonymous and tautological. Even within multicultural policies, the volatilities of race-based conflict cannot be medicated through nationalism. Because the nation state is an unstable formation, it needs to feed off more powerful discursive formations, such as race.[9] Nationalism juts an identity out over a landscape. Conversely, race is frequently applied conservatively rather than resistively, a difference to attack and demean, rather than affirm, celebrate and welcome. In such a divisive environment, formulating a nationalised people remains a challenge. It is a fascinating process to explore how a group of people, encircled by a territorial boundary, create a functional, dominant mode of belonging. Take away sport and language: the allegiance to the nation state appears unstable and shallow.

For marketing executives and politicians, the nation appears as the fulfilment of a project that stretches over centuries. Most have a recent origin in the 19th century — Australia, for example, only 'celebrated' a centenary of nationhood in 2001. There is a projection of individual diversity onto a collective narrative. Citizens never meet all members of the nation, so how is a consciousness of belonging established? How does an isolated person become a Samoan, Indonesian or New Zealander? As Anderson stated, 'communities are to be distinguished, not by their falsity/genuineness, but by the style in which they are imagined'.[10] Therefore, attention must be paid to representational systems such as education. While race feeds off binary oppositions (black/white, criminal/citizen), nationalism is an in-between formation, unstable, molten and malleable. Nationalism is the embodiment of ambivalence, being neither intrinsically reactive nor progressive. Through the international restructuring of capitalist economies, the role of the nation state has changed, dialoguing with regional, local and global formations.

Discussions of virtual communities only tangentially connect to Anderson's well-researched and considered work. Indeed, Howard Rheingold empties Anderson's research of content, arguing that 'people in virtual communities do just about everything people do in real life, but we leave our bodies behind'.[11] As I discussed in Chapter 5, digitised citizenry tends to be distanced from bodies; it is important to acknowledge that national communities are formed around language and the printed word, rather than corporeal performances. Therefore, the Internet forms a higher form of imagined community, a complex (re)interpretation of 19th century nationalism. My concern with Rheingold's interpretation is that he summons virtual communities as a new and innovative formation, rather than part of an ongoing semiotic stitching of self, identity and community. The Internet — and the communities formed within it — has a history. Cyberspace is not a 'social petri dish',[12] but merely the continuation of an experiment. The Internet-based community perpetuates its origins in the same way as the nation state continues the paradoxes of colonising capitalism.

Theorists of virtual communities ignore how the nation state transformed the performance of identity. Barry Wellman and Milena Gulia realised that:

Critics worry (mostly in print, of course) that life on the Net can never be meaningful or complete because it will lead people away from the full range of in-person contact.[13]

Belonging structures in the last 200 years have rarely been based on in-person contact. Significantly, Wellman and Gulia also ignore the irony of their position: that web-based communication is a textual, print-based culture. This continuum approach to the Internet is verified through the easy movement of print from the nation state into cyberspace. English was the language of 19th century British colonisation: it is the primary language of 21st century search engines. Frequently, (formerly) subaltern peoples express their resistance in the language of the colonizer.[14] As Anderson acknowledged, we need to monitor not only the authenticity of inter-personal relationships, real people building real relationships, but the imagining styles that allow connections to occur. That makes the systematic masking of nationalism within Internet theories even more odd. For example, Wellam and Gulia stated that 'virtual communities are simultaneously becoming more global and local'.[15] The (easy) absence in their statement is nationalism. The nation state does not magically disappear the moment an inbox is opened. It is time for an intellectual pause, to promote a discussion between the global and the national. Computer-based social relationships need to be understood beyond an economically rationalist framework of efficiency, productivity and the global movements of capital.

Identity is *always* multiple and emerges in a particular context. Who we are at work is different to the identity summoned when talking with a family member or friend. It is no surprise that our national affiliation is also gendered, classed and raced. A Sri Lankan citizen is also of a particular race, religion, class, gender and age. The style of identity changes when these other variables are considered. The important realisation is that not all communities exhibit this capacity for fluid flexibility. Empowered groups match offline movement with online behaviour. Such a judgment was confirmed by Robin Hamman's study:

My findings suggest that users taking part in this study are motivated to use AOL by the need to do research for academic or business purposes and to communicate with others within their pre-existing offline communities.[16]

Fresh online identities are not fashioned by virtual communities. Who we are online is synonymous with our offline selves. Both are a performance of both digital and analogue power. The next section demonstrates how these imagined differences of race return to the body via virtual communities.

RACE TO THE FUTURE

Differences in bodies or histories form subjectivity through language. Education positions students and teachers to write a culture, nation and race. An identity verbalises specific linguistic values. In formerly colonised nations, proficiency in a European language is considered to be the dominant, unchanging, stable and secure base of all cultural values. The European construction of knowledge is saturated with a very particular representation of modernity, industrialisation and culture. This strategy builds a network of values and differences that administer and police social space. Nationalism is powerful because it is woven with racism. We are different from them, because they *look different*. Rarely realised is that the eye is an ideological organ: we are taught to see differences, to obsess over differences in skin colour, eye shape and hair colour. Some distinctions are more significant than others. Nose shape is more important than ear shape. In this way, segregation and separation are perpetuated. Bauman has argued that there is a desire to 'protect' the citizens from cultural ambivalence. He recognised that 'identities may be safe and "unproblematic" only inside a secure social space'.[17] Internet and web spaces are volatile, unsettling and changeable. It is not surprising that there is an intense search for limitations, restrictions and boundaries, to create a stable anchor for identity.

Racial thinking is not marginal to contemporary thought. Racial difference is determined not by biology, but the meanings granted to somatic distinctions. This 'imagined biological differentiation'[18] not only creates dominant groups, but also triggers subordinate resistance. Categories like African American, disabled or lesbian are not only a way to label and demean others, but an apparatus to trigger political alternatives.[19] In other words, the very term that was used to ridicule and hurt can be the basis for community-based resistance. There is a unity and power gained from disempowerment. The process of colonisation does not end when the colonisers leave the country, but continues through language, media and technology. Truths and histories are relearned, and retaught. The aim of these new narratives of land and history is to ease the negotiation of ambivalence.[20] This tactic is moving from national imaginings to virtual communities.

A virtual community, like a national imagining, is built through stories of origin and the sharing of language. The Internet provides a context for identity politics. Importantly, for scattered diasporas such as Indians, Irish or Chinese, resistance can be activated beyond national boundaries. It is a way to prevent the desegregation of the 'other', the excluded, the different. But the electronic infrastructure has not developed in a uniform, ordered fashion. Nils Zurawski reminded us that 'the blessings of the information age have by no means reached all people and countries of the world'.[21] The argument that the Internet can correct race-based societal injustices or facilitate indigenous self-determination must be derived from a reading of economic and social conditions.[22] Disempowered communities find repeated patterns of exclusion and disempowerment moving from the non-electronic to the electronic sphere.[23] There is a need to activate a relationship between identity politics and e-democracy.

E-VADING THE REVOLUTION

A political imperative of Internet studies is to theorise, with both precision and rigour, the alignment between national and virtual communities. Racial differences and colonial infrastructures punctuate both the virtual and national environments. It is necessary to ponder whether the online discourse is creating a citizenship that formulates a different, and perhaps better, public sphere. If a virtual community is of political benefit, then those privileged with access must fight for the connectivity of the disempowered.[24] The empowered provide the rules, names and definitions that determine the disenfranchised. For virtual communities to create a more equitable imagining, the structure of European history — of accuracy, truth and citation — needs to be dislodged from its status as the primary skeleton of society.

The key is to ponder the social accountability of the Internet. After industrialisation, power and discipline rarely operated directly on the body politic. Schools remain one of the few sites where bodies are disciplined: through uniforms, exams and testing, sirens and bells. These complex mediations and protocols on the body have increased through cyberspace. This is not simply caused through a supposed retraction from bodies. There is an open mesh of selves and spaces. Allucquere Stone showed the consequences of this quilting of identity politics:

> In virtual systems an interface is that which mediates between the human body (or bodies) and an associated 'I' (or 'Is'). This double view of 'where' the 'person' is, and the corresponding trouble it may cause with thinking about 'who' we are talking about when we discuss such a problematic 'person,' underlies the structure of more recent virtual communities.[25]

The convoluted, repetitive and humorous application of multiple inverted commas in this passage initiates a stark intervention in the simple narratives of a fixed identity and location. A 'mother' or 'wife' moves into different locations to become more than these labels permit. This splice between body and subject is continuing the project of industrialisation and the nation state, creating alienation, unhappiness, compliance and resistance. Therefore, stressing the 'real world' or 'real life' is blocking a discussion of the constructed, artificial and political nature of *all* identity formations.

What makes a virtual community politically disconcerting is its capacity to mask societal inequalities.[26] The nation state has displaced a consideration of the class structure: virtual communities merely intensify this process. Sherry Turkle has discussed this avoidance of class, citing Thomas, a 24-year-old university graduate who was over-educated, under-employed and stripped of self. He stated that 'MUDs got me back into the middle class'.[27] His words verify either the inadequacy of Marxist economic determinism or the effective naturalisation of societal inequalities through virtual communities. I favour the latter interpretation.

The public sphere is a space of communication, where truths and structures are negotiated and maintained. For such a formation to function, it must be a site of universal access and rationality. Derived from Aristotle's polis, the aim is to promote communication between all citizens, regardless of rank or power. However, the saturation of the English language on the web makes such a dialogue difficult.[28] There is much desire to frame the Internet as 'a real leveler',[29] a new way to promote political activism or even cyber-terrorism. Colin Beckles attacked the suggestion that the next revolution will be virtual, stating the obvious: 'those primarily engaged in this type of

"Net" politicking will be whites'.[30] Attention is required not only on the text-based nature of this politics, but the race-based inequalities perpetuated through the prose.

NOW READ THIS

To theorise virtual communities requires an understanding of how language and print culture constitute subjectivity. Anthropologists, including Levi Strauss, defined civilization through the activity of writing.[31] To create a space between the colonised's 'culture' and the coloniser's 'civilization' renders the 'native' exotic and interesting for a European audience. In this context, to assess the imagining of virtual communities, consideration must be made of how print culture creates our understanding of democracy and citizenship.

For Anderson, print capitalism is a necessary determinant of nationalism. Latin, through much of the second millennium, was the language of a literate Europe, a population widely dispersed and few in numbers. Anderson recognised that 'relatively few were born to speak it and even fewer one imagines, dreamed in it'.[32] After 1640, when fewer books were printed in Latin, publishing was no longer a global formation. Dynastic borders were permeable, but this fluidity was undermined by the growth in vernacular languages. The decline of Latin's currency created spaces for new narratives of origin, community and belonging. Print became a commodity that also secularised the population. The decline of definitive manuscripts of knowledge transformed print-based information into a reproducible formation. At this point, print languages created the potential for national spaces and ideologies. New languages of power were formed.[33] In 19th century Europe, reading signified authority. Not surprisingly, the most significant site in forming a national imagining was primary education, where language and history were taught to a captive audience via *text*books.

The relationship between community and communication is obvious, with both words derived from the Latin root, *communis*, or 'common'. The word's dual meanings — of vulgarity and collectivity — carry through to the virtual environment, explaining the political and social tensions surrounding notions of community. Jan Fernback and Brad Thompson believe that 'virtual communities as a concept is still amorphous due to the lack of shared mental models about what exactly constitutes community in cyberspace'.[34] The narrative, ritualistic and communicative practices of these virtual communities are not yet providing the solid identity and saturating allegiances of the nation state. The MOOs and MUDs, and other interactive Internet worlds, are not the only sites for the text-based building of new spaces and identities. Flaming — the language of argument and agitation — can destroy communities.

Through the hostility, confusion and politics, much nostalgia pervades theories of virtual community. There is no reason why a more equitable system should emerge in the information age, when it did not surface in the agrarian or industrial eras. Further, through the hybridity and complexity of social structures, the nostalgic rendering of a virtual community is damaging. Marc Harris displayed the ruthless application of the new inequalities through a discussion of Panama, the 'new virtual nation'. He argued that the virtual corporation, which is a product of downsizing and a desire for economic efficiency, will produce the virtual state. The colonising imperative is stated overtly: 'Britain may have been the model of the 19th century, but Hong Kong and Panama could be the model for the 21st'.[35] The free market fuels a blunt and aggressive rebuilding of a national imagining into a virtual community. The language of the market and money is the universal translator of self, identity and community. I shop, therefore I am. The marginalisation and exclusion of the national narrative is only increased. Fictive capital has replaced Balibar's 'fictive ethnicity'.[36]

The nation is a shorthand bundling of traditions, histories and resistance. Such a grouping of ideas transforms a consciousness into a self-consciousness. This shared linguistic performance is rendered even more influential when entering text-based cultural formations, such as the Internet. American English predominates, and there are consequences for this linguistic hegemony. While idealists may present the virtual community as the social future, we need to recognise the limited new frontiers that are negotiable: sport, shopping and banking. We are all more than our football allegiances, shoe size and credit card. The virtual community creates an imagining that is actually national, specifically American. The modern past is (re)presented and (re)imagined as a simulacra nation.

Virtual communities retrace the histories of the nation state. There is much of the old world in this new world. Windows is not only an operating system, but a metaphor for identity. At any one time, a single window is open, but myriad other surfaces, texts and portals are available behind that solitary façade.

FAST FORWARD TO EDUCATION

The economic developments associated with the Internet create space for social and professional networks. Globalisation and digitisation have not triggered innovative models of community that substitute for a loss of geographical locality. These new modes of communication have grafted onto existing frameworks. One more community is sandwiched into other identity-building formations.

Virtual communities within education are saturated with theories of democracy. Through the Internet, the world may be educated. Such priorities undermine a detailed discussion of the ruptured, excessive expectations of both education and the workplace. Richard Cutler recognised that:

> The shift from body to mind is a reflection of the movement from factories to downsized businesses. Just as physical labour is displaced by intellective skills, in parallel fashion displaced workers transform work experience to intellectual equity as temporary consultants.[37]

Communities are difficult to organise, requiring rules of behaviour and conduct. The easiest mode through which this organisation can take place is the binding strategy of territory. If we share land, then the location provides us with information about race, age and class. If virtual communities are to become more than a metaphor, then the barriers will be sociological rather than technological. That means being able to use the Internet is not enough; sending emails is not sufficient. To build a community requires the sharing of stories, languages and context, rather than mastering the protocols.

The great advantage of the Internet for education is that it can be a site for collaborative learning. For off-campus students, it enriches the educational experience. Online tutor support — because of its 'timeshifting' nature — is highly beneficial for those matching education with taxing jobs and family responsibilities. This is probably the greatest gift that the Internet has given educators: the capacity for diverse students to slot education into their schedules. In discussion forums — particularly those that are threaded — the messages are sorted twice: through subject and by chronological order of response. It is an invaluable strategy for enabling complex communication flows. In this circumstance a virtual community, as a new model of social organisation, is effective if its purpose is precisely determined and actualised. Generating a sense of community for students external to the campus is profoundly important. Any contact is better than none at all. The problem is that web-based education still allows an isolated individual to contact other isolated individuals. This is an atomised social order, with communities of interest replacing and displacing communities of resistance and social justice. When considering virtual communities within an online environment, a capable moderator needs to be at least as able as face-to-face tutors. The skills required are diverse and include the capacity to use open-ended questions, to integrate student responses into the discussion, tolerate and reward opposition, and show respect for questions and comments.

For motivated, self-directed learners, Internet-based education is highly beneficial. While not creating a 'mesh of connectivity',[38] the Internet is a reasonable medication for the isolation facing students studying external to the university. It does not remedy the challenges to education, but it is a stopgap that prevents the system crumbling to its knees. Like the nation state, the Internet does not create equity, but a bandaid community. The last chapter of this book removes the plaster, to air these damaging issues.

8

META-TAGGING POLITICS: SOCIAL JUSTICE AND THE SOCIAL RESPONSIBILITIES OF UNIVERSITIES

What counts as knowledge, the ways in which it is organized, who is empowered to teach it, what counts as an appropriate display of having learned it, and — just as critically — who is allowed to ask and answer all these questions, are part and parcel of how dominance and subordination are reproduced and altered in this society.[1]

Michael Apple

The inequalities of education are not only revealed through the pathologisation of popular knowledge. The tensions of mediating between technology and pedagogy have both ruptured and revealed the politics of education. There is a fragile tissue that weaves technology through our commonsensical understandings of reality. A dark, gothic confusion enfolds the digital discourse: that the freedom to connect to the Internet and surf is somehow — intrinsically — aligned with democratic freedom. Privatisation and market forces will not solve the unstable, uneven passage of telecommunication in developing nations. It must be stressed — endlessly — that the major players in the development of the Internet have been white, middle-class, American men. Our gaze cannot be deflected from the long-term consequences of this origin. The immersion in sound and light — the dream of cyberspace — is a deflection from the inequalities that require gritty attention, not the 'inevitability' of cyber-democracy.

This chapter is fixated on social justice, a concern that has been pivotal to much of this book. I am interested in making our classrooms more effective for students rather than administrators, politicians and employers, and only using those components of the web that render education bolder, more textured and complex. Social justice, as a phrase and ideology, captures many interpretations: a deployment of fairness, recognition of personal differences, an affirmation of distinct needs and values, and a desire to overcome economic disadvantage. It is not the inevitable result of a 'safe' liberal democratic system. It is promoted only through the active, focused disruption of commonsense. In moderating and monitoring reactions to difference, the taken-for-granted values of the past are subverted. This chapter ponders the word 'netizens', then focuses on the 'new' virtual middle class, neo-colonialism and the (in)visibility of race, concluding with (de/over)sexed digital drag queens. Modernism and post-modernism play, converse and quarrel throughout the paragraphs, with the sociological mantras of race, class and sex being overlaid with the tropes of post-colonialism, cultural capital and transgression.

FROM CITIZENS TO CONSUMERS

One must admit that the mere fact of communicating
under the conditions of the new technology does not cancel
the marks of power relations constituted under the
conditions of face-to-face, print and electronic
broadcasting modes of intercourse.[2]

Mark Poster

My days are spent teaching 18-year-olds. Particular personal characteristics are necessary to the task. Patience is integral, as is a capacity to accept the blame for problems and inadequacies actually caused by the student. Surviving in such an environment means that I rarely become railed or agitated by the feel-good gurus of prime-time television. If we can handle 300 teenagers, then no self-help healer or aromatherapy peddler destabilises our identity. But I become a stressed shrew requiring medication when hearing the word 'netizen'. Michael and Ronda Hauben's *Netizens* is a naïve, tired and simplistic rendering of politics.[3] They argue that 'strangers are no longer strangers on the Net. People are free to communicate without limits, fears or apprehension'.[4] Their argument needs to be assessed in a careful and considered fashion, beyond the enflamed enthusiasm of easy egalitarianism. They believe that 'a new more democratic world is becoming possible ... Geography and time are no longer bound-aries'.[5] I challenge their premise, investigating if — and how — Net users transform into netizens.

The political and social aspect of the Internet summons a lexicon of change: plagiarism, intellectual property, anarchy, access and encryption. Continuities remain, though. Enlightenment narratives are attended by commentaries of liberation, and the Internet's 'decentralised' organisation continues this tale of social improve-ment. Definitions or representations of a public are difficult to claim, because of the volatility of words like citizens and 'the people'. There are political ramifications of electronic networking, most significant-ly atomisation and fragmentation of social structures. We cannot assume that a community is formed when we sit alone in our rooms, staring at a screen.

To build a community requires dialogue and debate, not access to information. Robert Putnam, in particular, has found a marked decline in the connectedness of American citizens. In a time of high levels of college education, he also determined a correlation between education and social responsibility:

> Education is by far the strongest correlate that I have discovered of civic engagement in all its forms, including social trust and membership in many different types of groups ... Well educated people are much more likely to be joiners and trusters, partly because they are better off economically, but mostly because of the skills, resources, and inclinations that were imparted to them at home and in school.[6]

Putnam argues that education plays an overt role in social con-nectedness. Cultural capital — and time — is required to arch beyond self-interest to wider social concerns. What happens to this social network if that education is attained over the web?

A part-answer to that question is found in a study conducted from October to December 1998. This survey demonstrated that most of those (American) web users surveyed held Republican polit-ical views. Ironically, while conservative on economic concerns, they were more self-assured in expressing a commitment to freedom and individuality in matters of sexuality and censorship.[7] Barney Warf and John Grimes reported that 'right-wing groups have harnessed the internet as readily as anyone on the political left, and perhaps more effectively so'.[8] Therefore, individual rights overwrite the opportunities for collective, social solutions.

Digital technologies alter the spaces and times of communication. This is of great benefit, providing a broader circuit and circulation of ideas. Through email, there is an added avenue for a nation's citizens to communicate with their political representatives. Dana Ott recognised that: 'the electronic media has given a larger percentage of constituents than ever before the ability to easily and quickly transmit their opinions on public policy issues to their representatives'.[9] The problem with Ott's analysis is that all citizens are already able to submit a letter to a politician or editor: the *capacity* to participate in this way does not guarantee that participation will take place. Once more, *access* to digital resources is not the only plank in the formation of social justice. More significantly, Internet literacy needs to be taught — overtly and clearly — as an embedded component of citizenship.[10] Democracy, like leadership, is learned. Phil Agre illustrated that 'there's a big difference between forwarding e-mail and building a political movement around your values'.[11] The domination of the English language also presents serious concerns for many regions, not only for Europe and Asia and the Pacific, but also the French- and Portuguese-speaking populations of Africa. Herbert Schiller declared that 'once the pre-eminence of English has been established, Anglo-U.S. ideas, values, and cultural products generally are received with familiarity and enthusiasm in the global arena'.[12] While the Internet may assist economic and political development, it will also increase and extend disparities.

The Internet initiates unique challenges for government. The desire to reduce the functions of national governments and grant the private sector ascendancy in the management of societal affairs is a way to increase commercialisation and decrease concerns with citizenship, social justice and responsibility. To reduce the power of the nation state is not intrinsically a problem. Throughout the 20th century, there have been radical shifts in the formation of identity, particularly when matched with the discrediting of the colonial system. Speaking to people as consumers rather than citizens reforms the body politic along commercial lines, while feeding off the aura of legitimacy gleaned through social democracy. While the content of the Internet is in the control of individuals, institutions and governmental organisations, government agencies and empowered institutions are still the determiners of how addresses and names are assigned. Similarly, the maintenance of hardware — cables, satellites and telephone lines — is in the hands of national governments.

Information does not circulate freely. Indeed, frequently there are significant reasons why silence is a necessary component of public life. Information is not integral to social justice. Instead, communication, community and collectivity are the pivotal planks for social change. There is no way to avoid the regulation of information. Life choices and changes are always regulated. Invariably, those who complain most about censorship have the greatest access to information. Jon Wiener realised that 'women's voices tend to get drowned out in cyberspace'.[13] The choices available through computerisation favour those already holding the most educational and economic resources. Troy Schneider offers the most potent and convincing critique of the netizen motif:

> Since at least 1996, technophiles have been promising that the Internet would revolutionize politics: that it would provide ... virtual town hall meetings to replace the six-second sound bite; real-time campaign-finance disclosure; cyber-coalitions; online voting; and more. In short, plugging in could offer purer, more productive politics and a more direct democracy ... The online world simply adds more tools to the political toolbox, and those tools — like television, talk radio and targeted mailings before them — play primarily into the hands of those already in power.[14]

Surveys verify this premise: netizens are more sexually progressive and politically active, but also more male than the non-digital population.[15]

The Internet has been highly beneficial for English-speaking academics — to a degree. Universities have gained enormously in research opportunities through the wired campus. The transcendence of time zones — that is, asynchronous communication — has made a major difference to the passage of ideas around the globe. For those of us who do not live in the Northern Hemisphere, but in highly divergent time zones from the United States, the ability to send an email has radically improved the ability to organise a work day. But it has also increased the quantity of correspondence. More intriguingly, power — academic power — is destabilised through web-based journals. As Poster — a prolific web-based writer — has recognised:

The Internet seems to discourage the endowment of individuals with inflated status. The example of scholarly research illustrates the point. The formation of canons and authorities is seriously undermined by the electronic nature of texts.[16]

So while conventional publishing times have slowed dramatically, taking years to pass from refereeing to print, electronic journals accelerate the time in which ideas are distributed and discussed. While credibility remains with significant publishers of books and journals, in the realm of ideas, e-journals are altering the intellectual landscape.

The Internet has destabilised many powerful institutions. This reshaping of the shopping mall and governments creates the potential for new affectivities and bonds of communication. As occurred during the industrial revolution, entire occupations are being lost: secretaries, bank tellers, postal clerks. Careers will be radically shortened for much of the population, increasing the pressure and importance of education and retraining. Therefore, notions of digital progress provide a way for political elites to ignore the personal loses from the information revolution. Tough criticisms have emerged from this environment. James Brook and Iain Boal staunchly affirmed alternatives:

We refuse to cede to capital the right to design and implement the sort of automation that deskills workers, extends managerial control over their work, intensifies their labour, and undermines their solidarity.[17]

Brook and Boal are accurate in their sketch of the post-industrial landscape. At its most neoliberal, their argument is verified by Marc Harris, who obviously intends to make money as the virtual state becomes the virtual corporation:

Downsizing has become an index of corporate efficiency and productivity gains. Now the national economy is also being downsized. Among the most efficient economies are those that possess limited production capacity.[18]

In pondering the precise nature of labour-saving devices, commodity fetishism replaces a commitment to collective wellbeing. The tropes of Internet egalitarianism and even anarchy are countered by significant inequalities in the decision-making process. By focusing on protocols, hypertext, emails and compression technology, analysts do not theorise the leap between individual and community, self and society.

There are places — in the alternative media — to find resistance and configure choices. The Internet provides the space for many of these proxy participations. At its best, we need to celebrate that the Internet is colour-blind and gender-blind. Both these utopic possibilities are critiqued later in this chapter, but the potential remains for a bodiless communication. There is also the opportunity to resist corporate capitalism. Mike Slocombe asserted that 'the Internet remains a place where big money doesn't always guarantee influence'.[19] While corporate sites provide another venue for shiny spin doctoring, the ease of DIY websites means that alternative presentations of products and policies can enter search engines in unexpected and important ways. The question remains, though: how does social change and collective public action move beyond the screen? Is an affirmation of difference and diversity a platitude, without ethical allegiance or learned responsibility? With corporate citizenship feeding commonsensical motifs — of access, privacy, quality and redress — competition becomes normative. This neoclassical model has not delivered — throughout its history — on wide-ranging social justice concerns, particularly in the areas of heath, education and disability.[20]

A public only exists when summoned. Unfortunately, the most effective social scaffoldings in our lives are shopping and work. Schneider recognised the consequences of this emphasis: 'As Americans become more wired, the wired world becomes more like America. And what do most Americans do — online and elsewhere? They shop'.[21] This superficial citizenship substitutes face-to-face communication with a passivity masked by the myth of interactivity. This interactivity is programmed within a narrow range of permutations. The dispersion of self and society makes social justice difficult to define, track, initiate and formulate. Public opinion is a fractured formation, carolled and exploited by balding men from the Rand Corporation. Similarly, Michael and Ronda Hauben asserted that 'the Net brings people together'.[22] Their argument is valid — but only to a point. Moran Lang's corrective is convincing:

> It is ... obvious that people who communicate via the WWW tend to be educated, middle-class white people, people who hardly

constitute a representative sample of any cultural affiliation other than that of a global association of individuals whose commonality originates in their ability to obtain and wield telecommunications technology.[23]

This critique is powerful, but not far-reaching enough in its application. These empowered individuals not only share Internet literacy: that is a symptom of a far deeper community affiliation. Importantly, they share a class, a race and all the advantages gained from speaking the English language. Those already possessing resources, cultural capital, education and the language have another channel to express their world view and politics. The place of the information poor in such a scheme of global capitalism is yet to be written.

VIRTUAL(LY) MIDDLE CLASS

The new virtual middle classes are dangerous to democracy because egalitarianism is the supposed communication matrix of the web. Feldman offers an off/backhand corrective to this ideological pseudo-utopia:

> The global reality is that 60 per cent of the world's population has never made a phone call and more than 50 per cent could not do so because of a lack of phone lines. So, while we glibly agree that the telephone is the most widely available form of network technology in the world, we should — in a small corner of our minds — remember the privileged position from which we make such judgments.[24]

Focusing attention on the massive potential bandwidth of cable over the telephone network is not tempered by a social awareness of those who may not be able to use the facilities for economic, geographical or political reasons. Internet usage — even more than access — is dominated by affluent, employed men under the age of thirty-five. Any happy discussion of networks, online forums and cable television needs to be offset by a coherent reminder of those who do not have regular access to a telephone. Telecommunication firms (even) in the United States, for example, bypass minority areas. The information rich and poor is the new division of societal disadvantage. This new inequality shadows and replays the older injustices. In other words, digitisation fortifies already existing disparities. Class remains the under-theorised variable in Internet studies, but is a focus of attention in both cultural studies and educational theories.

This lack of class-based research will initiate long-term political consequences. Because shopping is replacing citizenship, hegemonic notions of truth and value are reproduced and circulated without intent or malice. The question remains: how are resistive forces assembled to create a jurisdiction and influence for the disempowered or marginalised? Certainly some may be able to pull up the virtual bootstraps of social mobility; but too much of the on and offline system — of language, power, authority and resources — remains unchanged.

In terms of education, there is a very poor grasp of how class is revealed and applied in the workplace, schools and universities. This ignorance is particularly presented in documents from the United Kingdom. Not surprisingly, the Blair Labour government stressed the bearing of class on the educational discourse:

> The main motivating factor, which encourages potential students from lower social class backgrounds to enter HE, is a belief that a higher qualification will bring improved job and career prospects, and also improved earnings and job security.[25]

I have heard similar discussions in administrative briefings in Australia. There is a notion that working-class students do not have the right, desire or capacity to complete education like the middle class. They are only to be schooled in work-related skills, so that another generation of young people can service the needs of the middle classes — who are themselves educated at higher scholastic and critical levels. Speaking on behalf of the working class in this way means that they are disenfranchised from all but a few vocational courses, because job-related training serves the interests of the empowered. Actually, the interests of the middle class are perpetuated by reducing the choices and critical thinking of the weak, the poor and the underprivileged. Improving the job prospects of these young people merely 'value-adds' the workplace, and grants them neither ambition nor an intellectual trajectory. Imagine if such statements were made about indigenous students, the black community or women — for example, the notion that women's educational prospects should be limited to childcare, or that Aboriginal students should work in the health sector because that addresses a pressing need of 'their' community. To suggest that the working class want a quick, skill-based degree — that will attain them a job little better than those of their parents because of degree inflation — is class-based prejudice at its most ruthless.

Working-class children, adults and parents are able to attain less information about education than middle-class groups. Henry, Knight, Lingard and Taylor realised that 'the school assumes middle-class culture, attitudes and values in all its pupils'.[26] There is a gulf between the vocabulary, language and grammar spoken in working-class homes, and that spoken and written in the educational discourse.[27] Language, culture and identity stretch and shift between the distinct class modalities of these sites. Such a judgment is particularly problematic when fathoming female-headed households, which now dominate those families (with children) below the poverty line.[28]

Cultural or linguistic differences, determined via class or race in particular, are difficult to track because middle-class values frame educational institutions. Such a structure configures the behaviour and actions of teachers through habit. The dominant group holds a bank of resources, influential peer groups and family connections. This mesh of ideologies ensures that middle-class citizens are able to suture appropriate behaviour into context, and link economic capital with knowledge and linguistic resources. Cultural capital is therefore not available to all students. Every classroom holds diverse potentials. Unfortunately, too many schools and universities operate as if all students have access to the dominant motifs and motives within a society. Different backgrounds are not a problem for teachers: they contribute and improve the curriculum. To succeed in formal education is not a question of being gifted, bright or exceptional; it is a matter of being able to repeat dominant assumptions about language, knowledge and value in a way recognised by the dominant order. The information poor refers to the marginal citizens who are unable to align the educational and social worlds. Barriers are formed that block participation in the digitised network. Early adopters of technology are also the early adapters of technology, with the rest of society playing catch-up. Information becomes one of many commodities for sale, rather than an entity to be deployed for social good.

Rarely are discriminatory practices overt or intentional. They do not have to be. The structures — and the teachers/agents of those structures — simply impose their normalising standards that work to shun and undermine generations of working-class students. Explicit ideologies — of overt racism or sexism — are more easily resisted. When the naturalised class-based truths circulate in the level of structures and syntax, they are difficult to discredit. Ensuring social justice in a classed society is — in actuality — impossible. The inequalities and inelegances can be minimised through a three-stage process: check the curriculum, monitor the teacher's interaction with students and scrutinise the expectations that staff hold of students. A balanced, objective curriculum is not possible. For teachers desiring social change, there is a necessity to break the chain of associations that link indoctrination with multiculturalism, multi-literacies and political correctness, and truth with competition, standards and hierarchy. Through this rupture, teachers are no longer the pimps for the dominant discourse. Such a political imperative becomes more difficult in an environment of continual change in educational technology.

Technologies have diverse effects on students, dependent on their background, experience and learning styles. Angela Benson and Elizabeth Wright asked:

> which students embraced this new way of learning and which recoiled against it? Without a doubt, the most reliable predictor of the experience was the ownership of a personal computer with an up-to-date Web Browser and Internet access.[29]

Having a computer at home triggered a better performance by sudents in education. The world wide web, while designed to be user-friendly, is difficult to use and deploy with sophistication. The web — like the Internet — encourages decentralised participation.[30] The difficulties of the Internet — beyond the happy point-and-click intuitive interface — undermine those who already lack skills, time and opportunities for retraining. Technologies will reduce the potential of education to further social justice.

Class-based injustices have their origins in the unequal distribution of wealth, rather than a lack of technology. If technology becomes invisible, and is assumed to be prevalent and pervasive, then it becomes highly political. The most dangerous ideology is one that masquerades as a truth. Daniela Evans disclosed the destructive and pervasive impact of print on social structures:

> From the sixteenth century it became impossible for the illiterate to obtain either wealth or influence and this has largely occurred

due to the invention of print as a medium of communication in the fifteenth century.[31]

The Internet is integrated into the lives of the already empowered and multi-literate. It is yet to be revealed how the Internet will improve or address differences of nation, language, class, race, age, gender or sexuality. If the clichéd superhighway metaphor is actually extended, then it can be seen that highways are sites of differing size, power and hierarchies. Some roads are bigger, faster, better surfaced and serviced than others. Others are narrow, winding deathtraps. The task for teachers is to not only travail the safe, well-kept digital motorways, but to flag, critique and agitate about the technological injustices living in the crumbling crevices of working-class education.

(E)RACING TO THE FUTURE

To restate the point made from the previous chapter, the eye is an ideological organ. We do not see reality, but a version of real life that validates our truths and assumptions. Observing differences can result in either prejudice and discrimination or more effective communicative systems that acknowledge linguistic and national diversity. Similarly, there is an assumption that all computer users possess the same resolution and RAM capacity as the teacher's system. The over-familiarity with a personal computer and work-based network creates a misguided belief that all students and correspondents are utilising a compatible system. Through the Internet, differences are removed from view. Internet-based relationships are highly skewed, with users constructing others in their own image. There are profound consequences for this maligning of differences, particularly when considering the inequalities of race. Before 'build[ing] the internet into the very nature of our many democracies',[32] there is a necessity to establish alternative versions of its history. The knowledge taught in schools and universities has reinforced the construction of both race and racial privilege. To change and critique this intellectual pathway, teachers assume responsibility towards both the curriculum and the method.

While much Internet policy is fixated on questions of income and education level, more profound differences exist when pondering race. In the United States, white Americans are far more likely to own a home computer than African Americans.[33] When questions are asked of students who do not have wide-ranging access to computers at school and in the home, race is a major variable to consider. Communication technologies require consideration of how different groups are either permitted or denied sites of identity formation. The digital divide is racialised. The consequences of this demarcation for education are damning, and have a history. In a 1988 survey conducted by the US Department of Education, investigating the faculty members of 480 colleges and universities, there were an estimated 489 000 professors employed full-time in American higher education: 89 per cent of these were white.[34] At the same time as this race-based inequality saturates institutions of power, there remain what Colin Beckles described as 'utopian predictions about the internet as ... "colour-blind"'.[35] It is highly convenient to forget about race and colonialism when the structural differences are already embedded into the palette of power. In the LambdaMOO — a large virtual landscape in which 'characters' meet and interact — gender is chosen, but race is not a required choice or on the menu of permutated identities. While this identity tourism is a site of much literature and interest in the realm of gender cross-dressing, racial masking is more problematic. Lisa Nakamura realised the consequences of this closeting of race:

> While everyone is 'passing,' some forms of racial passing are condoned and practiced since they do not threaten the integrity of a national sense of self which is defined as white.[36]

She affirms that 'the Oriental' is an acceptable archetype in the MOO, being a character base of fetishism, eroticism and sexual lure. This crass orientalism only reinforces the normalising grammar of whiteness. Power structures and differences in and through the Internet are not being subverted.

Anonymity on the web carries a political difficulty. For disempowered groups, visibility and collectivity form the basis of empowerment and consciousness. To displace corporeality is to undermine community-building languages, identities and histories. These cultural links are important, as they create and deploy a useable past that mobilises injustices, histories and narratives of struggle. Through these shared narratives, a national history is rendered plural and fragmentary. Traces of information identify a chain of hosts through the transmission of email, for example, providing details about a university, company or government host. Other specificities are lost. These losses mean more for those who require an affirmation of difference to agitate for a better future. The uneven and under-developed nature of electronic communication infrastructure in some formerly colonised nations renders the easy summoning of a globalised information society inaccurate and dangerous. The global village has much of the colonial village resident within it.

Perhaps the most significant definition of social justice is fairness in distribution. Education — at its best — operates through relationships. These social affiliations are even more significant for those groups disenfranchised from empowered institutions. At best, students from distinct racial or linguistic backgrounds are encouraged to develop diverse competencies and multiple languages. At worst, great tensions emerge between school-based expectations and those of parents and peer groups. Education cannot solve the deep, dense and profound inequalities of race or colonialism. It remains implicated in the reproduction of dominant ideologies and the resultant inequalities. Teachers must consciously unravel these assumed narratives of justice, history and democracy.

ELECTRONIC MALE

Many men, it appears, are closet drag queens. The excitement of actually being able to choose to be a cyber-woman breeds much breathless excitement. For example, Mark Poster revelled in the 'challenges' of this new, sexualised environment:

> The fact of having to decide on one's gender itself raises the issue of individual identity in a novel and compelling manner. If one is to be masculine, one must choose to be so. Further, one must enact one's gender choice in language and in language alone, without any marks and gestures of the body, without clothing or intonations of voice.[37]

Drag queens have always mimed to disco. It seems appropriate that virtual drag queens mime to disco(urse). It is ironic that men's confidence and expertise in computer-based communication is being deployed to don a virtual frock.[38]

There is a systematic gender gap in the participation of girls in technology education. Many reasons for this disparity exist. Suzanne Silverman and Alice Pritchard's research showed that:

Girls who chose to take technology education were often reluctant to take classes where they would be one of the New Girls.
While only a few girls openly accepted stereotypes about appropriate careers for women, many of the girls felt uncomfortable
with the picture of themselves in nontraditional jobs. They lacked
confidence in their abilities and worried about the reaction of
friends and family.[39]

Unbelievably — considering the growth of information technology — the proportion of women entering computer studies in British
universities fell from 24 per cent in 1979 to less than 10 per cent in
1989.[40] This was, of course, during a period of high visibility of a
woman in power: Margaret Thatcher.

This inequality in educational structures is also observed in the
wider Internet environment. Janet Morahan-Martin reported that
'Online, when women try to have equal footing on male-dominated
lists, they are ignored, trivialized or criticised by men, again leading
women to drop out of online discussions'.[41]

While Rheingold has argued that individuals interact with equality and respect in the digital piazza, the Internet's 'social norms' are
actually replicating and reinforcing patriarchal disparities. The
National Coordination Office of Computing, Information and
Communications in the United States reported that 'the low participation of women, minorities, and persons with disabilities in the
Information Technology workforce is cause of concern and ...
alarm'.[42] The male-streaming of policy agendas means that there is
currently a mismatch between technology-based training and social,
curricula and web-based justice for women.

Women have the role of web shopper carefully sketched for them.
Whether they can be more than a consumer identity and attain edu-
cational goals beyond market imperatives is yet to be determined.
Jane Kenway remains suspicious, remembering that:

while happy to use (and abuse) them, neither the world of work
(paid or unpaid) nor the world of the commodity, market choice
and competition has ever been very kind to females.[43]

Women use the Internet differently and less frequently than men.
This distinction holds negative economic and educational consequences. There are not only the technical logistics for gaining access

to the online environment, but the flaming and harassment suffered while online.

To be fluid in an identity takes great power. To move between selves requires an agency enforced and fuelled by strong institutions. That is why disempowered communities load such emphasis on words like black, gay, woman or indigenous. These identities mean something — not because they are intrinsically real or significant — but because they are the basis and core of an alternative community. They form the foundation of political movements. The unmarked sign — the white, the middle class, the masculine, the coloniser — needs identity to be fluid and invisible. If those in power fix their identity, they can be easily located, attacked and critiqued. It is in the interests of the empowered to move, change and affirm multiplicity through online aliases or handles. Annalee Newitz revealed this most effectively:

> I would argue that our confusion about what constitutes 'real life' does not come from virtual and simulated technologies themselves, but something fundamental to the way capitalist ideology encourages us to structure our identities.[44]

It is in the interests of the disempowered to build a community on the basis of a historically-shared grievance. Therefore, the desire for teachers to be resilient and flexible, rather than committed and politically aware, can be viewed as an attempt to unsettle the identity of scholars, to block the building of a community fighting for rights, social justice and education.

The intricacy of feminine and masculine performances is naïvely marked with educational discourses, and appears strangely silent in the white noise of digital liberation:

> The social implications of CMC [Computer Mediated Communication] are vast, from its potential ability to overthrow centralized control of information to its potential ability to help people, no matter what their gender, race, or physical appeared, communicate with each other with fewer prejudices and misunderstandings than any other medium in existence.[45]

Within this statement, Gladys We has sealed the inequalities of the offline world from the Internet. Offline — as on — women are not oppressed because they have physical differences from men. Patriarchy, like racism, is not 'about' bodies or skin. It is based on linguistic and social systems, to verify the power held by the dominant culture, the unmarked sign, the normalised gatekeepers of negotiations over truth and value. Susan Herring recognised that, while the Internet may appear to democratise communication, 'women are discouraged or intimidated from participating on the basis of the reactions with which their posts are met when they do contribute'.[46] This harassment is not triggered in response to women's bodies, but to their presence in space. Whether this is textualised cyberspace, or corporeal occupation of the workplace and classroom, the result is the same. To maintain power, women's presence is undermined, ignored and decentred. Men then direct and determine the discursive frame. This is particularly the case in academic communications. Hierarchy and professional standing are not denied through the web. Instead, already existing male domination of the academy and higher educational echelons is perpetuated online.[47]

The question remains: should women adapt to the online discourse? As patriarchal institutions create and frame its languages, protocols and ideologies, women translate the directives and vocabulary to create more contextually appropriate knowledge. Some critics such as Lisa King advise women to mobilise women-friendly or women-only environments to learn and nurture online communication systems.[48] While creating a digital ghetto, such a strategy also allows a feeling of safety and confidence to be formed. An instrument for marginalisation and alienation simultaneously becomes a mechanism to build collectivity. Also, there is something significant about women bringing to the web diverse linguistic and relational tactics and styles. Patriarchy existed before the arrival of industrialisation, (post)Fordism or the market orientation of the economy. The Internet is causing new ruptures in the building of new feminine models. Sharmila Pixy Ferris reported that 'far from mitigating gender differences, CMC sometimes exacerbates them'.[49] The Internet is not a mirror: it does not reflect reality. Instead it actively circulates and remoulds the real for the political purposes of the present.

The attention to gender swapping on the web is excessive and tedious. Those with social influence and empowered literacies transgress the limits of the self and experiment with new languages, surfaces and bodies. For those groups that need a clearly determined and demonstrated identity to build and affirm consciousness and community, there is little to be gained from flexibility. Resistive political goals and agendas require a semblance of stability to actually intervene in governmental policy. A fly is easier to swat when it is resting than when it is flying. Fluidity cannot be the basis of political organisation and critique. Amy Bruckman asserted that:

> gender swapping is an extreme example of a fundamental fact: the network is in the process of changing not just how we work, but how we think of ourselves — and ultimately, who we are.[50]

The use of 'we' here is significant. It takes cultural capital to change identities, like changing shoes. For the disempowered, there is a need to grasp the building blocks of injustice and maintain rage and visibility on the narratives of inequality, to build an alternative society through resistance. Gender is not invisible — it is not discarded like a pair of high heels. Critics affirming the potentials of gender swapping need to ponder the following political question: what is the difference between doing nothing, with bad political intentions, and ignoring the gender question, with the best intentions in the world?

THE INFORMATION REDLINE

I've got so many friends on the Internet
I could never be alone ...
Lucky Me.

Bachelor Girl, 'Lucky Me'

Irony, humour and despair emerge from computer-mediated communication. Bill Gates stated in 1995 that 'already, anyone can send anyone else a message on the Internet — for business, education, or just the fun of it'.[51] Bill Gates' assertion that 'anyone' can access the Internet is ludicrous: global telephone networks are not universal.[52] Literacy in the protocols and ability to access the infrastructure are at a low level.[53] Amazon.com is not a digital library. The Internet is not a ballot box. There is no evidence to demonstrate that digitisation has permitted an education for those who have been excluded from the education system. There is little confirmation that the Internet has made a difference to poverty or powerlessness. The poverty line is being reinforced, rather than collapsed, by the information line. The allegorical flourishes of the Internet serve to unsettle and question notions of community and otherness. Therefore, it is easier — analytically, theoretically and politically — to mark technology as the primary marker of change. The key theory of the Internet yet to be presented is the history of silences: not only what is not being mentioned, but also who is not in the conversation. To ponder the inequalities of the Internet is to open the Pandora's box that few want revealed. Patrice McDermott affirmed the gross inequalities that exist even in the home of the Internet. In the United States, 31 per cent of the families receiving food stamps have no telephones.[54] The Internet is not an option in such a context.

HTML is the universal language of the web. It is soon to be replaced by XML (Extensible Markup Language). XML's great advantage is that tags attach to it; this grants the ability to view data in a way consistent with what the data represents. We need the political equivalent of XML. The meta-tagging of social justice is not simply a metaphor and motif of this section. It is a reminder that social concerns are not adjacent, tangential or irrelevant in the dawning new egalitarianism of the Internet. Technology does create enormous benefits, but for an elite few. The point of social justice in education is to intervene, to disrupt, dissociate and decentre the discourses of the great, advantaged and empowered. Therefore, meta-tagging politics is a reminder that technology without social awareness and consciousness is damaging, dangerous and destructive.

CONCLUSION:
SOCRATES IN THE SOFTWARE

The scholar is that man who must take up into himself all the
ability of the time, all the contributions of the past, all the
hopes of the future. He must be a university of knowledges.[1]

Ralph Waldo Emerson

The idea that the capitalist system wants a good many critical thinkers is simply absurd — it can only spell trouble
unless the thinkers are thinking for, not against, the boss.
Thus, the point is to produce a human as puzzle-solver, not
really as critical thinker.[2]

Monty Neill

Education reveals its benefits in the long term. It is a blue chip stock,
and superannuation for the mind. It does not create an easy, quick
return that can be assessed in terms of the first pay cheque, the first
bonus or a new car. Any society that is not prepared to invest in education is demolishing its future. It will take a generation, but if we lose the
capacity to create, desire, imagine and critique, we destroy the memory, intensity and inheritance of our history. Money must be set aside for
educational infrastructure. The imperatives of more hospitals, more
prisons and more warships will always appear more urgent and more
popular at election time. Politicians can never 'win' using education,
because the results are only revealed through a lifetime of social and cultural contribution to citizenship, rather than the quick fix needed for
the next political debate. But if education — in its sensuality, boldness
and breadth — is denied, then we foreclose our own potential.

Antonio Gramsci listed one of the most important political actions as 'renovating and making critical an already existing activity'.[3] He always spoke the language of possibility, even when imprisoned for his ideals. There are few more significant already-existing activities than education, and educators have a responsibility to speak out and resist those ideas that are destructive to the disempowered. The proletarianisation of teaching creates a technocratic consciousness in our institutions. This technocorporate matrix — a new, improved and different capitalism — transforms gimmicks into institutionalised strategic plans. In this world, teachers are digital butlers. Indeed, within the Australian Labor Party's election platform, the function of the humanities was to hold a role 'as a content provider for information-based industries'.[4] With such a profile emerging from the leftist/progressive party, questions of media literacy and intellectual leadership become redundant to national policy and education. Such ideologies are expressed even more overtly in the United Kingdom. The Enterprise in Higher Education Initiative (EHE) 'aimed to establish and embed the concept and practice of enterprise within universities, and to increase the effectiveness of higher education (HE) in preparing students for working life'.[5] The simplification of all teaching and learning considerations into the workplace is unfortunate, particularly in an environment of labour surplus. With such imperatives emerging from Labo(u)r governments, political debates about education have corroded what were already rusted, crumbling economic decisions. Martin Lawn's review of the Blairite Third Way has tracked the deep consequences of this political retreat:

> To speak of the 'teaching profession' is to speak the language of the past in England. The ideas and practices upon which the great post-war education system was built have been thoroughly demolished so that, in effect, a new vocabulary now has to be used to explain the purposes and practices of teaching.[6]

Teacher professionalism and public service were entwined by both the Beveridge Report and the post-war Attlee-led Labour Governments after 1945. Through the 1990s, the shift to the Right and the movement to post-Fordism and de-industrialisation have resulted in the market rate paid for public service. Teaching is a systematic list of competencies. Making teaching more efficient and evaluated triggers a loss of motivation, respect and responsibility. Without the goodwill of staff, the education system will fold like a deck of cards.

The arguments in this book may be framed as elitist and as an attempt to nostalgically hold on to an inappropriate model of literacy and education. I have been called idealistic, old fashioned and naïve at more meetings than I can count. It is ironic that to resist grinding corporate goals, the market, inequality, banality and mediocrity is framed as discriminatory. Economic rationalism and the commercial orientation of education is part of a far longer history of the powerful attempting to control schooling. There has always been a moral recalibration of the learning environment. Ian Hunter has offered a profound attack on those who claim such a critical intellectual status:

> The genealogies of the modern school and the critical intellectual thus turn out to be inseparable. It is only after we have freed ourselves from the spell of the latter's status-ideal — the self-reflective and self-realizing subject — that we can approach the former with the intellectual restraint necessary to do justice to its complex modernity.[7]

Hunter is suggesting that both the significant interpretations of the school — from liberal moral philosophy and Marxian social theory — are flawed because they oversimplify terms like choice and democracy. Both these theories empower the critical intellectual to perform critique. This book applauds the dissenting, questioning intellectual, while acknowledging Hunter's premise and arguments. The reason I assume such a stance is that the alternatives are disastrous. To remove the critical function from scholars at this time is to silence dissenting futures and alternative social truths. In a culture where the market is the primary vehicle of truth, it would be damaging for teachers to spend all their energy revealing — with consciousness and reflexivity, to be sure — the power they gain from the system while that system is crumbling around them.

While academics shun the description of teacher, other labels are used even less frequently, and with telling political consequences. The critical intellectual role has weathered off the limestone of our most prestigious universities. Instead of providing tough alternatives to tepid times, we live in an era of experts. Whenever a new economic policy, unemployment figure or an educational agenda is released, an old man in an over-stuffed reefer jacket is summoned to offer an opinion that, in the hands of an expert, becomes a truth.

There is a reason why educators are distracted from the issues of the day. We have our own problems, existing in an era of strategic plans, marketing meetings and endless governmental green and white papers. Not surprisingly, amid this political whirl, it is a tough time to be a teacher. It is an even tougher time to be an intellectual. That word — intellectual — sounds grandiose, odd and arrogant. Indeed, intellectual life is a verb rather than a noun: becoming, rather than being. This word, though, tends to make teachers in particular uncomfortable. In 1999, I was the guest speaker at a meeting of principals who head elite schools, having been asked to deliver a presentation about multiculturalism, indigenous rights, disability and notions of difference in education. As I have an obsessive-compulsive fear of lateness, I arrived thirty minutes before my speech. During this time, I (over)heard the assembled headmasters and one headmistress express their excitement at online technology, and the possibility of having individual classrooms connected to the Internet. The potential of computer-mediated education was reduced to the capacity to deliver emails to staff, therefore simplifying human resource management and professional development. Not only would these principals not have to see staff in person, but the amount of paper being used in the schools would supposedly decrease. The promise of the paperless schoolroom resonated from their lips.

Their attitudes were naïve and a little too excited by technology for my liking. PowerPoint was almost a religious experience for them. While the techno-enthusiasm was filling the air around me, I pondered the presentation that I was about to deliver. It was evaluating the nitty gritty of teaching — about how to manage diversity in language, physical capacity and socio-economic background. It was a speech about the social responsibilities of teaching. As their meeting continued, though, it became clear that none of the people in the room had actually taught anything, or thought about teaching, in the last ten years. Therefore, my speech was well placed. I argued for the necessity to move out of our comfort zones, to further social justice in our classrooms. Remember, Socrates was not Professor Popularity in Athens.

After arguing for the pivotal role of education in countering racist and elitist forces in society, the only female principal in the room remarked: 'I haven't thought about being an intellectual in twenty years, and I don't have the time to start now'. Her friend — the headmaster of the most expensive boys' school in the State — merely retorted that I needed to 'get into the real world'. This was the same group whose definition of a real world included using emails to simplify human resource management. These misconceptions should not have surprised me. Academics become the safe targets for ridicule and dismissal, taking from the public purse and living an easy, dream-like existence of writing, posturing and endless coffee breaks. Somehow, the university has become a place apart, distanced from time, space and life.

After my presentation to the principals, I tried to understand how these educational leaders, the very people responsible for training my future students, so misunderstood the work of universities. It was at this moment that I metaphorically stumbled upon CS Lewis. Having never entered Narnia from the world of the wardrobe, I was ignorant of his role in the childhood of millions. It was his critical writing and public commentary that grabbed my attention. His life, like that of his generation, had been composed of two wars, two reconstructions, rationing, sickness, grief and early death. His commitment to books, scholarship and public service left me hooked. While wildly different in our politics and belief structures, when reading his words I remembered why I became a teacher, writer and academic. Although a specialist in 16th century literature, his writing spoke of a desire to remind the public of education's place inside, rather than adjacent to, society:

> Those of us who have been true readers all our life seldom realise the enormous extension of our being that we owe to authors. My own eyes are not enough for me. Even the eyes of all humanity are not enough. In reading great literature I become a thousand men and yet remain myself. Like the night sky in a Greek poem, I see with a thousand eyes, but it is still I who see. Here, as in worship, in love, in moral action, and in knowing, I transcend myself: and am never more myself than when I do.[8]

In Lewis's words, there is a thirst for knowledge, a compulsive need to extend the self and test the limits of our world and truths. It is this passion for learning, reading and thinking that has dissipated from contemporary life.

The standardised nature of higher education has reshaped not only what is expected of graduates, but how students wish to be treated. This is no surprise. In 2000 the description of an innovative educator in an international education journal was 'the people who have incorporated PowerPoint into their Web page'.[9] Certainly, to understand the web's role in education we require an understanding of aesthetics, interactivity, vector map creation and visual communication in mixed media. But teaching requires something more: an integrated agenda of taste, sight and discovery. The words of John Henry Newman in 1852 attacked those with a simple notion of a university's purpose:

> they insist that Education should be confined to some particular and narrow end, and should issue in some definite work, which can be weighed and measured. They argue as if everything, as well as every person, had its price.[10]

In summoning Newman, socially-aware teachers need to state that we do not have a price, that the point of education is to arch beyond personal interest and into a greater good. Through the act of objection, a political vocabulary can be assembled beyond the technocratic and beyond the philistine. Competency is not good enough for our students, our education systems or our nations.

For all those horrified and despairing of the techno-abstainers and doubters like me, there is only one medication for that disgust: get off the cross. We need the timber. There is far too much technobabble and utopic posturing about the digital future of education. The aim of my words is to remind readers of what is already working effectively in our current system, what can be improved, and how the Internet can either assist or undermine that process. This is a project that unifies all teachers, regardless of our nationality or teaching level. It is a borderless advocacy.

Computer-mediated teaching is more than an adjunct to traditional teaching modes. Currently, it is a menace to the university sector. Do not read this threat as a trigger for hand-wringing and bitter tears. Like all political and social threats, it serves a unique purpose: to make us restate what we believe in, affirm what is worth fighting for and what needs protecting and nurturing. Online education has done us a service. It has reminded us how magical those intricate spindles of teaching and learning can be — and the potent force and imperatives of our actions. We know that those administrators and web 'experts' instructing us in the future of education do not have the skills to teach as we do — with consistency, rhythm and energy. Many educational managers could not run a bath, let alone a classroom.

Accomplished teachers are provocative thinkers. Socrates' method was so potent because he asked piquant questions that required answers that could potentially unravel the self and society. Personal experience is never enough, for teachers or students. The aim of teachers is to move students from the singularity of their own lives, through to observation and reflections on that experience. Only then may abstractions and generalisations be developed, which can then be tested through a process of experimentation.[11] The Internet will not replace the many roles of the teacher. Particular software packages may substitute for some well-defined and narrow classroom tasks. For drills and simulations, they are ideal. There are incredible advantages in indexing, editing and searching through the computer-mediated environment. The Internet is a site of production. It is not an autonomous site for thinking. The dependency on computers has been so rapid that we have forgotten the importance of experience: the necessity of failure, weakness and anxiety to the learning process. If a definitive answer can be given, then the wrong question has been asked.

This book has not been filled with stories of hardware development, miniaturisation or convergence. Neither has it welcomed a digital nirvana of individual libertarianism. Plenty of these books are available from the Amazon.com shopping trolley. I am suggesting that definitions of the real create real consequences. Intentions summon a reality. The Internet is framing our understanding of the real. The time has come to take that power back. A computer is not simply composed of hardware, software and data. It is not only a physical entity, but a running system — a social network — with permeable borders that spill into politics and ethics. The aim of education is to not allow another generation of citizens to be exploited in the casual workforce, living off tips and gratuities while dreaming of winning the lottery. Educators must stop being compliant in a system that transforms students into consumers and teachers into information traffickers. Summoning and changing a familiar refrain, online students make history, but not on their own terms. They do not choose the circumstances for themselves, but negotiate a system passed down from the past. Cultural studies imperatives and techniques assist in this new, interpretative journey.

In 1981, the Birmingham Centre for Contemporary Cultural Studies — the long-departed powerhouse of the field — published *Unpopular Education*. Authors Steve Baron, Dan Finn, Neil Grant, Michael Green and Richard Johnson sought to research the 'crisis' of educational policy and practice. They wished to focus cultural studies scholars on education as a site of struggle to organise a popular politics. The writers described 'the crisis of social democratic intellectuals'.[12] They demanded intervention, interpretation and activity from scholars, to ensure that middle-class parents and 'experts' did not engrain education into the directives of a capitalist schooling system. Their warnings over twenty years ago have not been heeded. Well-paid consultants have replaced intellectuals. Parents require league tables of the 'best schools' to ensure that middle-class children continue to gain middle-class employment. When discussing the crisis of intellectuals, we are actually discussing a crisis in social democratic intellectuals. What we are missing is the critical intellectual — the ratbag dissenter — whose ideas may not be popular, but offer a radical dialogue with the truths of the time. The best of intellectuals are able to determine how much of the past we can manage in the present. Indigenous rights and multiculturalism are not conversation fillers between chardonnays. They are deep and profound re-assessments of our history and our experience. These words and debates are part of an ongoing dialogue between our present selves and the ghosts of history.

The education sector plays an integral role in forging the social democratic connection. To affirm this significance is increasingly difficult, because of the convoluted relationship between education and training, teaching and learning, teaching and research. Donald Horne, in the 5th edition of *The Lucky Country*, restated his argument that intellectual life in Australia is second rate, and he held university scholars partly responsible for the frightening racism that erupted in the mid-1990s around Pauline Hanson's One Nation.[13] Similarly, McKenzie Wark affirmed that 'there has been too strong an emphasis on reading in Australia and not enough on thinking'.[14] I have rarely disagreed with anyone more than Wark: reading and thinking are not disparate entities. In fact, if I have one criticism of Australians, it is that we all read too little. Thought without research is opinion without depth, and therefore dangerous. As people involved in education, our responsibility is to teach a discipline of thought, alongside scholarly rigour and stylistic clarity. Again, Wark has misunderstood the role of the intellectual. He needs to read more. I know who should be at the top of his reading list.

The man I admire most is the late Edward Palmer Thompson. He did everything that is no longer fashionable. He was tough, spoke his mind, was ruthlessly intelligent and passionate. He did not fit anywhere, joining and leaving myriad political organisations and universities. But he was honest. He was tough. As a co-founder for the Campaign for Nuclear Disarmament, he tried to make the world safe. As the writer of *The Making of the English Working Class*, he changed the way history was researched, written and presented. By 1970 Thompson was bubbling with anger fuelled by the student revolts at Warwick University in the late 1960s. He was horrified at the corporatisation of education. He was worried about the loss of the critical intellectual tradition: to say what must be said, rather than writing and mouthing what others pay us to say.[15] By 1981 EP Thompson was voted among the four most admired people in Britain, following — unbelievably — Margaret Thatcher, Queen Elizabeth II and the Queen Mother.

Opinion is being managed so ruthlessly at the moment. Conformity and mediocrity anchor our thoughts. We need chronic objectors like Thompson. Not knockers, but teachers, writers and intellectuals who are prepared to offer alternatives. Politics is congealing around us, pushing us into crisis management and panic stations. That is why I like Thompson. He stated in one of his early teaching journals that:

> There is too little rebellion in the class ... and ... it looks as if the whole course of the class might be run without one good earnest row between the students.[16]

We need to bring back the good row: a debate about ideas and identities.

Teaching is an activity of innovation and problem solving. The joyous creativity of the best classrooms unravels the banal simplicity of workplace-related skills. The portability of the teacher, moving between reading, writing, interpretation and theory, organises thought and meaning. To write about teaching is to summon the spectre of theoretician and storyteller, in an attempt to flesh out the ephemeral into an experience. Education changes to provide what the society needs at a particular time. The humanities are important, though, as the memory of the educational system. Mathematics, medicine, economics, law and the biological sciences are noble pursuits. Alone, they are not an education. Alone, they do not make a scholar. Alone, they do not forge a citizen.

As a cultural system, education needs to be written about, and often. Through cultural studies, this book has offered a method to socially reconstruct the educational experience. In a classroom, both students and teachers carry forward prior understandings of learning and teaching, hoping to build a coherent sense of meaning, interpretation and identity. Education is frantic, ambivalent, exciting and creative. Through the digital barricades, dodging economic and political limitations, we are guided by Socrates' difficult questions, while confronting — head on — the social injustices we find.

NOTES

PREFACE: HEMLOCK IN THE HARDWARE

1   L Grossberg, 'The scandal of cultural studies', from L Grossberg et al., *It's a sin*, Power, Sydney, 1988, p 9.

I   DO YOU WANT FRIES WITH THAT? INTERNET TEACHING AND THE ADMINISTRATION OF KNOWLEDGE

1   M Apple, *Cultural politics and education*, Teachers College Press, New York, 1996, p 23.
2   J Dudley & L Vidovich, *The politics of education: Commonwealth Schools Policy 1973–1995*, Australian Council for Educational Research, Melbourne, 1995, p 145.
3   J Scigliano & J Levin, 'One-stop shopping in an online educational mall', *Technological horizons in education*, Vol 27, Issue 11, June 2000, [full-text].
4   A clear exploration of this process of academic development is presented by Tony Becher in *Academic Tribes and Territories*, Open University Press, Buckingham, 1993:1989.
5   D Whittle, *Cyberspace: The human dimension*, WH Freeman and Company, New York, 1998, p 37.
6   C Lucas, *Crisis in the academy: Rethinking higher education in America*, St Martin's Griffin, New York, 1996, p xi.
7   M Baily, 'Great expectations: PCs and productivity', from R Kling (ed), *Computerisation and controversy*, Academic Press, San Diego, 1996, p 21.
8   S Aronowitz & H Giroux, *Education under siege*, Burgin and Garvey Publishers, Massachusetts, 1985, p 28.
9   'Institutional vs. educational priorities', <http://www.curtin.edu.au/home/allen/we3/igt/tool35.html>, accessed 29 December 2000.
10 'Computer Mediated Communications: Teaching with CMC should be facilitation', <http://www.curtin.edu.au/home/allen/we43/igm/120402.html>, accessed 29 July 2000.
11 'IBL can involve increased academic workloads', <http://www.curtin.edu.au/home/allen/we3/igm/090204.html>, accessed 29 October 2000.
12 As Paul Rodes, Dennis Knapczyk, Carrie Chapman and Chung Haejin have realised, 'it should not be surprising … that many of the most successful

web-based courses are in computer science and other technically advanced fields where students are already comfortable and familiar with computer technology'. Therefore, the form and content relationship is even more significant when discussing Internet-based education. See 'Involving teachers in web-based professional development', *Technological Horizons in Education*, Vol 27, Issue 10, May 2000, [full-text].

13   This is an arduous task, and before Macromedia's Dreamweaver, very time-consuming. Yet the hypertext capacity (and strength) of the web means that maintenance becomes an unending process. Between one semester and the next, generally one third of the URL links no longer function.

14   S Brookfield, *Becoming a critically reflective teacher*, Jossey-Bass Books, San Francisco, 1995, p 6.

15   'Educational foundations: Education and Communication', <http://www.curtin.edu.au/home/allen/we3/igm/030108.html>, accessed 29 July 2000.

16   David Tripp has stated that 'teachers are being more rigorously assessed on ever narrower observable criteria', *Critical incidents in teaching*, Routledge, London, 1993, p 142.

17   'Student IBL Survey Report', <http://www.curtin.edu.au/home/allen/we3/igt/tool21.html>, accessed 29 July 2000.

18   A Smith & F Webster, 'Introduction: The university as imagined community', in A Smith & F Webster (ed), *The Postmodern University? Contested visions of higher education in society*, Open University Press, Buckingham, 1997, p 1.

19   A Benson & E Wright, 'Pedagogy and policy in the age of the wired professor', *Technological horizons in education*, Vol 27, Issue 4, November 1999, [full-text]. These results were confirmed through Curtin University's student surveys, where the major problems reported by students were technical and access concerns, 'Student IBL Survey Report'.

20   D Petre & D Harrington, *The clever country: Australia's digital future*, Lansdowne, Sydney, 1996, p 102.

21   For example, Deborah Padgett and Simone Conceica-Runlee, in 'Designing a faculty development program on technology: if you build it, will they come', *Journal of Social World Education*, Vol 36, Issue 2, Spring 2000, [full-text].

22   M Vachris, 'Teaching principles of economics without 'Chalk and Talk', *The journal of economic education*, Vol 30, Issue 3, Summer 1999, [full-text].

23   As Stephen Brookfield has stated, 'the concept of vocation serves the interests of those who want to run colleges efficiently and profitably while spending the least amount of money and employing the smallest number of staff that they can get away with', *Becoming a critically reflective teacher*, Jossey-Bass Books, San Francisco, 1995 p 16.

24   L Shrum, 'Introducing teachers to telecommunications: California's (ESTTI)', *Technological Horizons in Education*, Vol 15, No 8, April 1998, [full-text].

25   As Curtin's IBL Construction Kit offers, 'Basically, the Centre for Educational advancement and the IT Section of the University will provide much help: you will also have to learn more technical skills yourself'. 'Curtin's IBL Construction Kit: Questions answered and links for more', <http://www.curftin.edu.au/home/allen/we3/igq/index.html>, accessed 29 July 2000.

26 'Administering IBL: Choose from these options', <http://www.curtin. edu.au/home/allen/we3/igm/080000.html>, accessed 29 July 2000.

27 J Scigliano, J Levin, G Horne, 'Using HTML for organising student projects through the Internet', *Technological Horizons in Education*, Vol 24, No 1, 1996, [full-text].

28 T Kerry & J Tollitt-Evans, *Teaching in further education*, Blackwell Publishers, Oxford, 1990, p 120.

29 *Australian Literature (LCS12)*, 'Selection of online units', <http://www.curtin.edu.au/home/allen/we3/igt/tool18.html>, accessed 29 July 2000. A similar problem regarding student numbers was revealed by Geoff Rehn in 'The Western Australian networks for learning trial', <http://wwwtlc1.murdoch.edu.au/gen/aset/confs/edtech92/ rehn1.html>, accessed 19 September 2000. Rehn reported that after assembling a two-way video set-up at Kununurra, no students enrolled in the course.

30 As James Garton realised in 1997, 'despite the pervasive growth of electronic genres, and the equity issues that accompany them, recent Australian curriculum initiatives in the field of language and literacy education pay little attention to new online literacies', from 'New genres and new literacies: The challenge of the virtual curriculum', *Australian Journal of Language and Literacy*, Vol 20, No 3, August 1997, [full-text].

31 'Student IBL Survey Report', http://www.curtin.edu.au/home/ allen/we3/igt/tool21.html, accessed 29 July 2000.

32 'Teaching and learning online', <http://www.newcastle.edu.au/depart- ment/so/students.html>, accessed 29 July 29 2000.

33 'Institutional vs. educational priorities', http://www.curtin.edu.au/home/ allen/we3/igt/tool35.html, accessed 29 July 2000.

34 James O'Donnell described this process as 'Students do fill out evaluation forms, and these are read assiduously by chairs and deans, believing that the judgment of the unskilled is the only measurement we can make', *Avatars of the world: From papyrus to cyberspace*, Harvard University Press, Cambridge, 1998, p 171.

35 b hooks, 'Eros, eroticism, and the pedagogical process', in H Giroux & P McLaren (ed), *Between Borders: Pedagogy and the politics of cultural studies*, Routledge, New York, 1994, p 118.

36 R Atkinson, 'Going online: Infrastructures and services for Internet deliv- ered vocational education', 3rd International Conference Researching Vocational Education and Training, 14–16 July 1999, Bolton Institute, <http://www.leeds.ac.uk/educol/documents/000001047.htm>, accessed 19 September 2000.

37 G Rawlins, *Moths to the flame: The seductions of computer technology*, MIT Press, Cambridge, 1996, p 111.

38 'Improving lectures with technology', <http://darkwing.uoregon.edu/ `tep/technology/techlect.html>, accessed 29 July 2000.

39 C Oberman, 'Library instruction: Concepts and pedagogy in the electron- ic environment, *RQ*, Vol 35, No 3, Spring 1996, [full-text].

40 R Dennis Hayes, 'Digital palsy: RSI and restructuring Capital', in J Brook & I Boal (ed), *Resisting the virtual life: The culture and politics of informa- tion*, City Lights, San Francisco, 1995, p 173.

2 LET'S MAKE LOTS OF MONEY: DIGITAL DEALS AND TRAFFICKING TRUTH IN THE VIRTUAL CLASSROOM

1 'Opportunities', performed by the Pet Shop Boys, written by Neil Tennant & Chris Lowe, produced by Stephen Hague, from *Please*, EMI, London, 1986, track three.

2 P Willis, *Common Culture*, Westview, Boulder, 1990, p 147.

3 Both statements are derived from J Shurkin, *Engines of the Mind: The evolution of the computer from mainframes to microprocessors*, WW Norton, New York, 1996, p 93.

4 Ada Byron's remarkable algebraic contribution to the history of computer-mediated communication was discussed in Sadie Plant's *Zeros and Ones: Digital Women and the new Technoculture*, Fourth Estate, London, 1997, pp 5–32.

5 D Lowenthal, *The past is a foreign country*, Cambridge University Press, Cambridge, 1985.

6 'How does the net work?', [online], <http://www.cnet.com/Content/Features/Techno/Networks/ss02.html>, accessed 24 August 2000.

7 Please note that I am intentionally separating the Internet from the web for the sake of historical clarity and intellectual rigour. While the web is part of the Internet, it is based on hypertext transfer protocols (http) that allow the exchange of video, sound images and text. Web browsers and servers share http. The Internet can exist independently of the web. The web cannot exist without the Net.

8 The compression of digitised data, which utilises the MPEG international compression standard, allows 72 minutes of video to be delivered on CD Rom. This means that feature films are delivered on two or three discs. To place information — including the history of cinema and television — in a digitised form such as this makes it manipulable, shareable and interactive.

9 M Soules, 'The paradox of technology', January 1997, [online], <http://www.mala.bc.ca/~soules/paradox/paradox.htm>, accessed 24 August 1999.

10 M Soules, 'The paradox of technology'.

11 M Rosenthal, 'Futures and histories of the Book', [online], <http://www.mtbs.com/bkhist1.html>, accessed 30 July 1999.

12 Occasionally, this demarcation between the United States and other components of the network is expressed crudely: ROW (Rest of the World). To see an example of this tendency, please refer to Jonar Nader's *Illustrated Dictionary of Computing*, Prentice Hall, Sydney, 1998, p 26.

13 'Information Technology for the Twenty-First Century: A bold investment in America's future: Social, economic, and workforce implications of information technology and information technology workforce development', National Coordination Office of Computing, Information and Communications, <http://www.hpcc.gov/pubs/it2-ip/social.html>, accessed 16 August 1999.

14 Please refer to 'Who started the Net?' [online], <http://www.cnet.com/Content/Features/Techno/Networks/ss05.html>, accessed 24 August 1999.

15 Leonard Kleinrock wrote the first paper on packet switching theory from MIT, in 1961. For further information about this early publishing history of

the Internet, please refer to Robert Zakon's 'Hobbes' Internet Timeline v 4.2', [online], <http://info.isoc.org/guest/zakon/Internet/History/HIT.html#Growth>, accessed 24 August 1999.

16 B Sterling 'Internet', [online], <http://www.eff.org/pub/Net_info/Net_culture_internet_sterling.history>, accessed 16 August 1999.

17 Outside of defence concerns, the National Science Foundation (NSFNET) allowed scholars to use the network, and promoted educational access.

18 J Quarterman & S Carl-Mitchell, 'What is the internet, anyway?', 1994, [online], <http://www.mids.org/what.html>, accessed 16 August, 1999.

19 For an example of this myth building, please refer to Katie Hafner's 'The Creators', *Wired Archive*, 1.12-December 1994, [online], <http://www. wired.com/wired/archive/2.12/creators.html>, accessed 16 August 1999.

20 T Berners-Lee, 'Press FAQ', [online], <http://www.w3.org/People/Berners-Lee/FAQ.html>, accessed 16 August, 1999.

21 C Lucas, *Crisis in the academy: Rethinking higher education in America*, St Martin's Griffin, New York, 1996, p 24.

22 'Applications of learning', <http://connectedteacher.classroom.com/tips/resources/communicating.htm>, accessed 16 June 2001.

23 D Kember, 'Teaching beliefs and their impact on students' approach to learning', from B Dart & G Boulton-Lewis (ed), *Teaching and learning in higher education*, ACER, Melbourne, 1998, p 23.

24 L Porter, *Creating the virtual classroom*, John Wiley and Sons, New York, 1997, p 199.

25 Obviously a Doctorate in Education instructs the holder in pedagogy, assessment and curriculum. However, these students frequently obtain a Doctor of Education, rather than a Doctor of Philosophy.

26 A Morrison & D McIntyre, *Teachers and Teaching*, Penguin, Harmondsworth, 1969, p 45.

27 S Brookfield, *Becoming a critically reflective teacher*, Jossey-Bass Books, San Francisco, 1995, p xi.

28 For a discussion of the art of teaching, please refer to EW Eisner, *The Educational Imagination*, Macmillan, New York, 1985, pp 175–90.

29 J Heimlich & E Norland, *Developing teaching style in adult education*, Jossey-Bass Publishers, San Francisco, 1994, p 13.

30 D Tripp, *Critical incidents in teaching*, Routledge, London, 1993.

31 D Tripp, *Critical incidents in teaching*, p 131.

32 For an outstanding discussion of 'reconstructing action situations' through journals, please refer to Grimmett, MacKinnon, Erickson & Riecken, 'Reflective practice in teacher education', in Cliff, Housten & Pugach (ed), *Encourage reflective practice in education: An analysis of issues and programs*, NY Teachers College Press, New York, 1990, pp 20–31.

33 K Hafner, 'Lessons learned at Dot-Com U', 2 May 2002, <http://www.nytimes.com/2002/05/02/technology/circuits/02DIST.html?ex=1021310020&ei=1&en=bcb160867f6404b2>, accessed 2 May 2002.

34 These costings were cited in K Hafner, 'Lessons learned at Dot-Com U'.

35 T O'Shea, cited in G Davies, 'Going to college by logging on', *Guardian Weekly*, 2–8 May 2002, p 23.

36 J McCalman, 'Online learning fails the screen test', the *Age*, 17 January 2001, <wysiwyg://Body.46/http://www.theag...u/news/2001/01/17/FFXSAR6G0IC.html>.

37 J O'Donnell, *Avatars of the world: From papyrus to cyberspace*, Harvard University Press, Cambridge, 1998, p 120.
38 J Shiveley & P Van Fossen, 'Critical thinking and the internet: Opportunities for the social studies classroom', *The Social Studies*, Vol 90, No 1, Jan–Feb 1990, [full-text article].
39 L Porter, *Creating the virtual classroom*, John Wiley and Sons, New York, 1997, p 132.
40 P Cartwright, 'Technology and underprepared students — part two', *Change*, Vol 28, No 3, May–June 1996 [full-text article].
41 A Smith & F Webster, 'Introduction: The university as imagined community', from A Smith & F Webster (ed), *The postmodern university?* Open University Press, Buckingham, 1997, p 13.
42 Lynnette Porter reminds her readers of the many modes of distance education in *Creating the virtual classroom: Distance learning with the internet*, John Wiley, New York, 1997, particularly pages 19–23.

3   BONFIRE OF THE LITERACIES: :), :(, AND LITERACY IN THE INFORMATION AGE

1   D Marc, *Bonfire of the humanities*, Syracuse University Press, Syracuse, 1995, p 62.
2   S Weller, 'Let's return to more balance', *The Weekend Australian*, 18–19 May 2002, p 13.
3   M Stefik, *Internet dreams: Archetypes, myths and metaphors*, MIT Press, Cambridge, 1997, p 7.
4   For a presentation of this debate — at its most political and vitriolic — please refer to Deborah Hope's piece 'The literacy war', *Weekend Australian Review*, 16–17 July 1994, pp 1–2. She recognises that there is 'the wider philosophical dilemma of whether we want schools to act as process lines delivering citizens ready made for the workforce, or to produce culturally literate, well-rounded individuals', p 2.
5   A Borgmann, *Holding on to reality*, University of Chicago Press, Chicago, 1999, p 47.
6   Such a premise has been the foundation of the Whole Language Programme, much of which was derived from the ideas of Sylvia Ashton-Warner's Key Vocabulary. For a discussion of this scheme refer to L Limbrick's 'The literacy debases: What are the issues in New Zealand', paper presented at the British Educational Research Association Annual Conference, University of Sussex, Brighton, 2–5 September 1999. Also, for an evaluation of Sylvia Ashton-Warner's career please refer to 'Sylvia Teaches', T Brabazon, *Ladies who Lunge*, UNSW Press, Sydney, 2002.
7   C Lucas, *Crisis in the academy: Rethinking higher education in America*, St Martin's Griffin, New York, 1996, p 203.
8   For a magisterial and impressive analysis of language in/and its context please refer to MAK Halliday & R Hasan's *Language, context and text: Aspects of language in a social semiotic perspective*, Deakin University Press, Geelong, 1985. In this text, the three meta-functions of context are discussed; the field of discourse, the tenor of discourse and the mode of discourse. These three elements create the context of the situation in which a text functions.
9   This knowledge system has been described and explored by Robert Connell

as 'the hidden curriculum', from *Schools and Social Justice*, La Martreise de'ecole, Montreal, 1993, p 15.

10 R Connell, *Schools and Social Justice*, p 11.

11 M Nakata, 'History, cultural diversity and English language teaching', from B Cope & M Kalantzis (ed), *Multiliteracies: Literacy learning and the design of social futures*, Macmillan, Melbourne, 2000, p 106.

12 To view this debate in action, please refer to Patrick Lawnham's 'Unis cautious over soft marking fears', *The Australian*, 28 March, 2001, p 47.

13 D Marc, *Bonfire of the humanities*, p 67.

14 S Petrina, 'The civilization of illiteracy', *Journal of Technology Education*, Vol 11, No 2, Spring 2000, p 70.

15 I Duncan, cited in Wendy Morgan, *Critical literacy in the classroom: The art of the possible*, Routledge, London, 1997, p 203.

16 E Kirk, 'Information and its counterfeits: Propaganda, misinformation and disinformation', 16 May 2001, <http://milton.mse.jhu.edu/research/education/counterfeit.html>, accessed on 16 June 2001.

17 C Szymanski Sunal, C Smith, D Sunal & J Britt, 'Using the internet to create meaningful instruction', *The Social Studies*, Vol 89, No 1, 1998, p 13.

18 Kathy Schrock has assembled a strong model for interpretation of the Internet through 'The ABCs of Web Site Evaluation: Teaching media literacy in the Age of the internet', Connected Newsletter, [1999–2000], <http://connectedteacher.classroom.com/newsletter/abcs.asp>, accessed on 16 June 2001. Similarly, Alastair Smith, for his Department of Library and Information Studies in the Victoria University of Wellington, Aotearoa/New Zealand, has also fathomed a criteria of judgment: 'Criteria for evaluation of internet information resources', <http://www.vuw.ac.nz/~agsmith/evaln/index.html>, accessed on 16 June 2001.

19 For an excellent discussion of the power and potential of this process, please refer to Terry Flew's 'From demountables to foundations: Media studies, media convergence and the curriculum', *Metro Education*, No 10, 1997, pp 22–27.

20 R Hannam, 'Teaching large classes in higher education', paper prepared for the *Teaching large classes in higher education project*, University of Queensland, July 2001.

21 These three recognitions of change are derived from DN Rodowick's 'Audiovisual culture and interdisciplinary knowledge', [1994], <http://www.cc.rochester.edu/Colleg...ulture/AudiovisualCultureText.htlm>, accessed 24 August 1999.

22 H Duggan, 'Bootstrapping your community', <http://www.bigbangworkshops.com/html/from_site_to_community.htm>, accessed 8 April 2001.

23 T Taylor & I Ward, 'Introduction', from T Taylor & I Ward (ed), *Literacy theory in the age of the internet*, Columbia University Press, New York, 1998, p xvi.

24 N Postman, *The end of education: Redefining the value of school*, Vintage Books, New York, 1996, p 116.

25 J Valenza, 'Media specialists: Leading the way to information literacy', *Connected Newsletter*, March 1999, <http://connectedteacher.classroom.com/newsletter/mar99.asp>, accessed 16 June 2001.

26 C Harris, *An internet education*, International Thomson Publishing Company, Belmont, 1996, p 12.

27 The New London Group, 'A pedagogy of multiliteracies: Designing social

futures', from B Cope & M Kalantzis (ed), *Multiliteracies*, p 13.

28 C Luke, 'Cyber-schooling and technological change: Multiliteracies for new times', from C Luke, 'Cyber-schooling and technological change', p 71.

29 J Bolter, *Writing Space: The computer, hypertext, and the history of writing*, Erlbaum, Hillsdale, 1991, p 2.

30 It must also be acknowledged that there are major continuities between hypertext and 'conventional' reading. Reading a book can be as non-linear and cut-up as hypertext, and it is common to read a hypertext document through, without clicking to the 'interesting asides'. The level of control exercised by the reader of a hypertexted document can be overrated. The navigation bar and tools still play the role of page numbers, imposing a dominant reading strategy over the document.

31 'Improving lectures with technology', <http://darkwing.uoregon.edu/~tep/technology/techlect.html>, accessed 29 July 2000.

32 S Silverman, 'Linking technology standards to essential learning', *Connected Newsletter*, September 1998, <http://connectedteacher.classroom.com/newsletter/sep98.asp>, accessed 16 June 2001.

33 J O'Donnell, *Avatars of the world: From papyrus to cyberspace*, Harvard University Press, Cambridge, 1998, p 153.

34 Ilana Snyder confirmed this reading, stating: 'in Australia, at least, technology has never assumed a significant presence — neither in schools nor in post-school educational institutions. When television arrived fifty years ago, many believed that the new communication medium would transform education. It did not', from 'Page to Screen', from I Snyder (ed), *Page to Screen: Taking literacy into the electronic age*, Allen and Unwin, Sydney, 1997, p xxii.

35 S Kerr, 'Pale screens: teachers and electronic texts', from P Jackson & S Haroutunian-Gordon, *From Socrates to Software*, University of Chicago Press, Chicago, 1989, p 202.

36 N Postman, *The end of education: Redefining the value of school*, Vintage Books, New York, 1996, p 31.

4 DOUBLE FOLD OR DOUBLE TAKE? BOOK MEMORY AND THE ADMINISTRATION OF INFORMATION

1 N Baker, interviewed by Alexander Laurence and David Strauss, The Write Stuff: Alt-X [1994; cited 15 June 2001], available from <http://www.altx.com/interviews/nicholson.baker.html>. An outstanding history of the footnote that verifies Baker's claim for the potential of marginal stories and persuasive tangents is Antony Grafton's *The Footnote*, Harvard University Press, Cambridge, 1997.

2 L Miller, 'Lifting up the Madonna', *The Salon Interview*, <http://www.salon.com/10/features/baker1.html>, accessed 15 June 2001.

3 J Billington, cited in N Baker, *Double Fold: Libraries and the assault on paper*, Random House, New York, 2001, p 36.

4 The Double Fold test is derived from the MIT Fold Test, initiated by WJ Barrow, who demonstrated that books were vulnerable when a strip of its pages were turned back and forth through 270 degrees, at the rate of 175 Double Folds per minute. For a discussion of this text, please refer to Baker, *Double Fold*, pp 152–55.

5 There is also an error rate in digital scanning, averaging to three characters

out of 100. For a discussion of the difficulties of accurate scanning of print-based texts, pleas refer to Maggie McDonald's 'Don't rip it up and start again', *New Scientist*, Vol 170, No 2291, 19 May 2001, p 49. There are also qualitative issues to be discussed in relation to scanning. Most documents can be scanned at 200dpi, but for many texts — particularly those with sizeable image-based content — this standard is not sufficient.

6   As Baker argues, 'Newspaper pages are the most difficult of all printed artefacts to photograph (or digitize) well: they are very large, narrow-margined, and filled with tiny type and finely detailed line drawings and photography', *Double Fold*, p 26.

7   N Baker, *Double Fold*, p 16.

8   These figures are cited by Elaine Sciolino, 'Preserving books? It's easy on paper', *The New York Times*, 7 April 2001, <http://www.nytimes.com/2001/04/07/arts/07PAPE.html>, accessed 15 June 2001.

9   J Billington, cited in Baker, *Double Fold*.

10   Michael Dirda, 'Double Fold', *Washington Post*, 15 April 2001, p 15. Similarly, Julian Dibbell described an 'ongoing holocaust of books, journals, and newspapers', from 'The paper chase', *Village Voice Literary Supplement*, April 2001, <http://www.villagevoice.com/vls/174/dibbell.shtml>, accessed 15 June 2001.

11   J Billington, cited in J Conaway, *America's library: The story of the Library of Congress 1800–2000*, Yale University Press, New Haven, 2000, p 206.

12   M Jones, 'Paper tier: taking librarians to task', *Newsweek*, 16 April 2001, p 57.

13   As Baker stated, 'Library users did not like microfilm that was clear, and they didn't like microfiche any better', p 168.

14   N Baker, *Double Fold*, p 40.

15   N Baker, *Double Fold*, p 224.

16   M McDonald, 'Don't rip it up and start again', *New Scientist*, Vol 170, No 2291, 19 May 2001, p 49.

17   To view a trace of his operations, please refer to 'American Newspaper Repository — images from the *Chicago Tribune*', July 1911, <http://home.gwi.net/~dnb/ChicagoTribune1911.html>, accessed 15 June 2001.

18   RJ Cox, 'The great newspaper caper: Backlash in the digital age', *First Monday*, Vol 5, No 12, December 2000.

19   b.q., 'Don't burn books! Burn Librarians!', *Searcher*, 2001, p 16.

20   b.q., 'Don't burn books! Burn Librarians!', p 10.

21   C Sessions Stepp, 'Disintegrating into dust', *American Libraries*, April 2001, p 61.

22   Through the 19th century, for example, popular culture and ephemera were not rendered worthy of collection. For a discussion of the consequences of this decision, please refer to John Hamilton's *Casanova was a book lover*, Louisiana State University Press, Baton Rouge, 2000, p 214.

23   R Emerson, 'The American Scholar', from G Suriano (ed), *Great American Speeches*, Gramercy Books, New York, 1993, p 32.

24   Both these stories were told by John Maxwell Hamilton, *Casanova was a book lover*, pp 5–6.

25   G O'Brien, *The Browser's Ecstasy: a mediation on reading*, Counterpoint, Washington, 2000, p 65.

26 J Hamilton, *Casanova was a book lover*, p 5.

27 J Hamilton, *Casanova was a book lover*.

28 Cited in John Browning, 'Library without walls — for books without pages', [1993], <http://eff.org/pub/GII_NII/Regional_rural_edu/libraries_online.articles>, accessed 6 October 1999.

29 N Baker, *Double Fold*, p 135.

30 Plato, *Phaedrus*, translated with introduction and commentary by R Hackforth, Cambridge University Press, Cambridge, 1952, 274e.

31 H Martin, *The history and power of writing*, University of Chicago Press, Chicago, 1994:1988, p 507.

32 J Hamilton, *Casanova was a book lover*, p 45.

33 'Submission Guidelines', *Cultural Studies-Critical Methodologies*, Sage Publications, 2002.

34 'Lectern' of course comes from the Latin verb *legere*: 'to read'.

35 For an outstanding history of the bookshelf, please refer to Henry Petroski, *The book on the bookshelf*, Alfred A Knopf, New York, 1999.

36 F Lerner, *The story of libraries from the invention of writing to the computer age*, The Continuum Publishing Company, New York, 1999, p 11.

37 This description was used by Catherine Marshall, Gene Golovchinsky and Morgan Price in 'Digital libraries and mobility', *Communications of the ACM*, Vol 44, No 5, May 2001, p 55.

38 G Himmelfarb, 'Revolution library', *American Scholar*, Vol 66, No 2, 1977, pp 203–204.

39 Also, while the phrase 'full text database' may imply cover-to-cover coverage of participating/aggregated titles, this is an incorrect judgment. Editorials, letters, reviews and advertisements are often excluded. Full text access via aggregated databases is not equal to a print subscription. Further, once the institution ceases to subscribe to the product, access to past issues is denied. Electronic access to aggregated full text databases does not guarantee *ongoing* access.

40 For example, Alastair Smith researched the low level of WIF (Web Impact Factor) of Australian and New Zealand information, sites and ideas. Please refer to 'ANZAC webometrics: exploring Australasian Web Structures', <http://www.csu.edu.au/special/online99/proceedings99/203b.htm>, accessed 10 August 2001. Further, the few references in the dire 'research' tool, Microsoft Encarta, include very few references to Australia, indigenous Australians, Aotearoa/New Zealand and Maori peoples, or the myriad communities of the Asian and Pacific region.

41 M Gorman, 'The corruption of cataloguing', *Library Journal*, Vol 120, 15 September 1995, p 34.

42 Stewart Brand ponders why 'the burning of libraries is so universally regarded as a crime against humanity that it is instructive to examine the historical record. What exactly is the outrage about?'. *The clock of the long now: Time and responsibility*, Basic Books, New York, 1999, p 72.

43 F Kilgour, *The evolution of the book*, Oxford University Press, Oxford, 1998, p 130.

44 As Fred Lerner stated, 'even in those libraries founded specifically for the use of the common people, the book collections reflected the literary standards of intellectuals and cultural bureaucrats rather than the taste of ordinary readers', *The story of libraries from the invention of writing to the computer age*, p 150.

45 M Wilson, 'Understanding the needs of tomorrow's library user: Rethinking library services for the new age', APLIS, Vol 13, No 2, June 2000, p 81.

46 The Library of Congress started to sell its catalogue in 1902. The consequence of this action was that it became a centralised cataloguing agency.

47 Marion Wilson was very aware of the threat to libraries because they are significant, but not central, to a wide array of societal institutions. She stated, 'we risk our existence if we are not perceived as essential to society', from 'Understanding the needs of tomorrow's library user', APLIS, p 86.

48 F Fialkoff, 'Baker's book is half-baked', *Library Journal*, 15 May 2001, p·102.

49 H Schiller, *Information inequality: The deepening social crisis in America*, Routledge, New York, 1996, p 36.

50 'Off to the library', *The Economist*, Vol 348, No 8085, p 30.

51 M Dirda, 'Double Fold', *Washington Post*, p 15.

52 John Hamilton recognised this problem when he stated, 'strapped to meet rising prices, research libraries spend more money to buy less. The ARL study found that serial expenditures doubled, while overall purchases declined 6 percent; book purchases declined 14 percent', from *Casanova was a book lover*, p 239. Indexing databases provide information about printed sources with increasingly poor distribution, as the focus of collection managers becomes narrower, and authoritative journals without electronic equivalents are overlooked to advance the prospects of new electronic journals acquired by aggregators.

53 E Shreeves, 'The acquisitions culture wars', *Library Trends*, Vol 48, No 4, Spring 2000, p 877.

54 C Cody, 'Scandal in the stacks: a true story', Borders.com [14 June 2001], <http://go.borders.com/features/nbaker.xcv>, accessed 15 June 2001.

55 For an outstanding discussion of these diverse functions, please refer to Suzanne Gray's 'Virtual reference services: Directions and agendas', *Reference and User Services Quarterly*, Vol 39, No 4, Summer 2000, pp 365–75.

56 A search engine is not a catalogue of accessible holdings. The websites do not belong in any specific place, and no one is responsible for the management of these holdings. The Internet will never be indexed or classified in any standardised or meaningful way, because the Internet is not owned or managed by a single body.

57 G O'Brien, *The Browser's Ecstasy*, p 150.

58 S Brand, *The clock of the long now*, p 84.

59 PADI, 'Why preserve access to digital information?', [online], <http://www.nla.gov.au/padi.why.html>, accessed 1 August 2001.

60 PADI, 'Why preserve access to digital information?'.

61 F Lerner, *The story of libraries from the invention of writing to the computer age*, p 202.

62 S Florman, 'From here to eternity', *MIT's Technology Review*, Vol 100, No 3, April 1997, [Expanded Academic ASAP International Education, full-text].

5   RECLAIMING THE TEACHER'S BODY

1   D Tripp, *Critical incidents in teaching*, Routledge, London, 1993.

2   D Tripp, *Critical incidents in teaching*, p 44.

3   b hooks, 'Eros, eroticism and the pedagogical process', from H Giroux & P McLaren (ed), *Between borders: Pedagogy and the politics of cultural studies*, Routledge, New York, 1994, p 113.

4   Maryanne Dever commented directly on the threat to a feminist education. She stated that 'while it is fair to say that today many areas within the humanities and social sciences are increasingly subject to this kind of scrutiny, why should feminist work be singled out so consistently and so frequently for the "utility test"', from M Mayberry & E Rose, *Meeting the challenge: Innovative feminist pedagogies in action*, Routledge, New York, 1999, p 60.

5   A considered analysis of non-verbal communication is found in F Beisler, H Scheers & D Pinner's *Communication Skills*, Longman Cheshire, Melbourne, 1993.

6   b hooks, p 117.

7   b hooks, p 118.

8   S Shapiro, *Pedagogy and the politics of the body: A critical praxis*, Garland Publishing, New York, 1999, p 142.

9   William Kerrigan, from L Botstein, J Boswell, J Blythe & W Kerrigan, 'New rules about sex on campus: Should professors be denied admission to students' beds?', *Harper's Magazine*, September 1993, pp 35–36.

10 To view this rhetoric at its most brutal and banal, please refer to WE Halal & J Liebowitz, 'Telelearning: The multimedia revolution in education', *The Futurist*, Vol 28, No 6, November–December 1994, pp 21–25.

11 WE Halal & J Liebowitz, 'Telelearning', p 25.

12 For example, the Occasional Papers and Working Papers which emerged from the Birmingham Centre for Contemporary Cultural Studies during the 1970s rarely featured educational questions. However, in the mid-1970s an Education Working Group was formed, publishing *Unpopular Education: Schooling and social democracy in England since 1944*. There is also some focus on the transition from school to work in Paul Willis's *Learning to labour: How working class kids get working class jobs*, Saxon House, 1977.

13 L Grossberg, 'Introduction: Bringin' it all back home — pedagogy and cultural studies', from H Giroux & P McLaren, *Between Borders: Pedagogy and the politics of cultural studies*, Routledge, New York, 1994, p 3.

14 S Hall, 'Race, culture and communications: Looking backward and forward at Cultural Studies', *Rethinking Marxism*, Vol 5, 1992, p 18.

15 D Chandler, 'Biases of the ear and eye: "Great divide" theories, honocentrism, graphocentrism and logocentrism', [online], <http://www.aber.ac.uk/~dgc/litoral.html>, accessed 22 July 22, 1999.

16 A Bates, 'Technology for distance education: A 10-year perspective', in A Tait (ed), *Key issues in open learning — a reader*, Longman, Harlow, 1993, p 242.

17 E Meacham & B Butler, *Audio tapes for distance education*, Division of External Studies, Riverina-Murray institute of Higher Education, Riverina, 1988, p 1.

18 J Kenny, 'They're taking over', *Times Educational Supplement*, Issue 4269, 24 March 2000, p 2.

19 E Rose, 'This class meets in cyberspace: Women's studies via distance education', in M Mayberry & E Rose (ed), *Meeting the challenge: Innovative feminist pedagogies in action*, Routledge, New York, 1999, p 148.

20 A Benson & E Wright, 'Pedagogy and policy in the age of the wired professor', *Technological horizons in education*, Vol 27, No 4, November 1999, [Expanded Academic database, full-text article].

21 M Vachris, 'Teaching principles of economics without "Chalk and Talk"',

The Journal of Economic Education, Vol 30, No 3, Summer 1999, [Expanded Academic Database, full-text].

22 M Vachris, 'Teaching principles of economics without "Chalk and Talk"'.

23 B Readings, The University in Ruins, Harvard University Press, Cambridge, 1996, p 131.

24 Z Bauman, 'Universities: Old, new and different', in A Smith & F Webster (ed), The Postmodern University? Open University Press, Buckingham, 1997, p 21.

25 To observe Richard Bosworth's outstanding historical praxis in action — which conveys something of his first-year teaching experience — please refer to his Explaining Auschwitz and Hiroshima: History Writing and the Second World War 1945–1990, Routledge, London, 1993. In his preface, Bosworth states that 'this book has at least one claim to fame: it is more the product of "teaching" than of "research". It therefore runs counter to the assumption increasingly made in my home country, Australia, that only "researchers", elevated by grants above teaching, write books', p xi. Quite overtly, Bosworth creates and inscribes a political imperative within his teaching spaces.

26 H Giroux & R Simon, 'Popular culture as a pedagogy of pleasure and meaning', in H Giroux & R Simon, Popular culture, schooling and everyday life, Bergin and Garvey, Granby, 1989, p 3.

27 D Newlands & M Ward, 'Using the Web and E-Mail as substitutes for traditional university teaching methods: Student and staff experiences', unpublished paper, Department of Economics, University of Aberdeen, undated.

28 Z Bauman, 'From pilgrim to tourist — or a short history of identity', in S Hall & P du Gay (ed), Questions of cultural identity, Sage Publications, London, 1996, p 19.

29 S Talbott, The future does not compute, [online], <http://www. ora.com/people/staff/stevet/fdnc/indx.html>, accessed 10 August 2001.

30 S Turkle, from H Rheingold's 'Mr Rheingold's Neighborhood', Salon, [1999], <http://www.salon1999.com/12nov1995/departments.howard. htm>, accessed 6 October 1999.

31 H Rheingold, 'Mr Rheingold's Neighborhood'.

32 A Stone, 'Will the real body please stand up?', <http://www.rochester. edu/College/FS/Publications/StoneBody.html>, accessed 1 May 2001.

33 This phrase was used by Amy Bruckman in 'Gender swapping on the internet', presented at the Internet society, San Francisco, California, August 1993, <http://www.vcn.bc.ca/sig/comm-nets/gender-swapping.txt>, accessed 6 October 1999.

34 Gladys We presented this problem through 'Cross-Gender Communication in Cyberspace', Paper for CMNS 855, Simon Fraser University, 3 April 1993, <http://cpsr.org/cpsr/gender/we_cross_gender>, accessed 4 May 2001.

35 'Cross-Gender Communication in Cyberspace'.

36 L King, 'Gender issues in online communities', CPSR Newsletter, Vol 18, No 1, Winter 2000, <http://www.cpsr.org/publicaitons/newsletters/ issues/2000/Winter2000/king.html>, accessed 4 May 2000.

37 Grossberg, 'Introduction: Bringin' it all back home — pedagogy and cultural studies', p 20.

38 For an outstanding investigation of curricula justice, please refer to RW Connell, 'Social justice in education', Overland, No 157, Summer 1999, pp 18–25.

39 G O'Brien, *All the essential half-truths about higher education*, University of Chicago Press, Chicago, 1998, p 1.

40 A Morrison & D McIntyre, *Teachers and Teaching*, Penguin, Harmondsworth, 1969.

6 POINT, CLICK AND GRADUATE: STUDENT MOTIVATION IN THE INFORMATION AGE

1 Han Solo, played by Harrison Ford, *Star Wars*, written and directed by George Lucas, Twentieth Century Fox, 1977.

2 'Educational foundations: Education and communication', <http://www.curtin.edu.au/home/Allen/we3/igm/030108.html>, accessed 29 July 2000.

3 A Rogers, *Teaching Adults*, Open University Press, Milton Keynes, 1986, p 31.

4 Albert Borgmann, at his critical best, argued that 'schooling via lecturing culminates in the scholar. What kind of expert does distance learning aim at? ... The goal then of education in cyberspace is to produce the learner, the person who has learned how to learn but otherwise knows nothing', from *Holding on to reality*, University of Chicago Press, Chicago, 1999, p 206.

5 N Entwistle, 'Teaching and the quality of learning in higher education', in N Entwistle (ed), *Handbook of educational ideas and practices*, Routledge, London, 1990, p 675.

6 L Alley, 'Technology precipitates reflective teaching: An instructional epiphany', *Change*, Vol 28, No 2, March–April 1996, [Expanded Academic Database, full-text].

7 J Bang, 'Curriculum, pedagogy and educational technologies: Some considerations on the choice of technology for open and distance learning', *EADTU News*, Vol 18, December 1994, p 35.

8 This distinction was put in place by Bang, 'Curriculum, pedagogy and educational technologies', pp 38–41.

9 Bang, 'Curriculum, pedagogy and educational technologies', p 40.

10 S Newstead argued that the increasing level of school leavers entering higher education has not resulted in a reduction of standards. Please refer to S Newstead, 'Silk purse or sow's ear?', *The Psychologist*, Vol 13, 2000, pp 184–88. In the United Kingdom the data is difficult to read. The number of good degrees in Britain — attaining a first or upper-second class honours — has actually increased over the decade. Please refer to R Myron-Wilson & PK Smith, 'A matter of degrees', *The Psychologist*, Vol. 11 1998, pp 535–38.

11 N Small, 'Education in a uniting society', paper presented at SCUTREA, 30th Annual Conference, 3–5 July 2000, University of Nottingham, p 1.

12 A Cowan, 'Planning a history curriculum', in A Booth & P Hyland (ed), *History in higher education*, Blackwell Publishers, Oxford, 1996, p 25.

13 W McKeachie, 'Class size, large classes and multiple sections', *Academe*, Vol 66, 1980, pp 24–26.

14 T Tapper & D Palfreyman, *Oxford and the decline of the collegiate tradition*, Woburn Press, London, 2000, p vii.

15 Respondent, survey conducted by Zane Berge, 'Concerns of online teachers in higher education', <http://www.emoderators.com/zberge/iste98.html>, accessed 13 July 2001.

16 For a statement of this position, please refer to Malcolm McElhone's

'A methodological approach to educational innovation: A case study involving web-based learning', paper presented at the British Educational Research Association Conference, Cardiff University, 7–10 September 2000.

17 Z Berge, 'Concerns of online teachers in higher education'.

18 B Means, *Technology and education reform*, Jossey-Bass, San Francisco, 1994, p 5.

19 This problem is rarely recognised, but was hinted at by Michele Knobel, Colin Lankshear, Eileen Honan and Jane Crawford in 'The wired world of second-language education', in Ilana Snyder (ed), *Page to Screen: Taking literacy into the electronic age*, Allen and Unwin, Sydney, 1997. They stated that 'email appeared to increase student dependence on the lecturer', p 45.

20 K Feldt, 'E-learning: Still waiting for the first big thing', techLEARNING.com, [1 June 2001], <http://www.techlearning.com /db_area/archives/WCE/ archives/kenfeldt.htm>, accessed on 16 June 2001.

21 Knobel, Lankshear, Honan & Crawford, 'The wired world of second-language education', p 28.

22 There is also a suite of educational theory that promotes this notion. John Halliday, from the University of Strathclyde, described the 'mistaken conception of learning as something anterior to and distinct from work', from 'Lifelong learning and the world of work', paper presented at the European Conference on Educational Research, Lahti, Finland, 22–25 September 1999, p 1.

23 R Pithers & M Mason, 'Learning style preferences: Vocational students and teachers', *Australian Educational Researcher*, Vol 19, No 2, 1992, p 68.

24 D Presti, 'The world wide web as an instructional tool', *Science*, Vol 274, No 5286, 18 October 1996, p 371.

25 'Student IBL Survey Report', <http://www.curtin.edu.au/home/Allen/ we3/igt/tool21.html>, accessed 29 July 2000.

26 This reflexivity is termed double loop, or spiral learning. It is a meta-learning strategy whereby students reflect critically on their assumptions and imagine alternative learning trajectories.

27 S Brookfield, *Understanding and facilitating adult learning*, Jossey-Bass, San Francisco, 1987, p 11.

28 S Brookfield, *Understanding and facilitating adult learning*, p 12.

29 This modelling behaviour is termed exogenous constructivism. It differs from the Piagetian-inspired endogenous constructivism, which stresses the importance of child-directed exploration and discovery, rather than direct teaching. Dialectical constructivism lies between these two structures, emphasising the interpersonal dimension of learning, and the relationship between self-discovery and the guided tour of learning provided by a teacher.

30 M Vachris, 'Teaching principles of economics without "Chalk and Talk"', *The Journal of Economic Education*, Vol 30, Issue 3, Summer 1999 [Expanded Academic Database, full-text].

31 Z Berge, 'Concerns of online teachers in higher education'.

7   HOW IMAGINED ARE VIRTUAL COMMUNITIES?

1   J Gee, 'New people in new worlds: Networks, the new capitalism and schools', in B Cope & M Kalantzis (ed), *Multiliteracies: Literacy learning and the design of social futures*, Macmillan, Melbourne, 2000, p 50.

2   EP Thompson, *The Making of the English Working Class*, Victor Gollancz, London, 1968.
3   G Greer, *The Female Eunuch*, Paladin, London, 1971.
4   G Spivak, 'Can the Subaltern Speak?', in L Grossberg & C Nelson (ed), *Marxism and the interpretation of culture*, University of Illinois Press, Urbana, 1988.
5   B Anderson, *Imagined Communities: Reflections on the origin and spread of nationalism*, Verso, London, 1983, p 15.
6   B Anderson, *Imagined Communities*, p 12.
7   Please note that this consent is managed hegemonically. Empowered classes must reach beyond their own interest and organise disempowered groups so that they consent to their own oppression. As A Simon has stated, 'a class cannot achieve national leadership, and become hegemonic, if it confines itself only to class interests', *Gramsci's Political Thought*, Lawrence and Wishart, London, 1982, p 23.
8   P Chatterjee, 'Whose imagined community?', in G Balakrisihnan (ed), *Mapping the nation*, Verso, London, 1996, p 215.
9   As Anderson has suggested, 'nationalism thinks in terms of historical destinies, while racism dreams of eternal contaminations', *Imagined Communities*, p 136.
10 B Anderson, *Imagined Communities*, p 15.
11 H Rheingold, 'Introduction', *The Virtual Community: Homesteading on the Electronic Frontier*, <http://www.rheingold.com/vc/book/intro.html>, accessed 24 February 2001.
12 H Rheingold, 'Introduction', *The Virtual Community*.
13 B Wellman & M Gulia, 'Net surfers don't ride alone: Virtual communities as communities', <http://www.acm.org/~fccp/references/wellman/wellman.html>, accessed 15 March 2001.
14 To view the consequences of this process, please refer to Subramani's 'The Oceanic Imaginary', *The Contemporary Pacific*, Spring 2001, Expanded Academic Database.
15 B Wellman & M Gulia, 'Net surfers don't ride alone'.
16 R Hamman, 'Computer networks linking networks communities: Effects of AOL use upon pre-existing communities', <http://www.socio.demon.co.uk/cybersociety>,accessed 1 May 2001.
17 Z Bauman, 'Racism, anti-racism and moral progress', *Arena Journal*, No 1, 1993, p 16.
18 R Miles, *Racism*, Routledge, London, 1989, p 70.
19 This ironic, responsive representation to cultural domination was theorised by Edward Said in *Orientalism*, Penguin, London, 1978. As he stated, 'England knows Egypt; Egypt is what England knows', p 34.
20 Ambivalence is best theorised by Homi Bhabha in 'The other question: difference, discrimination and the discourses of colonialism', in R Ferguson, M Gever, Trinh Minh-ha & C West (ed), *Out there: Marginalisation and contemporary cultures*, MIT Press, New York, 1990, p 71.
21 N Zurawski, 'Ethnicity an the internet in a global society', <http://www.isoc.org/isoc/whatis/conferences/inet/96/proceedings/e8/e8_1.htm>, accessed 16 May 2001.
22 A solid study of 'Self-determination in the information age', was written by Scott Crawford & Kekula Bray-Crawford, <http://www.hawaii-nation.org/sdinfoage.html>, accessed 16 May 16, 2001.
23 Guillermo Delgado-P and Marc Becker stated that 'native activists and

scholars have observed the patterns of economic inequality which exist elsewhere have been reproduced in access to electronic media', from 'Latin America: The internet and indigenous texts', <http://www.cs.org/publications/CSQ/csqinternet.html>, accessed 16 May 2001.

24 Sarah Green and Penny Harvey express this political imperative very clearly: 'to fail to connect would be disastrous, and to fail to help those who can't help themselves to connect morally reprehensible', from 'Sealing place and networks: An ethnography of ICT "innovation" in Manchester', paper presented at the Internet and Ethnography Conference, Hull, 13–14 December 1999. Not surprisingly, Manchester — as the first industrial nation and the focus of Marx and Engels early studies — has been a site of negotiation of the new virtual communities. Please refer to Penelope Harvey's 'Social contexts of Virtual Manchester', <http://www.brunel.ac.uk/research/virtsoc/projects/harvey.htm>, accessed 1 May 2001.

25 A Stone, 'Will the real body please stand up', <http://www.rochester.edu/College/FS/Publications/StoneBody.html>, accessed 1 May 2001.

26 This problem was revealed in Troy Schneider's discussion of how leisure-based communities can actually block an involvement in governmental affairs. He discussed his virtual community for military vehicle buffs: 'we know each other by name; I've spoken to many directly and even met a few in person. We share hints and horror stories, swap parts, and commiserate over breakdowns. And not infrequently, someone mentions a political issue — anything from emissions control to government destruction of surplus parts. (Not exactly the stuff of revolutions, but most of politics isn't.) We're all online. Our elected representatives' e-mail addresses are just clicks away, as are most of the resources to help us get active. The networks and websites are there to leverage. But without fail, the online politics go no further than comments that someone really should do something', from 'Online in 2000: call off the revolution', <http://www.findarticles.com/cf_)/m1548/5_14/56065498/print.jhtml>, accessed 16 May 2001.

27 Thomas, quoted in Sherry Turkle, 'Virtuality and its discontents', *TAP*, Vol 7, No 24, <http://www.prospect.org/print/V7/25/turkle-s.html>, accessed 1 May 2001.

28 Dana Ott realised that 'access to the Internet will likely require literacy in English, for the most part, to enjoy the benefits', from 'Power to the people: The role of electronic media in promoting democracy in Africa', *First Monday*, No 3, 1998, <http://www.firstmonday.dk/issues/issue3_4/ott/>, accessed 16 May 2001.

29 M Slocombe, 'Community action goes global on the net', *New Statesman*, 18 December 2000, <http://www.findarticles.com/cf_0/mOFQP/4517_129/68644263/pring.jhtml>, accessed 16 May 2001.

30 C Beckles, 'Virtual resistance: A preliminary analysis of the struggle against racism via the internet', <http://www.isoc.org/isoc/whatis/conferences/inet/96/proceedings/e6/e6_4.htm>, accessed 16 May 2001.

31 Claude Levi Strauss, in 'A writing lesson', from *Tristes Tropiques*, Penguin, Harmondsworth, 1976, p 388, stated: 'It is unnecessary to point out that the Nambikwara have no written language, but they do not know how to draw either, apart from making a few doted lines or zigzags'. Significantly here, there is the assumption that *obviously* the Nambikwara do not write, and are therefore outside the structures of civilisation.

32 B Anderson, *Imagined Communities*, p 42.

33 A significant — and often displaced — argument is that this print-based knowledge system served to erode the plurality of languages. Indigenous languages were frequently undermined by the new print-based knowledge systems that provided the historical conditions for the formation of the nation state. As Anderson suggested, 'the convergence of capitalism and print technology on the fatal diversity of human language created the possibility of a new form of imagined community, which in its basic morphology set the stage for the modern nation', *Imagined Communities*, p 49. However, I would like to problematise Anderson's notion of 'fatal diversity'. Indigenous languages of the formally colonised have survived. The current boom (and revival) of Welsh and Maori in particular demonstrate that linguistic diversity is surviving — and frequently encouraged through the potentials of the Internet. The New Zealand government site performs the bicultural nature of the nation state by featuring both English and Maori.

34 J Fernback & B Thompson, 'Virtual communities: Abort, retry, failure?', <http://www.well.com/user/hlr/texts/Vcivil.html>, accessed 15 March 2001.

35 M Harris, 'Panama: the new virtual nation', <http://www.cyberhaven.com/offshorelibrary/panama.html>, accessed 16 May 2001.

36 E Balibar & I Wallerstein, *Race, Nation and Class: Ambiguous identities*, Routledge, New York, 1991, p 96.

37 R Cutler, 'Distribution and community in cyberspace', *Interpersonal Computing Technology* (IPCT), Vol 3, No 2, 1995, <http://jan.ucc.nau.edu/~ipct-j/1995/n2/cutler.txt>, accessed on 3 March 2001, p 16.

38 S Holtzman, *Digital Mosaics: The aesthetics of cyberspace*, Simon and Schuster, New York, 1997, p 38.

8   META-TAGGING POLITICS: SOCIAL JUSTICE AND THE SOCIAL RESPONSIBILITIES OF UNIVERSITIES

1   M Apple, *Cultural politics and education*, Teachers College Press, New York, 1996, p 23.

2   M Poster, 'Cyberdemocracy: Internet and the public sphere', <http://www.hnet.uci.edu/mposter/writings/democ.html>, accessed 1 May 2001.

3   For an online version of Michael and Ronda Hauben's *Netizens*, please refer to <http://www.columbia.edu/~hauben/project_book.html>, accessed 10 August 2001.

4   M & R Hauben, *Netizens*.

5   M & R Hauben, *Netizens*.

6   R Putnam, 'The strange disappearance of civic America', *TAP*, Vol 7, No 24, 1 December 1996, <http://www.prospect.org/print/V7/24/putnam-r.html>, accessed 1 May 2001.

7   For a discussion of this survey, pleas refer to Adam Marlin's 'Politics on the Web, why and where?' *Campaigns and elections*, Vol 20, Issue 3, 4 April 1999, pp 11–12.

8   B Warf & J Grimes, 'Counterhegemonic discourses and the internet', *The Geographical Review*, Vol 87, Issue 1, April 1997, p 259.

9   D Ott, 'Power to the people: The role of electronic media in promoting democracy in Africa', First Monday, Issue 3, 1998, <http://www.firstmonday.dk/issues/issue3_4/ott/>, accessed 16 May 2001.

10 There are some organisations assuming this pedagogic role. Please refer to the Washington-based Internet Education Foundation, <http://www.neted.org/>. It states its role as being 'dedicated to educating the public and policymakers about the potential for a decentralized global Internet to promote democracy, communications, and commerce'.

11 P Agre, 'Ralph Reed on the skills of democracy', *The Network Observer*, Vol 2, No 19, September 1995, <http://dlis.gscis.ucla.edu/people/pagre/no/september-1995.html#who>, accessed 24 August 1999.

12 H Schiller, *Information inequality: the deepening social crisis in America*, Routledge, New York, 1996, p 92.

13 J Wiener, 'Static in cyberspace: Free speech on the internet', [13 June 1994] <http://www.eff.org/pub/Net_info/Net_culture/Criticisms/static_in_cyberspace.articles>, accessed 6 October 1999.

14 T Schneider, 'Online in 2000: Call off the revolution', <http://www.findarticles.com/cf_0/m1548/5_14/56065498/print.jhtml>, accessed 16 May 2001.

15 T Schneider, 'Online in 2000: Call off the revolution'.

16 M Poster, 'Cyberdemocracy'.

17 J Brook & I Boal, 'Preface', in J Brook & I Boal (ed), *Resisting the virtual life: The culture and politics of information*, City Lights, San Francisco, 1995, p viii.

18 M Harris, 'Panama: The new virtual nation', <http://www.cyberhaven.com/offshorelibrary/panama.html>, accessed 16 May 2001.

19 M Slocombe, 'Community action goes global on the net', *New Statesman*, 18 December 2000, <http://www.findarticles.com/cf_0/mOFQP/4517_129/68644263/print.jhtml>, accessed 16 May 2001.

20 The trope of 'netizens' is most applicable when discussing the place of computer-mediated communication for those with differing physical capacities. These policies and programmes for digital prosthetics need to be implemented with care. Inaccessible print-based text is a barrier for the visually impaired, but effective mechanisms to verbalise keystrokes and the use of Braille printers can be profoundly useful. For the hearing impaired, the fax and email function on computers can overcome many of the difficulties with the telephone. Those with physical disabilities require computers that respond to spoken commands. Therefore, these assistive technologies are profoundly important for increasing the reach and clarity of diverse ideas and attitudes in a culture. This is a significant consideration, and adds depth to discussions of representation, equity and justice. For example, the Open University has placed great emphasis and attention on its disabled students, making up 4.1 per cent of the total undergraduate population. The opportunities of carefully-configured technologies have made a difference to distance education for these students. The use of ASCII is highly useful for converting text into either large print, Braille or speech. For further discussion of the initiatives instigated by the Open University, please refer to A Jones, G Kirkup & A Kirkwood, *Personal computers for distance education*, Paul Chapman, London, 1992, pp 83–85.

21 T Schneider, 'Online in 2000: Call off the revolution'.

22 M & H Hauben, *Netizens*.

23 M Lang, 'Futuresound: Techno music and mediation', <http://music.hyperreal.org/library/fewerchur.txt>, accessed 30 March 2001.

24 Feldman, *Introduction to digital media*, Routledge, London, 1997, p 76.

25 H Connor & S Dewson, with C Tyers, J Eccles, J Regan & J Aston, 'Social class and higher education: Issues affecting decisions on participation by lower social class groups', Research Brief No. 267, March 2001, Institute for Employment Studies, Department for Education and Employment, United Kingdom.

26 M Henry, J Knight, R Lingard & S Taylor, *Understanding schooling: An introductory sociology of Australian education*, Routledge, London, 1988, p 142.

27 Such a problem is obviously exacerbated when a language distinct from the national language is spoken in the home.

28 Patrice McDermott reported that 'telephone penetration for households headed by women with children, living at or below the poverty line is around 50%', in 'The unfortunates: Nonprofits and other hitchhikers on eh information superhighway', <http://ombwatch.org/www/ombw/info/infortun.html>, accessed 13 July 2000.

29 A Benson & E Wright, 'Pedagogy and policy in the age of the wired professor', *Technological horizons in education*, Vol 27, Issue 4, November 1999, [expanded academic, full-text article].

30 It is important at this point to make a more subtle distinction between the Internet and the web. The world wide web, while an important part of the Internet, is far more commercialised and corporate-based than the Internet. The ideology of ease of use is of benefit to companies trying to encourage more customers to use a web-based service.

31 D Evans, 'A critical examination of claims concerning the "impact of Print"', [March 1998], <http://www.aber.ac.uk/~eduww.Undgrad/ED10510/dleE701.html>, accessed 24 August 1999.

32 S Clift, 'An internet of democracy', Communications of the ACM (CACM), Vol 43, No 11, November 2000, <http://www.publicus.net/articles/net-dem.html>, accessed 16 May 2001.

33 Thomas Novak and Donna Hoffman reported this home computer ownership disparity in 1998 as 44.2 per cent of white Americans, compared to 29 per cent of African Americans, owned a home computer. Further, their research demonstrated that twice as many whites as African Americans had accessed the web in the week preceding their survey. This research was reported in 'Bridging the Digital divide: The impact of race on computer access and internet use', [2 February 1998], <http://ecommerce.vanderbilt.edu/papers/race/science.html>, accessed 16 May 2001.

34 This report is cited in Chrisopher Lucas, *Crisis in the academy*, St Martin's Griffin, New York, 1996, p 19.

35 C Beckles, 'Virtual resistance: A preliminary analysis of the struggle against racism via the internet', <http://www.isoc.org/isoc/whatis/conferences/inet/96/proceedings/e6/e6_4.htm>, accessed 16 May 2001.

36 L Nakamura, 'Race in/for cyberspace: Identity tourism and racial passing on the internet', <http://www.hnet.uci.edu/mposter/syllabi/readings/nakamura.htm>, accessed 6 October 1999.

37 M Poster, 'Cyberdemocracy'.

38 For a discussion of boys' privileged access to computers, please refer to Elaine Millard's 'New technologies, old inequalities — variations found in the use of computers by pupils at home with implications for the school curriculum', paper presented at the British Educational Research Association

Annual Conference, 11–14 September 1997, University of York, particularly pages 8–15.

39 S Silverman & A Pritchard, 'Building their future: Girls and technology education in Connecticut', *Journal of Technology Education*, Vol 7, No 2, Spring 1996, p 49.

40 Statistics cited in Jones et al., *Personal computers for distance education*, p 88.

41 J Morahan-Martin, 'Women and girls last: Females and the internet', IRISS '98: Conference Papers, 25–27 March 1998, Bristol, United Kingdom, accessed 24 August 1999.

42 'Information Technology for the Twenty-First Century: A bold investment in America's future — Social: Economic, and workforce implications of information technology and information technology workforce development', [online], <http://www.hpcc.gov/pubs/it2-ip/social.html>, accessed 16 August 1999.

43 J Kenway, 'Postmodern girls: Gender justice and restructuring education', *Education Links*, Vol 46, Spring 1993, p 5.

44 A Newitz, 'Surplus identity online', [January 1995], <http://wnglish-www.hss.cmu.edu:80/BS/18/Newitz.htm>, accessed 6 October 2000.

45 G We, 'Cross-Gender communication in cyberspace', paper for CMNS 855, Simon Fraser University, 3 April 1993, <http://cpsr.org/cpsr/gender/we_cross_gender>, accessed 4 May 2001.

46 S Herring, 'Gender and democracy in computer-mediated communication', *EJC/REC*, Vol 3, No 2, 1993, <http://dc.smu.edu/dc/classroom/Gender.txt>, accessed 4 May 2001.

47 Please refer to Herring, 'Gender and democracy in computer-mediated communication', for discussion of academic computer mediated communication, and its impact on female scholars.

48 L King, 'Gender issues in online communities', CPSR Newsletter, Vol 18, No 1, Winter 2000, <http://www.cpsr.org/publications/newsletters/issues/2000/Winter2000/king.html>, accessed 4 May 2001.

49 S Ferris, 'Women online: Cultural and relational aspects of women's communication in online discussion groups', *Interpersonal computing and technology*, Vol 4, No 3–4, October 1996, <http://www.helsinki.fi/science/optek/1996/n3/ferris.txt>, accessed 10 October 2000, p 37.

50 A Bruckman, 'Gender swapping on the internet', presented at the Internet society, San Francisco, August 1993, <ftp://ftp.media.mit.edu/pub/asb/papers/ender-swapping.txt>, accessed 4 May 2001.

51 B Gates, *The Road Ahead*, Wheeler, Rockland, 1995, p 136.

52 As Patrice McDermott has suggested, 'Telephone penetration directly correlates to income … telephone penetration for households headed by women with children, living at or below the poverty line is around 50%', in 'The unfortunates: Nonprofits and other hitchhikers on the information superhighway', 1999, [online] <http://ombwatch.org/www/ombw/info/infortun.htm>, accessed 30 July 1999.

53 As Charlotte Denny reported in 'Cyber utopia? Only the usual candidates need apply', *The Guardian*, 12 July 1999: 'The typical net user is male, under 35, with a university education and high income, urban based and English speaking, an elite minority', p 5.

54 P McDermott, 'The unfortunates'.

CONCLUSION: SOCRATES IN THE SOFTWARE

1   R Emerson, 'The American Scholar', in G Suriano (ed), *Great American Speeches*, Gramercy Books, New York, 1993, pp 35–36.

2   M Neill, 'Computers, thinking, and schools in the 'new world economic order', in J Brook & I Boal (eds), *Resisting the virtual life: The culture and politics of information*, City Lights, San Francisco, 1995, p 192.

3   A Gramsci, *Selections from the prison notebooks*, International Publishers, New York, 1971, p 331.

4   D Illing, 'Two cheers for Knowledge Nation', *The Australian Higher Education Supplement*, 4 July 2001, p 32.

5   S Burniston, J Rodger & J Brass (York Consulting Limited), 'Enterprise in higher education — changing the mindset', Research Brief No. 117, *Department for Education and Employment*, United Kingdom, September 1999.

6   M Lawn, 'Following the Third Way? Teachers and New Labour', in C Chitty & John Dunford (ed), *State Schools: New Labour and the Conservative Legacy*, Woburn Press, London, 1999, p 100.

7   I Hunter, *Rethinking the school: Subjectivity bureaucracy criticism*, Allen and Unwin, Sydney, 1994, p xxiii.

8   CS Lewis, *An experiment in criticism*, Cambridge University Press, Cambridge, 1996:1961, p 140.

9   D Padgett & S Conceicao-Runlee, 'Designing a faculty development program on technology: If you build it, will they come', *Journal of Social World Education*, Vol 36, No 2, Spring 2000, [Expanded Academic Database, full-text].

10 J Newman, *The idea of the university*, Regnery Publishing, Washington, 1999, p 139.

11 To monitor the Kolb learning cycle, please refer to DA Kolb, *Experiential learning: Experience as the source of learning*, Prentice Hall, New York, 1983.

12 Centre for Contemporary Cultural Studies (S Baron et. al.), *Unpopular education*, Hutchinson, London, 1981, p 246.

13 D Horne, *The Lucky Country*, Penguin, Melbourne, 1998.

14 M Wark, 'Who's afraid of the theory wolf?', *AQ*, Vol 70, No 4, July–August 1998, p 8.

15 Please refer to 'The Business University', in EP Thompson, *Writing by Candlelight*, Merlin, London, 1980, pp 13–27.

16 EP Thompson, cited in B Palmer, *E.P. Thompson: Objections and Oppositions*, Verso, London, 1994, p 67.

INDEX